SINGLE PARENTS

A Reference Handbook

Other Titles in ABC-CLIO's
**Contemporary
World Issues**
Series

Other Titles in ABC-CLIO's

Contemporary
World Issues
Series

Books in the Contemporary World Issues series address vital
issues in today's society such as terrorism, sexual harassment,
homelessness, AIDS, gambling, animal rights, and air pollution.
Written by professional writers, scholars, and nonacademic
experts, these books are authoritative, clearly written, up-to-
date, and objective. They provide a good starting point for
research by high school and college students, scholars, and
general readers as well as by legislators, businesspeople,
activists, and others.

Each book, carefully organized and easy to use, contains an
overview of the subject, a detailed chronology, biographical
sketches, facts and data and/or documents and other primary-
source material, a directory of organizations and agencies,
annotated lists of print and nonprint resources, a glossary, and
an index.

Readers of books in the Contemporary World Issues series will
find the information they need in order to better understand the
social, political, environmental, and economic issues facing the
world today.

SINGLE PARENTS

A Reference Handbook

Karen L. Kinnear

CONTEMPORARY WORLD ISSUES

ABC-CLIO

Santa Barbara, California
Denver, Colorado
Oxford, England

Library of Congress Cataloging-in-Publication Data
Kinnear, Karen L.
  Single parents : a reference handbook / Karen L. Kinnear.
    p.   cm.—(Contemporary world issues)
  Includes bibliographical references and index.
  ISBN 1-57607-033-6 (alk. paper)
  1. Single parents—United States—Handbooks, manuals, etc.
I. Title.   II. Series.
HQ759.915.K56   1999   98-47236
306.85'—dc21   CIP

05   04   03   02   01   00   99   10 9 8 7 6 5 4 3 2 1

ABC-CLIO, Inc.
130 Cremona Drive, P.O. Box 1911
Santa Barbara, California 93116–1911

This book is printed on acid-free paper ∞.

Typesetting by Letra Libre

Manufactured in the United States of America

To my mother,
Mildred Kinnear

Contents

Preface

The purpose of this book is to provide a survey of the available literature and other resources on the topic of single parents and to provide sources for further research. The number of single-parent families has grown in recent years. Concern for the problems that may be encountered by single parents as well as the problems caused by children growing up in single-parent families has grown as well. This book explores many of these concerns. This document provides a resource for students, writers, and researchers as well as professionals in the field.

In most societies, the ideal family is composed of a father, mother, and children. The increasing prevalence of single-parent families has forced many societies to consider this alternate family form and examine its strengths as well as its weaknesses. The most obvious problems can include financial problems, which can lead to poverty and the need for some type of welfare assistance; legal problems, including establishing paternity, determining child custody, receiving child support, and trying to adopt a child if the parent is single; and problems in finding child care, housing, health care coverage, and employment. There is also the moral aspect of single parenthood, especially for those women who decide to have a child without marrying the father. The prevailing opinion in many segments of society today is that single people, especially single girls and women, should not be having sex. They are viewed as morally corrupt if they choose to have sex and especially if they become pregnant. More and more single women are choosing to keep their children instead of giving them up for adoption. This practice also does not settle well with many segments of society. Most people agree that two parents are better than one, for all sorts of reasons, and that anyone who chooses to ignore this belief deserves the consequences.

Many people fear that the growing number of single-parent families proves that the family "ideal," that is, the two-parent family, is dying. As an indication of social disorganization, the mother-only family presents a problem to many in society. Others view the mother-only family as one of many alternative family forms; it is an indication of the growing economic independence of women. No matter what is believed about single-parent families, they are probably here to stay.

This book, like other books in the Contemporary World Issues series, provides a balanced survey of the resources available and a guide to further research on the topic of single parents. Chapter 1 reviews the literature concerning single parents, including how people become single parents, men versus women as single parents, single-mother families and poverty, problems and challenges facing single-parent families, the legal system and single parents, and contemporary concerns regarding single parents, such as the increasing numbers of single parents, father absence, welfare mothers, teenage pregnancy, gay and lesbian parents, and the effect on children of growing up in a single-parent family. The experiences of single parents in other countries are also discussed. Chapter 2 provides a chronology of the significant events in the history of single parenting. Chapter 3 offers biographical sketches of people who have played or are currently playing key roles in some aspect of the field of single parenting. Chapter 4 provides various facts and statistical information on single parenting, single fathers, teenage pregnancy, welfare participation, and homelessness. Federal government programs are described and the legal system and its effect on single parents, especially concerning paternity, child support, and adoptions, is examined. International experiences of single parents are presented. Supreme Court decisions that have had an impact on single parents are annotated, state statutes concerning child custody and adoption are listed, and the future of single-parent families is examined. Chapter 5 provides a directory of representative private and public organizations, associations, and government agencies involved in working with single parents. In Chapter 6, books that focus on single parents are annotated; the literature varies from popular accounts to primary research carried out and provides a perspective on the many issues of importance to single parents. Chapter 7 includes an annotated list of nonprint resources including films and videocassettes as well as relevant sources of information that can be found on the Internet.

Introduction and Overview

1

The number of single-parent families in the United States and throughout the world is growing. Professionals in the fields of family studies, social work, sociology, anthropology, and economics, along with educators, law enforcement personnel, politicians, lawyers, and judges, believe that this trend has had a major impact on society.

Given the current trend experts estimate that between 25 and 70 percent of all children in the United States will live with only one parent before they reach the age of 18 years. With numbers like these it is important to examine who becomes a single parent and under what circumstances. This chapter briefly discusses the factors related to the growing number of single-parent families, the problems that single parents face, the legal system and single parents, and contemporary concerns regarding single parents—such as absent fathers, moral issues, welfare mothers, gay and lesbian parents, teenage pregnancy and motherhood, the effects on children of growing up in single-parent families—including the probability that these children will grow up to be single parents themselves—and societal problems that are frequently blamed on growing up in a single-parent family. The experiences of single parents in other countries are also discussed. Statistics on single parents are briefly mentioned here; they are discussed in more detail in Chapter 4.

Single-parent families are created by divorce, separation, desertion, out-of-wedlock births, and adoption, as well as through other exigencies, such as when one parent has died or is in the military, incarcerated, working out of state, or in the hospital for a long period of time. While single-parent families are found in every racial, economic, and cultural group, the image most often associated with a single parent is that of a poor unwed mother, often African-American, on welfare, or a teenager pregnant before she finishes school. Neither of these images reflects reality. Approximately two-thirds of all single parents are white, although among all African-Americans single-parent families are the most common family form (Dowd 1997). For specific statistics on single-parent families, please see Chapter 4.

Definition of Family

A variety of beliefs exists concerning what constitutes the typical or "ideal" family. Definitions have been discussed by experts in this field, as well as by groups as diverse as members of the U.S. Congress and religious organizations. Most agree that the "ideal" family comprises a father, mother, and child(ren). According to Skolnick and Skolnick (1971) characteristics that are central to definitions of the family include:

1. The nuclear family—a man, a woman, and their children—is universally found in every human society, past, present, and future.
2. The nuclear family is the building block of society. Larger groupings—the extended family, the clan, the society—are combinations of nuclear families.
3. The nuclear family is based on a clear-cut, biologically structured division of labor between men and women, with the man playing the "instrumental" role of breadwinner, provider, and protector, and the woman playing the "expressive" role of housekeeper and emotional mainstay.
4. A major "function" of the family is to socialize children; that is, to tame their impulses and instill values, skills, and desires necessary to run the society.

5. Unusual family structures, such as mother and children, or the experimental commune, are regarded as deviant by the participants, as well as the rest of the society, and are fundamentally unstable and unworkable. (pp. 7–8)

The family type described above is an idealized type—what a family is expected to be—as much as a description of the existing reality of family life. This family type is part of a system of beliefs concerning female and male roles, describing the structure and functions of the family.

For better or for worse, the typical family may not be the same as this "ideal." Children live in a variety of environments and different family groups. In addition to the "ideal" family, children are raised in single-parent families as well as extended families. Some of these families are adoptive or foster families. Some of these parents are gay or lesbian.

Changes in family law, such as the passage of no-fault divorce laws, have made it easier to dissolve a marriage. This is one factor that has contributed to the growing number of single-parent families. The increasing acceptance of cohabitation without marriage has also created a new type of household and family. However, without a formal commitment and especially after a child is born, such relationships may end and one of the former partners—usually the woman—is often left with the child and no support. In addition, growing gender equity has helped women become financially independent and less likely in some instances to need husbands in order to raise children. Many women today, along with some men, do not see why they must be married or be with someone to raise a child. Finally, the stigma associated with premarital sex and out-of-wedlock births has lessened considerably over the years, leading to an increase in single parents.

Although being a single parent is becoming more acceptable in today's society, many people still do not believe that it is a viable family form. Arguing against single motherhood, critics contend that children need fathers for adequate financial support and in order to develop normally. They cite the importance of a responsible male role model to help children stay out of trouble. As regards single fathers, many people still believe that men should be out working and filling the role of provider, rather than staying at home raising children. According to these critics, children need mothers and will be stigmatized by living with their fathers. Another fear for many people is that men may pose a sexual threat to children, that they will sexually abuse their children. Although this fear is not grounded in reality, the threat is believed to be real by all too many people.

Becoming a Single Parent

People can become single parents in one of four ways: through unplanned pregnancy, divorce, death of a spouse, or by choice.

Unplanned Pregnancy

When we think of women who become pregnant without planning to become pregnant, we often picture teenage girls, although this can happen to any woman of childbearing age. Teenage girls are more likely to become pregnant without planning the pregnancy than women of any other age.

Years ago teenage girls who became pregnant usually gave up their babies for adoption or married the father. Today, most teenage girls keep their babies but do not marry the father, thereby becoming single mothers (Kamerman and Kahn 1988). Today the public as well as many professionals in the field see adolescent pregnancy as a social problem primarily because of the growing number of births to young unmarried girls. The popular belief is that births to these young girls are responsible for the high rates of welfare participation among young mothers. It is also believed that children of young single mothers will themselves become young single parents. These beliefs are discussed in more detail in the sections on welfare mothers and teenage pregnancy found later in this chapter.

Divorce

In recent years the number of divorces has increased and has created increasing numbers of single-parent families. Most often, the mothers are given custody of the children or share joint custody with the fathers. Less common, but with increasing frequency, the father receives custody of the children. In many cases, the lone parent with custody faces an uncertain future, often with little or no financial support to help raise the children.

The number of divorces has increased for many reasons. Some researchers (Wilson and Neckeman 1986) believe that this increase is due to the decreasing availability of jobs for males, especially those living in the inner city with few job skills. This lack of jobs has led to stress on many marriages, resulting in divorce for some families. Another reason suggested is that more women are working and have many career opportunities not previously open to them. When women can support themselves financially, they are more likely to leave a bad marriage (Rodgers 1996; Garfinkel and McLanahan 1986; Ellwood and Bane 1985). A third reason for the increasing number of divorces is the lessening stigma associated with divorce. Societal attitudes toward divorce have moderated in recent years.

Some researchers believe that passage of the no-fault divorce laws in 1970 contributed to the growing number of divorces in the United States. Covering the time that statistics on divorce have been available, since 1867, the rate of divorce has increased by over 1,700 percent; the greatest growth in numbers came between 1970 and 1979 (Burns and Scott 1994). Until 1975 men and women who divorced generally remarried quickly. After 1975 the number of remarriages dropped sharply.

Finally, some experts believe that the availability of welfare has led to more divorces and out-of-wedlock births. Several studies have shown a modest relationship between availability of welfare and higher numbers of divorces and out-of-wedlock births. For example, Garfinkel and McLanahan (1986) found that the increasing availability of welfare between 1960 and 1975 led to an increase of 15 percent in single-mother families. Other researchers have found a relationship between receiving welfare and divorce (Ellwood and Bane 1985; Bassi 1987).

In the United States supporters of liberalized divorce laws in the 1960s and 1970s believed that both men and women would be better off if allowed to cleanly end their marriages. Many also believed that women would soon be on an equal par with men economically and therefore men would no longer need to financially support their ex-wives and children (Weitzman 1985). Many experts now believe that in reality no-fault divorce has been extremely harmful to women and children. The number of single-parent families, often headed by the mothers, increased, while economic equality, adequate child care, and other support systems for families did not materialize. According to some studies, only 30 percent of ex-husbands are willing to pay child support (McDonald 1986).

Another country with liberal divorce laws is Sweden. Divorce was fairly common in Sweden until the numbers declined in the mid-1970s. Many people believe this reduction was due to the declining popularity of marriage. Sociologists suggested that because children of single parents are guaranteed a home and income, women had no reason to stay in an unhappy marriage. With the advent of these social support laws, marriages declined because women did not need husbands to support them and their children (Burns and Scott 1994).

Among the divorced women who become single mothers are women who are victims of domestic violence. Battered women who leave their husbands often find themselves in shelters, trying to get their lives back together and find ways to support themselves and their children as single parents. These parents often have a difficult time because they are dealing with the lingering effects of the physical or emotional abuse they have suffered, while at the same time trying to rebuild their lives as single parents and support their children, physically, emotionally, and financially. These mothers may be less prepared to support themselves and their children than other divorced mothers.

Death of a Spouse

Some people become single parents as a result of the death of a spouse. In the past fathers frequently became single parents when their wives died in childbirth or as a result of complications of pregnancy or childbirth, while women were more likely to become widows as a result of their husbands dying in war, or in workplace accidents. In the past a person was more likely to lose his or her spouse early in marriage than today.

In many areas of the world, especially in developing countries, the majority of single-mother families result from the death of the husband. War, other acts of violence, and the fairly popular practice of older men marrying young women contribute to the high number of widows with young children (Burns and Scott 1994).

In some countries, primarily in Europe and other developed nations, widows with young children are supported by government subsidies. These governments realize the importance of helping to support these women and their families. Some countries, such as Israel, have an extensive support system for widows and their children. War widows, women who have lost their husbands in wars and other hostile actions, receive many benefits along with an elevated social status. They receive a monthly allowance, child support, and fringe benefits. Widows whose husbands did not die during war actions are covered by a dependent's pension or survivor's pension and their children are also covered, although war widows and their children receive the most generous benefits (Lopata 1996).

In many developing countries widows (both young and old) are customarily taken care of by their extended families, at least in theory. In many cases, however, these women are asked to leave their homes, their household possessions, and sometimes even their children. The husband's family often has the right to remove the widow from the premises. In other cases these women may be forced to move back to their parents' homes or to fight for survival in any way they can. Some women may be forced by local custom to marry the brother or other male relative of the husband. Most developing countries do not have a formal government-supported system for providing help to these women and their children. For specific details of single mothers and their children in other countries, see the section concerning single parents in other countries later in this chapter and a similar section in Chapter 4.

Single Parents by Choice

During the past three decades the structure of the American family has changed. A growing number of single people, men as well as women, are becoming single parents. In the case of women McLanahan and Sandefur (1994) believe that three factors are responsible for the growing number of women choosing single parenthood. First, women are becoming financially independent from men; they are able to support themselves outside of marriage. Women can be selective about whom they marry or whether they marry at all. They can leave a bad marriage, and they can raise children on their own. A second factor in women choosing single motherhood is the decline in men's earning power relative to the earning power of women. Although women still earn less than men in comparable positions, the gains they have made have helped more women support themselves. For example in 1970 women earned 59 cents to every dollar men earned, while in 1990 women earned 74 cents for every dollar earned by men. Third, the stigma associated with having a child outside of marriage has lessened over time. In the 1950s a young father was expected to acknowledge his responsibility and marry his pregnant girlfriend or the young woman was spirited off to relatives until she gave birth and the child was then given up for adoption. In American society today the expectations are quite different; unmarried parents are less likely to resolve a pregnancy by getting married than they were 30 years ago.

The newest group of single parents are those that consciously choose to become single parents. Most often women, these parents decide that they don't need a spouse to raise a child, or they have not been able to find a compatible person to marry. Women and men may adopt a child or become the legal guardian of a child not their own. A woman may choose to become pregnant through artificial insemination or by having sex with a male friend. Many single parents decide to adopt a foreign child, in large part because some foreign countries do not have stringent rules against single people adopting children.

The decision to have a child without getting married is a difficult one for many people. This decision is a personal and individual choice, often made because this is the only way many people can have a child. Some segments of society believe the decision is made for political, not personal, reasons; that the people making this decision do not believe in the institution of the family or do not believe in following the basic morals of society. Others believe that this decision is selfish, that the parent does not want to share a child with someone else, or that the child will be hurt by having only one parent.

Older Women

In the past several years a growing number of older women have decided to bear children or adopt children without being married. Older women are generally considered to be those women over 40 years old, but may also include women over the age of 30 or 35. In 1994 over 209,000 unmarried women over the age of 30 had a baby (in 1984 only 84,000 unmarried women over the age of 30 had a baby) (National Center for Health Statistics 1995). This increase over 10 years may be due in large part to the improving life situations of many women. Well-educated women are often financially able to support a child. They have more freedom to choose if and when they will marry, and may choose to have one or more children without being married.

Very little research has been done on older never-married mothers. Most research on single mothers focuses on those mothers who are poorer, younger, and less well educated. These mothers are the ones who are more likely to be on welfare, go to public health clinics, or in other ways interact with government agencies. Much of the research on single parents draws study participants from lists of families dealing with public agencies. Older never-married mothers are more likely than other single mothers to blend into the mainstream of society.

What is known about older never-married mothers is that many of them have chosen to have a child, are well educated, have promising or already well-established careers, are financially secure, own their homes, and are confident that they can raise a child on their own. They blend into middle-class communities and tend to guard their privacy (Ludkte 1997).

When older unmarried women decide to bear children by themselves they face a major decision concerning how to become pregnant. They can choose to be artificially inseminated or can have sex with a man they know and would like as the father. If they choose artificial insemination, they can go to a sperm bank and choose an unknown person to be the father or they can ask a male friend to donate sperm. If they do not want to bear a child themselves, they can adopt. Many never-married older women choose to adopt a child from a foreign country, where the laws concerning single-parent adoption are not as strict as in many states in the United States.

When a woman decides to become pregnant, especially with sperm from a male friend, she is faced with another set of decisions to be made. She must decide whether she wants the father to provide financial support to the child, whether she wants to tell the child who the father is, and whether she wants the father to be involved in the child's life.

The reasons for wanting a child without being married are diverse. Early research concerning older single mothers focused on the belief that these mothers could not find a husband for one of two reasons: first, that these women were "undesirable" marriage material, and second, that the number of available men was inadequate. Little research has been conducted concerning these women, but the number of studies is increasing. Merritt and Steiner (1984) looked at motherhood without marriage and found that most women wanted to have a child but had not been able to find a man with whom they wanted to spend their lives. Similarly, many of the women in Siegel's (1995) study could not find a man they wanted to spend their lives with, but saw no rational reason to let their marital status prevent them from having children.

Siegel (1995) also found that most of these mothers expected to be the sole support of their children. Half of the women were satisfied with their marital status and many believed that marriage was too demanding and they wanted to do things their own way, without a lot of conflict. Other studies of unmarried women have found similar results concerning the theme of avoiding compromise and a desire to be in control. Englestein and her colleagues (1980) studied women who chose to bear a child on their own. These researchers found that the eight women they interviewed feared marriage, based on what they observed during their parents' marriages. They also believed that these women wanted and needed a child in order to have someone to control. Miller (1992) interviewed women who chose to bear or to adopt a child on their own and believed that these women viewed romantic relationships as restricting their independence and autonomy. Based on research results, single women choose to become mothers for a wide variety of reasons. In each individual case, the reason is personal and generally well thought out.

Men versus Women as Single Parents

The majority of single parents are mothers. Although the number of single fathers is increasing, the proportion of single-father families among all single-parent families is decreasing. As a result of this high number of single mothers, most literature concerning single parents focuses on single mothers. Single fathers do not get much attention, although the literature on single fathers is growing. However, both single fathers and single mothers face many similar problems in parenting. Greif (1985) believes that single mothers and fathers have similar problems because it is the task to be accomplished that creates the problem, not the sex of the parent.

The experiences of single mothers differ from the experiences of single fathers for two major reasons. First, the attitudes and expectations of society are different for fathers and mothers.

Second, men tend to have access to better jobs and earn more than women; therefore, single fathers often are more able to support children financially than single mothers.

In recent years fathers are almost as likely to get custody of their children following a divorce as mothers. Attitudes have slowly changed, providing fathers with some hope that they can get custody of their children. Custody, in particular, sparks much debate with strong opinions on both sides of the issue. Although some people believe that fathers should receive custody more often than they do, many people believe that mothers should receive custody in most cases. Reasons for mothers to receive custody include:

- Mothers are the ones who generally get custody; at least this was true in the past. Courts often still believe that mothers are the better parent because of their maternal instinct and therefore should raise the children.
- Mothers want custody. Many people believe that fathers don't care to have custody of their children.
- Fathers don't have a paternal instinct and therefore can't be good parents.
- Men are more career oriented. They would find it difficult to balance a career and a family.
- Men can't work full time and raise children.
- Mothers are more suited to care for children, with their maternal instinct.
- Men are usually the ones to disappear when children appear, not women. Men don't have to carry and give birth to the children and therefore can't be stuck with the children.

Fathers do gain custody of their children, despite many of the above beliefs. Reasons that fathers gain custody include:

- Mutual agreement with the mother.
- The children are allowed to choose with whom they want to live and they choose their father over their mother.
- Fathers can offer a more secure home and can better provide financially for the children.
- The wife could not handle the children.
  The wife deserted her family.

- The father is the better parent.
- The wife did not want a court fight, which would hurt the children.
- The wife wanted her own career.
- The wife was too ill to care for the children.
- The wife remarried, and the children would be better off with the father.
- Children need a male role model.
- The father abducted the children.

Society doesn't usually expect men to care for children, and when they do, they often are admired and believed to be extraordinary. Women are expected to care for children and even when mothers do not have custody of their children, they are expected to continue in their role as nurturers. Even though some mothers may be unfit to be parents to their children, society continues to see them as nurturers. Fathers are still seen by many as the financial supporters of their children, but not as nurturers. Slowly this attitude is changing.

Single Fathers

Men usually become single fathers as a result of divorce. In some cases, they become single fathers as a result of the death of their wives. Some single men adopt children, but this is still not a common occurrence. In general single fathers are better off financially than single mothers. However, in other ways, primarily relating to child care, many single fathers find they have a lot to learn. Research by Buehler (1988) and Tillitski (1992) has found that fathers can be successful parents and they are able to adjust to various situations as they arise.

Single fathers are usually better able than single mothers to provide financially for the children. In a study of single-parent families (60 mothers and 11 fathers), Richards and Schmiege (1993) examined the problems that single parents face in raising their children. The mothers were much more likely to report financial problems than were the fathers; 78 percent of the mothers compared with 18 percent of the fathers reported financial worries. Both mothers and fathers reported problems related to workload. Most of the men thought their experiences were different from single mothers. Men most frequently mentioned the fact that men have greater job flexibility and income as well as greater feelings of security and satisfaction. The men interviewed were aware that, while they encountered problems as single fathers, single mothers often faced greater difficulties in raising children alone.

Greif (1985) has conducted several studies that focus on single fathers. He found that single fathers were more likely than single mothers to hire someone to do the cooking and cleaning, although most fathers do the cooking and cleaning themselves, or have their children help out. Single mothers are less likely to hire someone to do these things because women are supposed to know how to cook and clean, have more experience with cooking and cleaning, and because they have less income to spend on this activity. Greif found that fathers who did hire someone to help out were earning over $33,000 yearly.

Fathers face many of the same problems that single mothers do in finding adequate child care. Greif (1985) found that several factors influence fathers' decisions concerning child care. The age of the children has a bearing on the decision to find child care. The older the child, the more likely he or she is to be left home alone. Teenagers are left alone the most. The father's income plays a role in deciding on child care; the more a father earns, the more able he is to hire someone to care for the children in his home. If the father has a support system, including family, friends, and neighbors, he can call on them to help out with child care. The father's beliefs regarding the type of home in which the children should be raised also has a bearing on child care decisions. If the father believes that family relationships are more important than anything else, he is more likely to find some way to spend more time at home with the children. Finally, the father's work schedule plays a major role in child care decisions. Fathers with more flexible work schedules are more likely to spend more time at home with their children.

For many fathers balancing the demands of work and raising children is difficult. Most men have been socialized to focus on their careers and let their wives coordinate their home activities and raise their children. When a father gains sole custody of his children, his priorities change. For example, he is more likely to have difficulty balancing work and home life because he has not had to do this prior to a divorce. Now he must focus on the children instead of his career. Instead of working overtime, traveling on the job, or working when his children are sick, the father must change his view of work and home. Greif (1985) found that many fathers experienced changes at work when they became single fathers. For example, 35 percent of the fathers in his study found that they got to work late or had to leave early because of the children, 34 percent had to miss work, and 32 percent had to reduce work-related travel. Over one-quarter (27 percent) reported no changes in their work routine. Many of the fathers believed that a flexible work schedule was the most important thing that would help them balance their responsibilities.

Some of the fathers in Greif's study, as well as other studies, found that they received special treatment because they were taking care of the children. Apparently, they are seen as extraordinary because they are able to take care of their children, and they are seen as exceptionally caring and sensitive. Some fathers like this preferential treatment; others do not. According to Greif (1985):

> When a father has custody, people assume he is an extraordinary man. They think he must be incredibly dedicated to his children, and they believe his children must be dedicated to him. They wonder how he can do all the things he has to do: work, run the house, cook, take care of the children. Socially, he is often seen as a good catch, especially to the single mother, because he is good father material.
>
> At the same time, dichotomously, he is seen as someone who needs help. How can he know how to discuss sexuality with an adolescent daughter? People feel sorry for him and run to his aid. They feel sorry for his children. They offer him assistance in the form of recipes and lectures on hair braiding. (p. 3)

Life is different for children living with their fathers from what it was when they were living with both parents, according to Greif (1985). Girls living with their fathers believe that they generally get away with more, but that they also have to do more housework than when they were living with both parents. Boys believe that they generally get away with less. In all cases, both boys and girls are responsible for more housework when they live with their fathers.

The legal system and child support received a great deal of criticism from the fathers that Greif (1985) interviewed. They complained that they often had to spend thousands of dollars to protect what was theirs and to fight for what they wanted. Mothers appeared to be favored by the courts, and even if the fathers did win custody, their ex-wives could always find another court to reverse the award. In recent years, many people believe that the court system has become more balanced; more equitable criteria are being used to determine custody. However, some women think that men are the ones receiving more favorable treatment by the courts (Polikoff 1982; Woods, Been, and Schulman 1982). Greif's research found that many fathers came before judges who clearly believed that children should be raised by their mothers. These fathers believed that they have to "go further than a mother to prove their competence, but they often are strapped with large alimony payments, and their ex-wives are exonerated from paying child support" (pp. 122–123).

Nieto (1983) studied single Hispanic fathers who had custody of their children. The men lived in four cities in Texas and one large city in Mexico. Two hundred questionnaires were completed and 50 interviews were conducted. The single fathers were determined to have a better relationship with their children than their fathers had with them. The men reported that their fathers had been aloof, distant, and lacked warmth. These fathers believed they had a more caring sensitive relationship with their children.

Single fathers who find fewer problems in parenting generally have several characteristics in common. These common characteristics include higher incomes that make them comfortable financially; participation in housework and child rearing while married; belief that both spouses bore responsibility for the marital breakup; satisfaction with child care arrangements; ex-wives who are involved with the children; and a desire for sole custody of the children (Greif 1985).

As more men become single fathers and their experiences are communicated to others, more fathers may seek custody of their children following a divorce. Some men may decide to adopt a child without being married. As men gain more experience in running a household and raising children, they may be more encouraged to fight for custody. As women see men gaining this experience, they may be more comfortable in sharing custody or in relinquishing custody to the father.

Single-Mother Families and Poverty

Single-mother families are more likely than single-father families to live in poverty. Because women in general earn less money than men, many single mothers have a difficult time finding jobs that pay enough to support their families. Despite the impression in recent years that most single mothers are receiving some type of social welfare assistance, research may indicate that this is not true. According to the U.S. Bureau of the Census (1988) in 1986 and 1987 less than half of all single mothers received Aid to Families with Dependent Children (AFDC), while approximately one-half of never-married mothers received these benefits.

Three major reasons may explain why many single-mother families are poor: First, many women do not receive any child support from the fathers of their children. Others do not receive the entire amount that has been awarded to them in court. Second, a woman's income is often not adequate to support a family. Single mothers often find themselves working in service, blue-collar, and pink-collar jobs that offer low pay and little chance for advancement. These jobs may not provide health benefits and may not be stable or provide a future. Third, inadequate social welfare programs and the strains on federal and state resources cannot provide adequate economic support for many single-mother families.

Women are often hurt more economically by a divorce than men for several reasons (Terdal and Kennedy 1996). First, women bear the major responsibility for the care of the children and the home despite the advances in "women's liberation." In many families, the husband's career takes priority over the wife's career. Second, women generally earn less money than men in comparable positions. According to some researchers, married women earn, on average, only 50 percent as much as married men. Third, with the passage of no-fault divorce in the 1970s divorce settlements are often designed to provide a clean break. In many cases women are expected to become self-sufficient even when they haven't developed their careers to the same extent as their husbands. Finally, child support payments, even with passage of the federal Child Support Enforcement Amendments of 1984, are not large enough to help many mothers support their children. And in many cases women are not awarded child support by the courts. According to Chambers (1997) 44 percent of all single mothers were not awarded child support by the courts in 1991.

A change in family structure does not always change a family's socioeconomic status. In some cases following divorce a mother and her children drop into a lower socioeconomic status. However, some single mothers were living in poverty before a divorce or death occurred. According to Bane (1986) approximately

65 percent of all African-American single mothers were poor before a divorce. For white women the number was 25 percent. Finding a job does not necessarily help a single mother get off welfare either (Zill et al. 1991; Schein 1995). The low level of women's wages, especially in jobs that require little education, does not help lift a single mother out of poverty. According to a report by the U.S. General Accounting Office (1991) single mothers are more likely than other employees to experience layoffs, they receive fewer fringe benefits, and they pay higher expenses for child care. Even with full-time jobs many single mothers will remain at or below the poverty line, the report's authors believe. Single-mother families, more often than single-father families, must weigh the economic benefits of work against the costs of child care, health benefits, transportation to and from work, role strain, and loss of time with their children (Garfinkel and McLanahan 1986).

In an essay reviewing the literature on single mothers McLanahan and Booth (1989) explored the problems that single mothers face, as well as prospects for their future. They found that single-mother families have little economic security, primarily because of the low earning power of women in general and single mothers in particular, the lack of child support from nonresidential fathers, and limited public benefits. Reviewing the literature, they also found that children from single-mother families are more likely to be poor and to become single parents themselves than are children from two-parent families.

Today's consumer-oriented economy may also play a role in family finances. Some researchers have found that many families today have a difficult time supporting themselves without two wage earners. In fact, over one-third of all two-parent families would be considered poor if both spouses did not work (Coontz 1997). The higher poverty rate of single-parent families is not caused so much by divorce or unwed motherhood but rather by the increasing requirement for more than one income per household (Gowan, Desimore, and McKay 1995). Other researchers (Lichter and Eggebeen 1994) agree that most poverty is caused by the changing earnings structure rather than a changing family structure.

Challenges Facing Single-Parent Families

Many single parents are faced with several problems that create stress in their lives. Societal attitudes toward single parents are not always positive. Single parents often live with the economic insecurity that can occur when they have a low-paying job or no job at all, as well as when—in cases of divorce—the payment of child support by the ex-spouse is unreliable. Finding a job may be difficult, especially one that provides flexibility as well as fringe benefits for the single parent. Quality child care is often hard to find, and in some cases impossible to afford when a secure well-paying job cannot be found. For many single parents getting off of welfare means finding a job, often low paying, which may not provide health insurance for the parent or the children. If financial resources are not reliable, single parents live with the real fear of being evicted from their housing if they cannot pay the rent. This section discusses several of the major stressors in the lives of single parents.

Societal Attitudes toward Single Parents

Early customs and practices regarded women as male property and marriage as the ideal goal for all women (and men). Women were expected to stay home and care for the home and the family. In most cases marriage was the only rite of passage into adulthood for women. Women were encouraged to marry by all major social institutions—the family, church, school, and community. Most women were discouraged from working. Young women who became pregnant while unmarried were quickly shuttled off to live with distant relatives or to a home for unwed mothers. They were often forced to give up their babies for adoption.

Even today a conflict exists in attitudes toward women and their role in caring for the family. Women in middle- and upper-income families are often encouraged to stay home with their children, especially when the children are young. They are viewed by many people as shirking their responsibilities if they go back to work too soon after their children are born or if they spend too much time at work. When President Richard Nixon vetoed the Comprehensive Child Development Act of 1971, which would have provided day care for all children, he proclaimed that government policies that encourage mothers to work outside the home threaten the existence of the traditional family. He believed that any government policy that encouraged the decline of the family would also encourage a breakdown of morality (Mulroy 1988). On the other hand poor mothers are encouraged, often pushed, into finding work, even when their children are still infants. In their case work and income are more important than caring for their children.

When poor single mothers go to work, they may leave their children alone at home, without any adult supervision, either because they cannot find someone to care for their children or because child care is too expensive and they cannot afford to pay for it out of their salaries. They are viewed as neglectful, but are really caught in a tough situation: they cannot afford to pay for child care but they need to work. The jobs many poor single mothers can find pay only minimum wage, making it difficult to support a family. According to Elizabeth Mulroy: "When the single mother then stays home to provide full-time supervision of her children and needs to rely on public assistance in order to do it, she is branded as unmotivated" (Mulroy 1988, 5).

While many people believe that single mothers are not capable of raising children—especially boys—without a father in the home, single fathers are usually viewed sympathetically. Some fathers receive a great deal of help, including suggestions for meals, help with shopping, and support with housekeeping decisions. On the other hand, society still views a single father with some fear and concern; the issue of child sexual abuse has not gone away for these men. Many people cannot understand why a man would want to care for children unless he has some ulterior motive. These attitudes are slowly changing as more men are caring for their children successfully.

Financial Problems

The most common, and perhaps the most profound, effect of growing up in a single-parent family is financial. Following a divorce, especially in families in which both parents work, loss of one parent's income can have devastating effects. Some of these effects include a lowered standard of living, loss of home and friends, and loss of status in the community. The death of a parent can also have an immediate financial impact on a family. But families don't have to experience a death or divorce in order to find themselves in financial trouble. Never-married mothers or fathers can also experience financial difficulty in trying to raise their children.

Several researchers have examined the problems, specifically financial problems, that many single mothers face (Hanson 1986; Mednick 1987). Many single parents, primarily single mothers, rely on government support or help from family and friends to survive. According to a study conducted by Hao (1995) approximately 35 percent of young single mothers received AFDC payments in 1985. Ellwood (1988) found that over 75 percent of all poor female-headed families in 1984 received AFDC payments. The amount of time these families typically spend receiving some type of government support varies widely. However, according to most estimates between 48 and 69 percent of all AFDC participants receive benefits for less than two years (Harris 1993).

In addition to cash payments from the government or financial help from family or friends, some single mothers find other ways to ease their monetary woes. For example, single mothers and their children may move in with other family members to save money. Mothers may depend on other family members for child care. Several studies have shown that many mothers receiving AFDC must supplement their government payments with private support in order to support their children (Uehara 1990; Edin 1991). Using a national survey Schoeni (1994) found that in 1987 28 percent of single-mother families received financial support and transfers from family and friends and 39 percent received help in the form of household work or child care from friends or relatives.

Using data from the Panel Study of Income Dynamics, McLanahan and Sandefur (1994) examined poverty rates between single-parent and two-parent families. In general single-parent families are more likely to be living in poverty than two-parent families, no matter what the race of the family. They found that 26.5 percent of single-parent families lived in poverty, compared with only 5.3 percent of two-parent families. Broken down by race 13.6 percent of single-parent white families lived in poverty compared with only 3.6 percent of two-parent families. For African-American families, the numbers are 48.8 percent and 19.3 percent, respectively. When the researchers examined parental education and family structure, they found that 40 percent of single-parent families in which the parent had less than a high school education lived in poverty, while only 12.1 percent of two-parent families in which the parents had less than high school education lived in poverty. By comparison 14.4 percent of white single parents with only a high school education lived in poverty, while only 3.1 percent of two-parent families with only a high school education lived in poverty.

Employment

Both single mothers and single fathers may have a difficult time trying to balance the demands of work and raising a family alone. Mothers and fathers often experience these challenges in different ways.

Single motherhood often limits a woman's ability to pursue a career. Unless a single mother has developed a career before having children or before ending a marriage, she may have trouble balancing work and the care of the children. Single mothers do not usually have the resources, both economic and emotional, to help them cope with the problems that working mothers face. If a mother has been supported by a husband who expected her to stay at home and not develop a career, she may not have any job experience. This lack of experience severely limits her ability to find a job that will pay enough to help her support her family.

Single fathers face other challenges. For many single fathers who have devoted their time to building successful careers, becoming a single father can create many different difficulties. Jobs may require overtime, travel, and other activities that are easy to accomplish for a man whose wife is available to take care of the children. But these job requirements are more difficult to deal with for a single father. Single fathers may find that their jobs are not flexible. Overtime and travel may still be required. Time off for children's visits to the doctor, dentist, and other appointments may not be readily available, except in emergencies. Many fathers have found that they have had to change jobs in order to take care of their new responsibilities as single parents.

Child Care

Tied in with the problems that single parents, especially single mothers, face in finding employment is finding child care for the children. Not only do mothers have to find child care, they must find affordable child care. Single fathers also may have trouble finding child care, but many single fathers are more able to afford such care than single mothers.

Single parents, especially those living in poverty, may not be able to afford adequate child care. Jobs may not pay enough to justify the need for the parent to work. Child care may not be available close to the parent's home or workplace. Some single parents find that their social support systems can help them with child care, while others find that although they receive some types of help from family and friends, these people are not able to help out with child care (Ercole 1988; Kurdek 1988; Thompson and Ensminger 1989). Some parents feel that the only way to work is to leave their children home alone.

Many researchers and other experts believe that providing affordable quality child care is the most important factor in helping single mothers get off and stay off of welfare. Kristin Moore, an expert in adolescent pregnancy and childbearing, believes that high-quality preschool child care and education are the most important factors in reducing the number of single mothers on welfare (Ludtke 1997).

Health Care

For single parents living in poverty health care can be a major problem. Under the new welfare program guidelines passed in 1996 these families will eventually lose their government-provided health care coverage, even though many of the jobs that are available to them do not provide health care coverage.

These single parents are under added stress. In addition to being anxious about supporting their children, they may be depressed over their situation. Their diets may not be as healthy as they should be. Living in poor neighborhoods may also expose them to more physical dangers. Many of the stresses experienced by these parents can lead to physical problems, thus increasing the need for health care that is unavailable to them.

According to Angel and Angel (1993) the most compelling mental health threat that single mothers face is poverty. In addition to lack of financial resources, poverty also means

> social and political powerlessness. The poor are not only denied many of the basic necessities of life and most of its luxuries but they often lack the basic sources of self-esteem. Many of the roles that single mothers occupy, like unwed mother, welfare recipient, or charity case, are stigmatized. They are not the sort of roles that are likely to enhance one's sense of mastery and control over one's environment. Single mothers must often bear the burden of such stigma alone. (p. 146)

Many of the health disadvantages that children face are related to poverty and limited accessibility to health care, especially preventive health care services and those services that focus on mental and emotional care. Minority children and the poor are more likely to experience illness as a result of infectious diseases and environmental toxins, such as lead (Children's Defense Fund 1990). Tuberculosis rates are rising in poor and minority communities, along with growing rates of AIDS (Children's Defense Fund 1991). Young pregnant unmarried mothers are less likely to seek out prenatal health care, especially in the early stages of their pregnancy. Many single parents do not even think about preventive care; they can only respond to emergencies.

Housing

Single parents often have difficulty finding suitable housing. Many reasons exist for these problems. Lack of an adequate income is the primary reason for most single parents, especially single mothers. In a study of 73 single mothers from a variety of backgrounds and situations Mulroy (1995) found that women were usually on the margin of the housing market, frequently uprooted unless they were financially independent and thus able to afford housing. Mulroy found that the major factors contributing to these housing problems included irregular, insufficient, or nonexistent payments of child support; frequent moves in attempting to maintain consistent employment; and physical or emotional abuse from a live-in partner that led them to search for alternative housing.

Single parents generally rent, rather than own, their living space (Holme 1985; Harrison 1983). They are also more likely to be homeless than two-parent families. According to Mulroy (1995) two-thirds of single parents rented housing compared with only one-third of two-parent families. In a study conducted by Dreier and Applebaum (1992) in 1989 over half of all poor renters paid at least 50 percent of their incomes for housing. Specifically, the typical single mother is paying approximately 70 percent of her income for rental housing. This expense often pushes single mothers into sharing housing with other family members or other single-parent families, creating overcrowded living arrangements.

Young single mothers appear to be the worst off in terms of housing, while single fathers and widows live in better homes. Divorced and separated mothers find themselves somewhere in the middle (Holme 1985). Other studies in England have estimated that between 25 and 33 percent of single parents share their housing with other adults (Millar 1987; Pascall 1986). Young never-married women often tend to live with their parents (Leonard and Speakman 1986; Walker 1988).

When single mothers cannot find affordable housing in areas that offer promising employment opportunities, they often find themselves excluded from these opportunities because they either cannot afford the transportation required to get to these jobs or public transportation is not available to them. Some public and subsidized housing programs do exist to help ease the burden of rent on poor families, but they have not been very effective, according to Mulroy (1995). Most low-income families do not live in public housing or receive any type of federal, state, or local rent subsidy, according to a report issued by the U.S. Bureau of the Census (1991).

Single parents living in the inner city are not the only ones who experience problems with housing. Separated and divorced mothers must often cope with the problems encountered in moving their families to a new home. Discrimination by banks and other lending institutions may keep single mothers from owning their own homes, even if their incomes are sufficient to make the loan payments. State and federal government policy makers may make decisions that affect the availability of affordable housing in good neighborhoods. Zoning regulations in suburban areas may not allow affordable rental and home ownership opportunities. The decisions that judges make in property settlements can also affect the housing situation of single mothers (and fathers), depending on which spouse is awarded possession of the family home and whether that spouse is able to afford the home mortgage payments (Mulroy 1995).

Homelessness among Single-Parent Families

Families with children are the fastest growing category of the homeless; they constitute approximately 40 percent of all people who become homeless (Shinn and Weitzman 1996). In rural areas the proportion of homeless families is probably higher; researchers believe that families, single mothers, and children make up the largest homeless population in rural areas (Vissing 1996), contrary to the popular belief that most homeless are single men or women who are drunks or drug users.

Several studies document the problems of homeless families and examine family homelessness as a social problem (Bassuk 1991; McChesney 1990; Weinrub and Buckner 1993). Letiecq and her colleagues (1996) studied the social support systems of 92 homeless and 115 permanently housed low-income single mothers and their children. They found that homeless mothers, compared with permanently housed single mothers, had significantly less contact with friends and relatives, had fewer people they could count on to help them with child care and other needs, and believed that their social networks were less helpful in raising their children.

Some studies have shown that many of the single-mother families had been receiving AFDC benefits when they arrived at the homeless shelter. Even though they were receiving AFDC benefits, many of these families found themselves below the poverty line (91 percent of those studied in Massachusetts, 82 percent in Los Angeles, and 89 percent in Atlantic City) (Steinbock 1995).

The effects of homelessness on children can be serious. Homeless children tend to have more physical ailments, psychological problems, developmental delays, and problems in school than children who have a home. Single mothers often lose their ability to nurture their children in homeless shelters. The children of some homeless families may be at risk for being placed in foster care. Some studies have indicated that homeless women with children are more likely to be substance abusers than women who have some type of housing available to them.

Mothers with substance abuse problems are more likely to see their children placed in foster care, until they get help and overcome their addictions and other problems. Other mothers, especially homeless ones, may also have their children placed in foster care if they are unable to care for them. The Stewart B. McKinney Homeless Assistance Amendments Act of 1990 attempted to prevent foster care placement by authorizing demonstration grants that would encourage cooperation between child welfare agencies and local housing assistance programs. Other federal laws have also attempted to break the link between homelessness and foster care. These laws include the Adoption Assistance and Child Welfare Act of 1980, the Family Preservation Act of 1992, and the Adoption and Safe Families Act of 1997. All of these efforts help to keep homeless families together, but one of the best ways to prevent foster care placement of homeless children is to make sure that more affordable housing is available to families living in poverty, according to Steinbock (1995).

Domestic Violence

Acts of domestic violence also lead to the creation of single-parent families, most often single-mother families. Women who leave a violent home environment with their children face a multitude of problems, which usually hit with sudden certainty. They must quickly find a place to live, a source of income, and a way to put their lives back together. Finding affordable housing is often quite difficult for a woman and her children, especially when the woman has left an abusive situation with nothing but her children and the clothes on her back. According to a 1990 study by the Ford Foundation, approximately 50 percent of homeless women and children were escaping abusive homes or spouses (Zorza 1991). Other researchers believe this number is between 25 and 35 percent (National Coalition for the Homeless 1997).

When a woman leaves an abusive spouse and decides to seek a divorce, she faces a legal system that does not always favor her. The issues of child custody and visitation are among the most controversial topics in family law when applied to families involved in domestic violence. Many researchers and policy makers believe that abuse of the mother is not always considered as seriously as it should be when determining custody. For example, Berry (1995) cites courts in Illinois and New York that have actually "ruled that a man cannot be considered an unfit parent 'merely' because he has murdered the mother of his children!" (p. 153). Berry suggests that while courts focus on what action is in the best interests of the child, a violent parent is not considered unless the violence is directed at the child.

Courts in many states believe that joint custody is the best solution for the family; both parents should play an active role in raising their children. However, in cases of domestic violence, the battered spouse is left to convince the judge that it is not in the best interest of the child to award joint custody. Many people believe that joint custody is not a good idea in cases of domestic violence. When the father has been the batterer, the mother and children can encounter major problems with joint custody. The women may be viewed as weak and unfit to be good parents. Berry (1995) suggests that many women find themselves in a paradoxical situation. If the mother protected the child from the violence, the judge could decide that the child was not harmed by the violence and therefore award joint custody. However, if the child was present during the violence, the judge could ask the mother why she didn't protect the child from viewing the violence.

However, attitudes are changing. Most states have enacted laws that require courts to consider domestic violence when making custody decisions. The U.S. Congress in 1990 passed a resolution that requires "each state to create a presumption in its law that spouse abusers should not get custody of their children, but only supervised visitation" (Berry 1995, 156). Judges may award sole custody to the mother, at least until the father completes a treatment program and shows "that he can obey the law, refrain from further violence, and follow court orders" (Berry 1995, 156).

The Legal System and Single Parents

Single parents often feel abused by the legal system in the United States. Both single mothers and single fathers, especially following a divorce, may believe that justice was not done. Access to the courts, division of property, alimony, child support, and custody are issues of concern to single parents following a divorce. For other single parents, the desire to adopt a child leads to an encounter with the legal system.

Custody

Custody of the children can be a problem for many parents following a divorce. There are two components of custody: legal and physical. Legal custody provides the authority to make major decisions concerning the children, including what school the children will attend, what medical care they will receive, and what religion they will follow. Physical custody concerns the right to raise the children, that is, to care for the children on a daily basis. Both legal and physical custody are divided into two categories: sole and joint. Sole custody assigns one parent exclusive rights; joint custody requires that parents share responsibility. Therefore, sole legal custody authorizes one parent to make all the major decisions for the children; this parent becomes the legal guardian of the children. Under joint legal custody, both parents share authority for all major decisions. Sole physical custody gives the daily child care responsibilities to one parent; the children usually live with this parent. Joint physical custody parents usually share the day-to-day responsibilities of raising their children. In some states joint custody is presumed or preferred, that is, joint physical custody is automatically decreed, unless it is proved to be not in the best interests of the child. Some states make it optional, while others allow a judge to award joint physical custody even though both parents do not agree that it is in the best interests of the child.

When sole custody is awarded, mothers are most often the ones who receive custody. Many researchers estimate that mothers receive custody approximately 90 percent of the time, and most of the time it is determined by agreement of the two parents, not by a court order (Mnookin et al. 1990; Dowd 1997). A court is required to enter a custody decree when parents divorce; however, when parents agree in advance on custody issues, the court will usually ratify such an agreement.

When custody is contested, fathers are often successful in attaining custody of their children (Polikoff 1982). When fathers do not receive custody, many of them give up their relationship with their children, usually within two years of a divorce according to Czapanskiy (1989). Furstenberg and Cherlin (1991) conducted a study of fathers' relationships with their children following divorce, and found that half of the children had not seen their fathers in the past 12 months, 17 percent saw their fathers from less than once a month to more than once a year, and that another 17 percent saw their fathers at least once a week. When fathers give up their relationship with their children, not only do they stop seeing them, but they also frequently stop making child support payments (Dowd 1997; Pearson and Thoennes 1988).

In some cases custodial parents are forbidden to move out of state, even to advance a career or improve the family's financial situation, so that the noncustodial parent can continue to have meaningful contact with the children. Witnesses appearing before the New York Task Force on Women in the Courts in the mid-1980s testified that women have a difficult time receiving permission from the courts to move out of state with their children for job opportunities. Courts believe that moving out of state will lessen the opportunities that fathers have for visitation. For example, in 1983 a female attorney from Louisiana wanted to move with her daughter out of state for a position with the National Labor Relations Board, a government agency. The judge claimed that she was more interested in her career than in her family and awarded custody to the father (Mulroy 1988).

However, courts are more likely to allow fathers to move for work-related reasons (Mulroy 1988). Judges, along with the rest of society, still view fathers as needing to support a family financially, while mothers are more likely to be viewed as providing nurture and emotional support to the children. Along similar lines fathers who do not have custody of their children are not required by the courts to remain in the community in which their children live in order to spend time with them.

Child Support

Most literature concerning child support focuses on mothers with custody because mothers have historically been the ones granted custody, unless the mother was believed to be unfit. Prior to this time mothers generally received a support award by the courts because they were the primary caregivers and maternal custody made sense.

One of the major problems facing single parents, primarily single mothers, is the inability to support themselves and their children. Receiving adequate and timely child support payments can go a long way toward relieving this situation. Because mothers are still most frequently given primary custody of the children following divorce, fathers are generally the ones who are required to pay child support to the mothers. However, fathers who have been awarded custody of their children may also have trouble when the mothers refuse to pay child support or do not pay enough. In most cases, however, the father is assumed to be the one paying support and most studies that have been conducted have focused on delinquent fathers rather than delinquent mothers.

Most research concerning child support has found that women who are awarded child support have a more difficult time financially than men who are awarded child support. In general, most men have developed careers and earn more money than women do; many women have stayed home to care for the children or have found work to supplement family income, never intending to have to support themselves and their children. Even though more mothers than fathers have difficulty supporting themselves and their children, custodial fathers can encounter financial problems.

States began passing no-fault divorce laws in 1970. Before these laws were passed, one spouse had to prove that the other spouse was somehow "at fault" in causing the marital breakdown before a judge could grant a divorce. Fault could include such things as infidelity, abandonment, and physical or mental abuse. Often spouses who mutually wanted their freedom had to invent some reason for their marriage to end, even though neither had done anything "wrong." Believed to simplify divorce cases, these no-fault laws ended the practice of perjured testimony and other false evidence that was engendered by the need to prove one spouse at fault in order to dissolve the marriage. While these laws helped solve many of the problems associated with obtaining a divorce, they also hurt many custodial parents, usually women. When one spouse wanted to leave the marriage, he or she could claim the marriage was irretrievably damaged. The other spouse in effect had no way to refute this. Thus, a divorce could be granted merely on the wish of one spouse alone. Prior to no-fault, a spouse unwilling to have the marriage end could at least bargain for a better financial settlement by threatening to put the spouse wanting a divorce to his or her proof—that is, make the moving spouse prove the grounds or "fault" for a divorce. This was often extremely difficult, as it would frequently involve hiring private detectives, arranging clandestine photography, or presenting strings of witnesses to attest to perceived infidelities, abandonment, alcohol or drug addiction, moral lapses, or cruel treatment by the nonmoving spouse. Thus, if one spouse wanted a divorce and the other did not, the spouse who wanted the divorce often found it advantageous to agree to a generous financial settlement with the other spouse in order to obtain his or her acquiescence in the split, rather than go to the effort and expense of a protracted trial. With the advent of no-fault, however, the nonmoving spouse lost his or her bargaining chips. After all, if one partner to a marriage believes that the union is irretrievably broken, then it is. Because women were usually the ones to gain custody of the children following divorce, they were often the big financial losers. If the woman initiated the divorce by claiming that the marriage was irretrievably broken, she risked appearing irresponsible by throwing away her and her children's "meal ticket" and thus not deserving of financial help. If the man initiated the divorce, the woman had to be content with what the judge believed "fair" to support her and the children. She had lost her leverage to insist on generosity in exchange for granting her husband his freedom with a minimum of court expense.

The federal government has enacted several laws over the years to help custodial parents gain child support payments that have been awarded but that are not being paid. These laws are briefly listed here, and described in more detail in Chapter 4:

- The Uniform Reciprocal Enforcement of Support Act (URESA), passed in 1950, helped custodial parents enforce child support awards across state lines. The Revised Uniform Reciprocal Enforcement Act (RURESA) updated URESA, providing a national procedure for establishing and enforcing child support across state lines. Both of these model laws have been replaced by the Uniform Interstate Family Support Act (UIFSA), which strengthens enforcement across state lines by preventing the second state of residence from changing the amount of support ordered by the home state. These laws are model laws that state legislatures are encouraged to adopt, making them uniform across states.
- In 1975, Title IV-D of the Social Security Act was enacted. A federal agency, the Office of Child Support Enforcement, was established and all states were required to establish similar local offices.
- The Child Support Enforcement Amendments of 1984 attempted to resolve some of the problems created by passage of Title IV-D. States were required to establish mechanisms to enforce child support and to set quantitative guidelines for levels of child support. If states did not establish these guidelines, they would lose federal funding for the AFDC program. The New York State Child Support Commission was set up to investigate the state child support collection system according to the 1984 Amendments. The Commission, in a 1985 study, reported that most complaints about the system revolved around the unwillingness of judges to demand compliance or impose penalties for noncompliance (Mulroy 1988).
- The Family Support Act (1988) focused on improving the services provided for child support enforcement and helping families collect child support payments. Each state was required to develop specific statutory

guidelines to determine child support awards. In fiscal 1988 the federal-state child support enforcement program collected $4.6 billion (Spencer 1989).

- The Child Support Recovery Act of 1992 makes it a federal crime for a noncustodial parent living in one state to fail to pay child support to dependent children living in another state. According to Boumil and Friedman (1996) an estimated 500,000 cases of willfully failing to pay child support could be prosecuted based on this law. However, lack of judicial resources makes it difficult to prosecute guilty parents. In some cases, however, the threat of criminal prosecution may be more effective in getting the parent to pay child support than any other method.
- The Omnibus Budget Reconciliation Act was passed in 1993 and one provision required that states establish expedited or streamlined procedures for determining paternity, or risk curtailment of federal funding.

States have also set up their own services to help custodial parents locate absent parents through a variety of sources, including motor vehicle and property records, employment, and other sources of information. Specific tactics have been developed to collect and distribute child support payments and to get delinquent parents into court. Some states use information from the department of motor vehicles, credit bureau reports, listings of property, and quarterly wage statements from the Internal Revenue Service to help gather appropriate information.

Criminal laws enacted in individual states vary, but generally have similar characteristics. They usually view abandoning a minor child without providing reasonably for his or her support as a crime. Willfully failing to comply with a support order for any reasons other than inability to pay is also considered a crime. Some states consider the failure to comply a misdemeanor; others consider it a felony. Penalties can include fines and/or imprisonment.

Many critics find fault with the current child support system in the United States. Payment of child support has increased in recent years, although it still does not adequately support most children. Passage of the Child Support Enforcement Amendments has helped improve collection, but some question the extent to which payments by noncustodial parents can fully and adequately support children. Stricter enforcement may help some children, but many parents already find it difficult to maintain separate households and fully meet all the needs of their children. According to McLanahan and Sandefur (1994) fewer than one out of three children receive the full amount of support that they are owed, according to the court decree.

Garfinkel (1992), among others, believes that the current child support system is unfair because fathers in similar circumstances are treated differently; child support for some fathers is a large portion of their income, while for others it is a smaller proportion of their income. The system also condones parental irresponsibility because all efforts are not made to collect child support from fathers who are uncooperative.

Women who were never married to their children's fathers have an even harder time collecting child support than women who at one time were married to the father of their children. Fathers who never marry their children's mothers often do not seek visitation and are not willing to pay child support. They did not intend to have a child, they do not want to have a child, and they do not feel obligated to pay child support.

Nichols-Casebolt and Garfinkel (1991) examined the extent to which changes in policy at the federal government level have actually helped in establishing paternity and gaining child support awards for children of unmarried mothers. Their research found that an increasing number of children born outside of marriage are awarded child support. However, they also determined that many children born outside of marriage do not have fathers who have been legally identified and have not been awarded any child support. Some states were better than others in determining paternity. The researchers were uncertain as to why this was so. They speculate that some may view paternity determination as a complicated legal process that is not worth the effort, or some policy makers may believe that children born to unmarried mothers deserve less than children born to married women.

In the past an unmarried mother often turned to welfare, specifically AFDC, to help support her child; few attempts were made to establish paternity or pursue the father for child support. However, today all jurisdictions are required by law to help single mothers establish paternity. Even though this requirement has helped many mothers establish paternity, there is no guarantee that the father will help support the children financially. For example, for the few unwed mothers who received some child support in 1989, the average payment was only $150 per month, according to Boumil and Friedman (1996).

Adoption

Adoption of a child by a single person has become easier over the years, but the practice may still be discouraged in many localities. Legislation in all states now allows a single person to adopt a child, although in the past this practice was banned or discouraged in many jurisdictions. As recently as 1970 adoption agencies did not allow single men and women to adopt children. However, attitudes have changed, contributing to the changes in legislation and to the growing numbers of single adults who are adopting children. According to the National Adoption Information Clearinghouse (1990), approximately 5 percent of all adoptions are by single men and women and 25 percent of all adoptions of children with special needs are by single men or women.

At least three reasons exist for this change in attitude toward single-parent adoptions. First, because of birth control, decisions by unwed mothers to keep their babies, and legalized abortion, there are fewer healthy babies available for adoption. Many of the children available for adoption are older or have disabilities and not very many people are willing to adopt them. However, because many single people who want to adopt a child are willing to adopt an older or disabled child, the adoption agencies have relaxed their rules because their ultimate purpose is to find homes for all the available children. Second, single parents who have adopted have been successful in proving their ability to raise children. Third, single-parent families are becoming more prevalent in society, for reasons already discussed. Because so many children are living in single-parent families, adoption agencies are more willing to allow single parents to adopt.

Some researchers have concluded that single-parent homes may be the best homes for children who are in need of a close relationship with an adult and require plenty of attention. Older children in foster care may be especially suited to being adopted by single parents (Shireman and Johnson 1985). Single mothers often have an easier time adopting a child than single fathers. Agencies are more likely to question a man's motive in wanting to adopt a child. They may ask the man questions about his sexuality, motives, and living arrangements. However, attitudes are changing. More fathers are gaining custody of their children following divorce and men are becoming more comfortable in taking care of children. These changes, which have contributed to society's changing attitude toward single fathers, will probably help increase the number of adoptions by single fathers.

Many single people find that adopting a foreign child is easier in many ways than adopting a child in the United States. Some U.S. agencies do not want to allow a single person to adopt a child. Others only have older or disabled children available for single-parent adoption. So single parents may find that foreign adoption agencies are more likely to have young healthy children available for adoption. However, most people find this route expensive and time-consuming. The cost of a foreign adoption also may be higher, especially if travel is required to complete the adoption or if an extended stay is necessary. The language barrier and cultural differences may also be a challenge, especially for a single parent with no one else to help.

Contemporary Concerns Regarding Single Parents

Single parents are the focus of many discussions, conferences, and political debates. The issues surrounding single parenthood and the problems created by single-parent families are described almost on a daily basis in the media and by those in public office.

Single parents are blamed for a variety of society's ills, from child delinquency to the proliferation of youth gangs. The increasing number of single-parent families is blamed for contributing to the demise of the traditional family—for suggesting to many people that the two-parent family is not necessary for a child's healthy development. Single parents are criticized for not spending enough time with their children, for not knowing what their children are doing, and for not being able to control their children. Unmarried mothers, especially teenagers, are blamed for the growing numbers of single-mother families on welfare. Single mothers are criticized for being immoral, for having sex without marriage, and for wanting to keep a child who will not have a father. Gay and lesbian single parents are seen as endangering a child's sexual and moral development. This section describes the major issues and explores reasons why the topic of single parents is of major concern to many people today.

Increasing Number of Single Parents

American society, like most cultures, highly values the two-parent family. "Family values" is the rallying cry of many groups that want to strengthen the family, encourage mothers to stay home with young children, and promote activities for the entire family. Many advocates of reviving and strengthening the two-parent family believe that communities will be strengthened by supporting two-parent families. Encouraging premarital counseling, increasing maternity and paternity leave, and improving child care will strengthen two-parent families, along with discouraging out-of-wedlock births and divorce, according to these groups. Many people and groups also believe that mothers should stay home to raise children and they advocate for policies that will encourage this practice (Etzioni 1993; Anderson and Davey 1995).

Most people will agree that encouraging two-parent families is a worthy and important goal. Society does benefit from two-parent families and what they are able to provide to their children. However, it is not always possible for a child to have two parents. The increasing number of divorces is contributing to growing numbers of single-parent families. More single people are becoming interested in having children but do not want to get married or cannot find someone they want to marry.

The double standard that encourages mothers who are financially able to stay home with their children, while forcing mothers on welfare to go to work will not easily change. Society still values the care and nurturance that a mother can provide to a child, unless society is required to help support that child. Then nurturance is not seen as important as requiring the mother to work. Many researchers believe the "family values" movement and others are attempting to restore the two-parent, male-headed family, to give men back the ultimate power in the family. By forcing many women to find a job and leave their children at home, some people suggest that many women will be less likely to have children without the benefit of a father and will be more likely to marry, thus restoring the two-parent family.

The White House Working Group on the Family was appointed by President Reagan to explore the reasons for the decline in the two-parent family. In a 1986 report the Working Group blamed government welfare and other public assistance programs for this decline and the decline in "family values." The

White House group believed that by shrinking social welfare benefits, the "two-parent, male-headed heterosexual family" would be restored. "Deprived of cash assistance, women would be less likely to turn to public aid as an alternative to work or as an alternative to marriage and economic dependence on men" (Abramovitz 1996, 350–351).

It will be difficult to stop the growth of single-parent families. As the numbers grow, society is becoming more accepting of single-parent families. Many people see this growth as a fact of life, something that cannot be changed overnight. While the goal may be to have fewer single-parent families, the reality may be harder to achieve. A movement to encourage two-parent families may help slow the growth somewhat, as some two-parent families are working harder to stay together, but the momentum will be difficult to stop. Moving many single mothers and their children off the welfare rolls will not force or encourage many of these women to marry. They will just be forced to make different plans for their own and their children's survival.

Father Absence

Many people have written or commented about the state of fatherhood in America today. Some blame fathers who walk out on their family responsibilities as the main cause of the increasing number of single parents today. In *Fatherless America*, David Blankenhorn writes that "fatherlessness is the most harmful demographic trend of this generation" (p. 1). He believes that fatherlessness has contributed to many social problems, including crime, adolescent pregnancy, and domestic violence.

Historically, father absence was caused primarily by the death of the father. According to Uhlenberg (1978) in 1900 only slightly over one-half of all children reached the age of 15 with both of their parents still alive. In 1977 more than 90 percent of children reached the age of 15 with both of their parents alive.

Growing numbers of fathers are leaving their families to fend for themselves. Whitehead (1993) notes that in "1976 less than half as many fathers as in 1957 said that providing for children was a life goal. The proportion of working men who found marriage and children burdensome and restrictive more than doubled in the same period" (p. 58). Whitehead believes that today many people are more interested in themselves than in others and their pleasure and happiness come first. For fathers this may mean that it is easier to leave a pregnant partner or a spouse with children than to take responsibility for them. Some fathers may believe that their children are better off without them, while others may believe that they are better off without their children.

Blankenhorn (1995) suggests that a culture of fatherlessness exists because all human societies encounter problems with fatherhood. Most societies have established legal requirements and moral encouragement for fathers to maintain a connection with their children because most men do not volunteer for fatherhood. Laws have been passed in the United States that require states to develop ways to determine paternity as well as require fathers to provide financial support to their children. Groups such as the Promise Keepers encourage men to take back their responsibilities for their families. The Promise Keepers believe that men have given up their role as providers and head of their families for the more egalitarian role of cospouse and coparent. This abdication of their role has contributed to the problems found in society today and men are encouraged to provide moral guidance and leadership to their families.

Moral Issues

Many people in the United States as well as other countries believe that single women should not be having sex. And women who have sex outside of marriage definitely should not be "allowed" to have children. These women, many believe, cannot be good parents because they are not setting a good example for their children. If a woman becomes pregnant without benefit of marriage, she is viewed as irresponsible and unfit to be a mother because of her immorality.

During the 1992 presidential campaign one of the major topics debated was the lack of morality in today's children. Vice President Dan Quayle claimed that young people, especially those in the inner cities, were becoming increasingly desperate due to a crisis in family values. Single-parent families were being glorified in the media, for example, on the television show *Murphy Brown*, which some suggested promoted the view that children did not need fathers. Today fathers have virtually disappeared from the poorest neighborhoods throughout the country and gang leaders are becoming the primary role models for young boys (Mack 1997).

Barbara Dafoe Whitehead (1993), a family researcher, claims that one of the many trends endangering children is illegitimacy. The growing divorce rate among parents with young children is also a factor. She believes parents, primarily many baby boomers, are focused more on individualism and self-realization and tend to put themselves and their needs above the needs of their children. These parents are not teaching their children about good morals and values.

The Christian Coalition, along with several other similar groups, has played a major role in the growing attempts to put the country back on what they believe to be a "moral" course. They frequently look to legislators to help improve Americans' morals. The Coalition was one of the major groups to propose that legislators should make the concept of personal responsibility the central theme in welfare reform. A common belief is that, by providing welfare to single mothers and their children, the government is encouraging single motherhood, illegitimacy, and immorality. Conservatives believe that welfare is the cause of many of the country's social problems, including the increasing dependency and illegitimacy that is "rampant in our cities" (Stefancic and Delgado 1996, 92). According to Rector (1992) the provision of welfare erodes morality, which leads to a deterioration of social norms and ethics. Many people believe that eliminating government-provided welfare benefits would force many women to find husbands to marry and support them and their children and would encourage others to think twice before having a baby without being married. In either case, according to these advocates, the number of single mothers would decrease and moral standards would be strengthened.

Welfare Mothers

Single mothers, the welfare system, and the relationship between the two are among the most debated topics in the United States today. Welfare programs are said to reinforce patriarchal norms, perpetuate poverty, encourage promiscuity, promote laziness, and lower general standards of morality. This section explores the debates concerning single mothers and welfare.

Society's expectations have changed since public assistance of single mothers was first instituted. Up through the 1960s and 1970s most mothers with young children did not work outside the home and were not expected to find jobs. This attitude applied to both married and unmarried mothers. Therefore, a public welfare program that allowed single mothers to stay home and care for their children was not controversial. However, since the early 1980s attitudes toward women in the workplace have changed. More women began working at that time and most Americans believed that it was appropriate for mothers to be working outside the home. As a result a public welfare program that allowed single mothers to stay home became controversial (Reischauer 1989).

In recent debates concerning welfare's effect on helping families get back on their feet and alternative ways to help families survive poverty, many people believe that too many women are having children just to receive additional welfare benefits. The common image of a young black woman with no husband, no education, and no job does not represent the majority of welfare recipients (see Chapter 4 for statistics concerning welfare and single families). In fact, according to many researchers in the field, no evidence exists to show a relationship between unmarried pregnancies and participation in welfare. Stephanie Coontz maintains that the belief that "welfare benefits cause unwed motherhood, especially among African Americans, is one of the most ill-founded notions in contemporary political discourse" (Coontz 1997, 89). Coontz noted that 76 leading researchers on welfare and unmarried childbearing recently issued a public statement claiming that few studies have found any kind of correlation at all between women receiving welfare and unwed motherhood. In a report on unmarried childbearing to the U.S. Congress in 1995 Robert A. Moffitt of Johns Hopkins University explained that the welfare system has not been responsible for increases in unmarried childbearing. He also said that in those cases in which welfare has produced an increase in childbearing, it has done so more among white women than among African-Americans (Ludtke 1997). According to Rank (1994) the typical woman who is receiving welfare has 1.9 children; this number is fewer than for women not on welfare. The longer that the woman stays on welfare, he found, the less likely she is to have additional children.

Welfare does provide many benefits, both to single mothers and to society. The availability of welfare benefits helps young single mothers decide whether to live with their parents or set up their own households, helps women in bad marriages decide whether to obtain a divorce, helps women refuse marriage to the father of their child(ren), and prevents some young women from placing their babies for adoption, or aborting the fetus. Most research on welfare participation does support two findings: First, welfare participation is very fluid; many women and their families move on and off welfare. Many stay on welfare for only a short time. Second, most welfare recipients want to work and many of them do find work (Harris 1997).

Several studies have shown that single mothers turn to public welfare when they are divorced, when they are unmarried and have a child, or when they experience some other financial crisis (Bane and Ellwood 1983; Duncan 1984; Blank 1989). Some studies have demonstrated that single mothers spend an average of two years on welfare before they are able to find a job or get married (Bane and Ellwood 1983; Harris 1991, 1993; Fitzgerald 1991; O'Neill, Bassi, and Wolf 1987). Other studies have found that young unmarried mothers stay on welfare for longer periods of time and are more likely to return to welfare than are unmarried women who became mothers when they were older (Bane and Ellwood 1983, 1994; Ellwood 1986). Ellwood (1986) found that mothers who had never been married received AFDC benefits for an average of 9.3 years, compared with divorced mothers who received these benefits for an average of 4.9 years. London (1996) studied the difference in the participation rates in the AFDC program between divorced and never-married mothers. She found that never-married mothers participate at a higher rate than divorced mothers, and that never-married mothers are more likely to need help from AFDC for a longer period of time than divorced mothers.

Harris (1993) examined the extent to which work can provide a way to get off welfare. She found that over time, half of all single mothers on welfare have some contact with work and the labor market. These women appear to get off welfare either by finding a job that pays enough money to get them off welfare, or by combining work and welfare until they are able eventually to move off welfare through additional work experience or training opportunities. She also found that, for poor single mothers, investing in an education or training provides greater benefits than investing in work experience. In a later study Harris (1996) looked at single mothers who had moved off welfare and then back again. She examined the processes by which they moved from welfare dependence to independence and back to dependence. She discovered that women found themselves back on welfare most often because of social isolation, child care responsibilities, and family economic status. Other researchers have found that single mothers who live in inner cities are more likely to have a difficult time finding jobs that pay living wages than single mothers living in other areas (McLanahan and Garfinkel 1989; Reischauer 1989; Wacquant and Wilson 1989).

Many women with children seek the support of welfare because they are divorced and receiving little or no financial help from their ex-husbands. Other women leave violent homes and find that welfare is their first and only option for survival. Once many of these women get back on their feet, receive education or training and other support, they become productive members of society. U.S. Congresswoman Lynn Woolsey from California found herself on welfare after she and her husband divorced and he refused to pay child support or alimony. Many other women have needed and used welfare only as a temporary measure until they are able to become productive members of society.

Rank (1994) examined the experience of people on welfare in a longitudinal study of approximately 3,000 welfare households in Wisconsin from 1980 to 1988. He found that 30 percent of the respondents were female heads of household (households headed by unmarried women pregnant or with children) and 1 percent were male heads of household. Recipients (female heads) were evenly divided among major metropolitan, other metropolitan, and rural areas. Seventy percent were whites, 23 percent black, and 7 percent were of other races. Among these women 38 percent had never been married, 60 percent were separated or divorced, and the remainder (2 percent) were widowed. The majority had one or two children (69 percent) while 12 percent were pregnant with their first child, 12 percent had 3 children, 6 percent had 4 children, and only 1 percent had 5 or more children. In terms of education, 41 percent had less than 12 years, 48 percent had high school diplomas, and 11 percent had at least some college education. Monthly income ranged from none (77 percent) up to $499 (12 percent), with 11 percent having monthly incomes over $500. Rank found that many female heads of household were unable to find affordable child care that would enable them to go out and find jobs. Most of his respondents were embarrassed when they applied for welfare, disliked being on welfare, and were actively trying to get off of it.

African-American women on welfare, especially single mothers, are especially burdened by negative societal attitudes.

They are often perceived as unable to find men to marry, as willing to bear children without marriage, and as straining the welfare system with hordes of their children. This perception is not true. Many black women live in poverty before they become single mothers (Bane 1985). The growth in black single-mother families is a fairly recent phenomenon, although their poverty has a longer history (Brewer 1988). The economic dynamics that influence the black family are complex. In a study by the Center for the Study of Social Policy (1986) researchers suggest that the increasing number of black single-parent families is a result of the deteriorating economic status of black men. Expectations for marriage for black single mothers are low, thus resulting in diminished opportunities for such women and their children to get off of welfare, according to many researchers (Rank 1987; Wilson 1987; Lichter et al. 1992).

Brewer (1988) suggests that the household arrangements of black families should not be the issue, but rather the prevalent poverty in all black households—even those with an adult male present. "Essentially, black women's poverty is reflective of and complicated by interrelated forces involving culture, politics, and economics, as well as race, gender, and class inequality. Understanding black women's poverty requires a hard look at political and economic changes in urban inner cities, in rural southern towns, and in the marginalization of black men and women from the labor market" (pp. 334–335).

Many researchers have examined the relationship between welfare and racial discrimination. The long-standing belief, described earlier, that many welfare recipients are young black females who have children without being married has promoted many attempts to curb welfare use and abuse. Some of these attempts have bordered on discrimination; others have been outright discriminatory. According to Piven and Cloward (1993) many welfare departments, especially in southern states, developed mechanisms to reduce welfare payments to black mothers. The "employable mother" rule, first passed in Louisiana in 1943, required that mothers with children seven years old or older who were on AFDC were to be denied benefits if the mother could be employed in the fields. Georgia passed a similar law in 1952 that allowed welfare officials to deny benefits to mothers with children over the age of three years if the mothers could find suitable employment. The state also directed officials to deny all benefit applications and to close all existing cases during periods of seasonal employment, when many people were needed to help pick cotton. According to Piven and Cloward the "employable mother" rule "has been more characteristic of states in the South than in the North and it has been applied in a discriminatory fashion against black women: when field hands are needed, Southern welfare officials assume that a black woman is employable, but not a white woman" (Piven and Cloward 1993, 138).

Another welfare rule that has been applied disproportionately against black women is the so-called man-in-the-house rule, in which states have traditionally denied benefits to a mother and children when there is a man living in the house or the woman is associated in any way with a man. While some people argue that these rules chase away men and force them to deny responsibility for their children, others believe that the rule reinforces the need to establish some moral standards for these families (Piven and Cloward 1993). The stories of welfare officials hiding outside of the homes of welfare recipients to watch for a man in the house are well known. A 1968 study of the attempt by the state of Florida to remove families from welfare provides additional evidence of discrimination according to Piven and Cloward (1993). Adverse reports were filed against 14,664 families; 91 percent of these families were black. Over 7,000 families lost their benefits, according to Chilton (1968), even though "all of the eligibility requirements for ADC were met but where one or more of the children was illegitimate . . . or where the welfare worker reported that the mother's past or present conduct of her sex life was not acceptable when examined in light of the spirit of the law" (p. 65).

Other researchers have examined the ways in which the welfare system has reinforced society's attempts to promote the two-parent family and to keep women and children in their place as second-class citizens. Abramovitz (1996) believes social welfare policy is preoccupied with the nuclear family: a male as the wage earner and a female who is a dependent homemaker. She claims that

despite the continued presence of many types of families, social welfare programs have consistently favored the conventional family model that uncritically freezes women and men into rigid gender roles. The rules and regulations of social welfare programs benefit those who live in traditional family structures while penalizing alternative family forms where poor women and women of color tend to predominate. . . . Despite changes in the definition of women's economic role, the family ethic has, throughout history, placed women in the home, subordinate to men. It has made them the guardians of family and community morality, expected them to remain pious and chaste and to tame male sexuality, and defined them as weak and in need of male protection and control. (Abramovitz 1996, 2–3)

In most debates about welfare few people mention the role of the absent fathers and their responsibilities in helping to support their children. Elizabeth A. Mulroy (1995) questions this attitude of ignoring the father's role. She says:

Despite the $34 billion in uncollected child support, nobody is proposing a work requirement for the fathers, only for the mothers. This is the worst kind of misogyny on the part of politicians who are tapping into the outrage many working people feel about the notion that welfare permits people to get something for doing nothing. As usual, the political debate over welfare reform focuses on the women; rarely, if ever, do the politicians talk about the responsibilities of the men who fathered the children on AFDC. (Mulroy 1995, xv)

With the passage of the Personal Responsibility and Work Opportunity Reconciliation Act of 1996, specifically the Temporary Assistance to Needy Families (TANF) program, more single mothers will be forced to find work than under the old AFDC program. Although—on the surface—this program is a good idea, in reality it causes many problems for single mothers. Working single mothers will have to pay for child care, which may be difficult to find in their neighborhoods and also may be expensive. Working single mothers will probably have to pay the costs of transportation to and from work. If they are not on a public transit route or live in a city that does not have a good transportation system, they will have to buy cars. Working mothers may also lose some of their food stamp allotment, as well as any housing subsidy they may be receiving. Finally, a working single mother may lose Medicaid benefits for herself and her children.

Her job may provide health benefits, although most single working mothers will likely receive no health benefits (Edin and Lein 1997). These welfare-to-work programs may get single mothers off welfare and into the work force, but may not provide any real benefits to them. Preliminary statistics from several states indicate that the number of people receiving welfare benefits is decreasing. However, statistics do not indicate what happens to those people going off welfare. Studies will need to be conducted to determine whether this program is successful, not only in moving people off welfare but also in providing real improvement in the lives of the families affected.

Teenage Pregnancy and Motherhood

Years ago a young pregnant girl usually either married the father of the child or gave birth to the child and gave it up for adoption. Today more young pregnant teenagers are deciding to keep their babies but not marry the fathers. This practice is creating a large number of single-parent families, many of which are living in poverty. Researchers, legislators, and other policy makers are concerned about this trend because of its impact on society. The growing number of single mothers who are teenagers contributes to the growing number of people living in poverty, which adds to the number of people applying for welfare and other public benefits.

Teenage pregnancy is seen as a social problem by many people. One of the major problems faced by teenage mothers is poverty. The relationship between being an unwed teenage mother and living in poverty is strong, although whether poverty causes teenage pregnancy or is caused by teenage pregnancy is debatable. Many researchers and policy makers believe that teenage motherhood leads to participation in the welfare system. Others believe that growing up in poverty in deteriorating neighborhoods and attending inferior schools contribute to the growing number of teenage pregnancies.

Several theories exist concerning teenage mothers and welfare. The structural theory of poverty suggests that inner-city teenagers see no reason to postpone having children because their chances of getting good jobs and getting married are poor. These teenagers believe that becoming a mother provides them with social status and psychological fulfillment (Geronimus 1991; Nathanson 1991). Some observers (Wilson 1987 and 1991) agree that marriage is not a viable option for many black women because most young black men have little hope for a promising economic future.

The cultural theory of poverty suggests that adolescent motherhood is indicative of deviant norms and values among the poor. These unwed teenage mothers, their families, friends, and neighbors ignore sanctions against premarital sex, ignore the institution of marriage, and reject the traditional structure of two-parent families (Harris 1997). Unwed teenage mothers rely on public assistance and then teach their children that the same beliefs and behaviors are expected of them.

The "opportunity costs" hypothesis suggests that the family background of the teenage mother affects her opportunities, not her age at childbearing (Geronimus and Korenman 1992). A teenage girl is much more likely to become pregnant if her future marital and employment opportunities are few (Duncan and Hoffman 1990; Lundberg and Plotnick 1990). Some research indicates that the costs of having an out-of-wedlock child are much greater for whites than for blacks (Lundberg and Plotnick 1989).

No one disputes the fact that teenage mothers often face many problems. Research has indicated that teenage mothers

- Are more likely to drop out of school either before or after giving birth.
- Earn less money than teenagers who do not have a child.
- Work less than other teenagers.
- Have less support from the fathers of their children.
- Are more dependent on public welfare as a result of earning less money and receiving less support from their children's fathers.
- Have more children.
- Spend a longer amount of time as single mothers.
- Are more likely to experience unstable marriages when they do get married.

Many people believe that teenagers who are on welfare are more likely to become pregnant and have children than teenagers not growing up in poverty. Most studies, however, demonstrate few if any effects of welfare policies on adolescent pregnancy (Ellwood and Bane 1985). Singh (1986) conducted a state-by-state analysis of adolescent pregnancy and welfare payments and found that "welfare payments to teenage mothers are negatively associated with both black and white teenage birthrates, and higher maximum payments are associated with relatively high abortion levels" (p. 210). Robert Moffitt (1992) reviewed the literature on the relationship between welfare benefits and births to unmarried women. He found that most research found no relationship; that is, women—including teenagers—do not have babies in order to increase their welfare benefits. When examined by race, researchers have found that black women are not likely to have additional children in order to increase benefits, while the effect on white women has been found to be small or nonexistent (Duncan and Hoffman 1990; Harris 1997; Plotnick 1990; Lundberg and Plotnick 1990).

Researchers have shown that even though levels of spending on welfare and other social benefits have been decreasing since the 1970s the percentage of teenagers becoming single parents has increased (Burtless 1994; Danziger and Weinberg 1994). According to a report to the U.S. House of Representatives the average income of a woman with two children and no other source of income was $900 per month in 1972; in 1993 a woman in similar circumstances received $658 (U.S. House of Representatives 1994). Some authors suggest that the increase in the number of teenage single parents is in part caused by fewer teenagers marrying; the number of teenage marriages has dropped significantly since the 1960s (Vinovskis 1988; Moore et al. 1987; Saluter 1994). This drop in teenage marriages makes it appear that the number of teenage girls giving birth while unmarried has grown tremendously.

Corcoran and Kunz (1997) in fact have found that single teenage mothers are not more likely to be economically dependent on welfare in later life. Using data from the Panel Study of Income Dynamics (see Sources of Research Data, below), they studied sisters to investigate the relationship between unmarried teenage births and adult poverty. They found that most of the correlation between teenage out-of-wedlock births and adult poverty and welfare is due to family background and neighborhood factors.

Despite the evidence, many sectors of society are still concerned that the availability of welfare enables girls and young women to stay at home and have children. Welfare reform legislation, most recently the Personal Responsibility and Work Opportunity Reconciliation Act of 1996, is one indication that U.S.

society is less tolerant and supportive of women who have children outside of marriage and need financial and other help to survive. The American values of education, hard work, and marriage are being threatened, according to many observers, especially by teenage mothers. According to Harris (1997) "unwed teenage mothers appear to have broken all the rules, and the public mood is somber. Welfare reform is focused on unwed teenage mothers and seeks to eliminate public assistance to families formed by nonmarital teenage childbearing in the hopes of discouraging future unmarried teens from becoming mothers before adulthood" (p. 7).

Some researchers, such as Hogan and Kitagawa (1985) and Franklin (1988), have found that adolescent girls who have older sisters who have become pregnant while young and unmarried are more likely to become pregnant themselves while still adolescents. Other studies indicate that higher rates of teenage pregnancy are more likely to be found in areas of high unemployment and inferior schools (Billy and Moore 1992; McCrate 1992).

McLanahan and Sandefur (1994) found that girls from single-parent families are more likely than girls from two-parent families to become teenage mothers. Using data from the National Longitudinal Survey of Youth (see Sources of Research Data, below), they found that 22 percent of white, 40 percent of black, and 46 percent of Hispanic teenage girls from single-parent families become pregnant as teenagers. For teenage girls from two-parent families the percentages are smaller: 8 percent of white, 26 percent of black, and 24 percent of Hispanic teenage girls.

Kamerman and Kahn (1988) propose several strategies that are showing promise in preventing teenage pregnancy. The provision of sex education and contraceptive supplies works best when delivered by a variety of programs, including health clinics, private physicians, school medical services, family planning programs, community social service agencies, and pharmacies. School dropout prevention efforts help keep teenagers in school and sometimes less likely to get into trouble. Part-time as well as full-time job opportunities help young people gain valuable experience, provide them with some income, and, when affiliated with school training programs, keep them in school. Mentoring programs sponsored through community agencies offer positive role models and additional adult guidance for children and young adults. Peer-support groups help young people develop higher self-esteem, offer ideas and options for their futures, and work toward community change. These programs can be organized through churches, schools, theaters, and sports, music, and other activity groups. Media campaigns can help change community perceptions of and attitudes toward teenage sex and irresponsible parenting.

Some schools have attempted to keep teenage mothers from receiving academic honors. In the news recently are a school in Ohio that does not allow teen parents to be listed on the honor roll and a school district in Kentucky that recently ruled that two teen mothers cannot join the National Honor Society even though their grade point averages are high enough to join.

Gay and Lesbian Parents

Many homosexual men and lesbian women who make known their sexual orientation following a failed marriage have been awarded custody of their children from that marriage. Public recognition of the ability of gays and lesbians to be good parents to children is growing. However, these parents face some unique problems, as well as the usual difficulties common to all single parents.

Gay and lesbian parents who were divorced from a heterosexual spouse were often denied custody of their children. Reflecting the prevailing view in society, courts typically believed that children needed to live in a heterosexual environment in order to be socialized into the dominant society. Many people believed that children living in gay and lesbian families would exhibit many adjustment and behavioral problems. In some cases judges granted custody to the gay parent only if she or he agreed to refrain from any sexual activities and relationships. Visitation was often controlled in similar ways, allowing no overnight visits, requiring visits to be supervised, and forbidding same-sex partners to be present at the same time as the children (Benkov 1994).

Many countries also restrict the ability of gays and lesbians to become parents. For example, in Victoria, Australia, in vitro fertilization services are denied to lesbian and gay couples as well as to single women. Many U.S. state legislatures (California, Iowa, Maine, Nebraska, New Mexico, Mississippi, Utah, Tennessee, South Carolina, and Washington) have recently introduced legislation that would ban gays and lesbians from adopting children and/or becoming foster parents (Gay and Lesbian Parents Coalition International 1997).

Another concern is that children of gay fathers or lesbian mothers will become gay themselves, that they will choose to emulate their father's or mother's behavior. Research does not support this belief (Green 1978; Miller 1979).

Lesbian Mothers

The number of lesbians given custody of their children following a divorce is increasing. However, many lesbian mothers still lose custody of their children. The court system often finds that same-sex sexual orientation does more damage to the children than an alcoholic or violent father (Chesler 1986). Some lesbian mothers who are awarded custody of their children may not pursue child support payments, because they are afraid of losing custody if a court explores their personal lives (Lewis 1986).

Some studies have shown that lesbian mothers tend to have significantly lower incomes than gay fathers, are less likely to live with a lover, are more likely to tell their children about their sexual orientation themselves, and are more likely to have a difficult time reconciling their gay and parenting roles (Turner, Scadden, and Harris 1989). Some lesbian single mothers have also found that other, heterosexual single mothers are not very supportive (Chesler 1986).

As with unmarried heterosexual women, the number of lesbians who want to have children is growing. A study conducted in 1979 found that most doctors (90 percent) would not artificially inseminate unmarried women. Many of these doctors believed that single women and lesbians were not fit parents and that children needed fathers in order to grow into healthy productive adults.

Gay Fathers

Many segments of society still believe that gay fathers are more likely to sexually molest their children than heterosexual fathers. While the research on gay fathers is limited, earlier research has indicated that gay fathers are no more likely to sexually abuse their children than heterosexual fathers (Geiser 1979; DeFrancis 1976; Richardson 1981).

Several studies have shown that gay fathers tend to be more nurturing and less traditional in paternal attitudes than heterosexual fathers. Gay fathers sometimes appear to be more concerned that outsiders are watching how they parent their children, in large part because of their sexual orientation. However, many men, both gay and heterosexual, feel that society keeps a close eye on their parenting to ensure that their children are safe and are not being neglected or molested (Robinson and Barret 1986).

Effect on Children

Many people believe that children who grow up in single-parent families are less well-off than children from two-parent families. For example, McLanahan and Sandefur (1994) have studied single-parent families for over 10 years and, based on their findings, believe that children who grow up with both their biological parents are better off, in general, than children growing up in single-parent families. Family characteristics and circumstances make little difference; children in single-parent families are worse off "regardless of the parents' race or educational background, regardless of whether the parents are married when the child is born, and regardless of whether the resident parent remarries" (McLanahan and Sandefur 1994, 1).

The benefits that children in two-parent families receive are broader than just what an additional parent can provide. Growing up with a single parent can often deprive a child of economic and community resources, in addition to the loss of parental resources.

Children growing up in single-parent families may be forced to accept adult responsibilities at an early age (Glenwick and Mowrey 1986; Wallerstein 1985). Some researchers, however, do not see this occurrence as negative. Amato (1987) found that children in single-parent families reported higher levels of autonomy; these children were more likely to have assumed many household responsibilities. Amato believes that the skills learned by these children will help them as adults. These children mature more quickly and learn to take care of themselves at an earlier age than other children.

Several studies suggest that single motherhood is associated with less parental involvement in schoolwork, less supervision, and less parental influence (Dornbusch et al. 1985; Hogan and Kitagawa 1985; Matsueda and Heimer 1987; McLanahan et al. 1988; Steinberg 1987). These effects and others of living in a single-parent family are discussed below.

Educational

The research on the effects of growing up in a single-parent family on a child's educational achievement varies widely. Several researchers have indicated that children from single-parent families have a more difficult time in school, tend to drop out of school more frequently, and display lower levels of achievement even when they stay in school. Others argue that because many of these children live in poor communities, the quality of schools found there is lower, and more distractions occur.

In a study of single mothers who have never been married Gringlas and Weinraub (1995) examined the effects of growing up in a single-parent family without experiencing the trauma of going through a divorce. The study sample consisted of white, employed, financially independent, older, never-married mothers and their children. The authors found that young children of never-married mothers exhibited characteristics similar to children from two-parent families. However, as the children became adolescents, differences between the two groups appeared. Mothers and teachers reported that children from single-mother families exhibited greater social-emotional and academic problems than did the children from two-parent families. Other researchers studying the effects of divorce on children have made similar findings (Amato and Keith 1991a; Hetherington and Clingempeel 1992; Wallerstein 1987).

Several studies have shown that children from single-parent families have lower levels of educational and economic achievement and tend to drop out of school more frequently and at an earlier age than children from two-parent families (Amato and Keith 1991; Keith and Finlay 1988; Krein and Beller 1988; McLanahan 1985; McLanahan and Bumpass 1988; McLanahan, Astone, and Marks 1988; Shaw 1982). For example, Krein and Beller (1988) found that children from single-mother families are more likely to drop out of high school and, in general, spend fewer years in school than children from two-parent families. Using statistics from the National Longitudinal Survey of Youth and the Panel Study of Income Dynamics (see Sources of Research Data, below), McLanahan and Sandefur (1994) found that children from single-parent families are almost twice as likely as children from two-parent families to drop out of school. They also examined the mothers' level of education, which is generally regarded as the single best predictor of the children's school achievement. The results indicated that children who have a mother with less than a high school education are twice as likely to drop out of school as children whose mothers have at least a high school education.

When their results were broken down by race McLanahan and Sandefur (1994) found that the average white child from a single-parent family is more likely (28 percent) to drop out of high school than a black (17 percent) or Hispanic (25 percent) child from a two-parent family. The rates for black and Hispanic children from single-parent families are 30 percent and 49 percent respectively. Other researchers believe that the reason that some children from single-parent families leave school early is that they must help out with family finances and responsibilities. They may quit school to take care of younger siblings or to find a job to help make ends meet.

Some researchers believe that children from single-parent families have lower levels of educational achievement primarily because of the low level of parental income. Single mothers who have less time and less money to invest in their children may have children who achieve less. Higher-quality schools are usually not found in poor neighborhoods and therefore those mothers living in poor neighborhoods may have trouble motivating their children to achieve in school (Becker 1981; Krein and Beller 1986; Michael and Tuma 1985).

When children from single-parent families stay in school, they are more likely than children from two-parent families to achieve in their academic studies (Boyd and Parish 1985; Lewis 1986).

Emotional

Several researchers have found that children from single-parent families are more likely to have lower levels of emotional development and have more emotional problems than children from two-parent families. Several studies have shown that the effects of a divorce on children include depression and emotional distress (Hetherington, Cox, and Cox 1985; Wallerstein and Kelly 1980). Because living in poverty can be stressful children in single-parent families may also experience behavioral and learning difficulties in school (Astone and McLanahan 1991; Hetherington, Cox, and Cox 1985).

Financial

Children in single-mother families have been found to be more likely to have lower earnings as adults and are more likely to be poor both as children and as adults (Hill, Augustyniak, and Ponza 1987). Many of these difficulties encountered by children of single-parent families can also be traced to and linked with the financial difficulties that most single-parent families face (Richards and Schmiege 1993; McLanahan 1985; Acock and Kiecolt 1989).

Societal

Many people blame single-parent families for causing many societal problems, including high crime rates, gang activities, and out-of-wedlock births. Most of the blame is directed at young, single, never-married mothers.

Some studies have indicated that a relationship exists between living in a single-parent family and committing delinquent acts. Matsueda and Heimer (1987) found such a relationship. A study commissioned by the Progressive Policy Institute in 1990 found a strong relationship between crime and single-parent families. The researchers found that the relationship is "so strong that controlling for family configuration erases the relationship between race and crime and between low income and crime" (Kamarck and Galston 1990, 14). Children from divorced families score higher on measures of problem behavior (Pillay 1987, Hetherington and Clingempeel 1992).

These children also have been found to have a higher susceptibility to peer pressure (Steinberg 1987) and are thus more likely to get into trouble. Emery (1988) has demonstrated an increased occurrence of substance abuse among children of single parents.

Becoming Single Parents Themselves

Many people believe that children from single-parent families have an increased likelihood of forming single-parent families themselves (Glenn and Kramer 1985; McLanahan 1988; Mueller and Cooper 1986). Hogan and Kitagawa (1985) also found a relationship between daughters growing up in a single-parent family and becoming single parents themselves. They found that black adolescent girls from single-parent families were more likely to be sexually active and to have a child while unmarried than girls from two-parent families. McLanahan (1988) found the same strong relationship, although Hill and her colleagues (1985) examined the same data and did not find such a relationship. Wallerstein and Blakeslee (1989) have demonstrated that children from single-parent families are more likely to have difficulty in establishing intimate relationships and are more likely to become single parents themselves.

Three theories seek to explain why children from single-parent families may themselves become single parents (McLanahan and Bumpass 1988). One theory focuses on the economics of single parenthood. Single parents have less time and money to spend on their children, which can affect the lives of the children. Children may adopt adult roles to help out the household; some may drop out of school to help out financially. By adopting adult roles, some may come to believe they can act like adults in other ways, for instance, by having a child. Some adolescent females may see parenthood as a way of establishing an adult identity. If the family is poor, parenthood may appear to be a way out of poverty, especially if the young girl plans on getting married (Becker 1981; Krein and Beller 1986).

A second theory focuses on the importance of childhood and adolescent socialization, specifically the important part that role models can play in the lives of children and the necessity of parental supervision. This theory argues that the absence of the father in children's lives can affect their behavior. For example, Hetherington (1972) found that girls whose parents were divorced were more likely to have a greater interest in and dependency on males. Daughters in single-mother families also are more likely to see their mothers coping with life as single parents and believe that they, too, can handle single parenthood.

The third theory, or explanation, is based on stress theory, which examines family events and their effect on family organization and family dynamics. Stress theory argues that the effects of marital disruption occur because of the change in family structure, not as a result of the conditions associated with single parenthood. Events such as marital disruption produce an imbalance in the family that can push children into the assumption of adult roles, including becoming pregnant and having children themselves.

McLanahan and Bumpass (1988) studied the intergenerational consequences resulting from family disruption using data from the 1982 National Survey of Family Growth (collected by the National Center for Health Statistics through interviews with 7,969 women between the ages of 15 and 44 and of all marital statuses). McLanahan and Bumpass found that women who spend at least part of their childhoods in single-parent families are more likely to marry and have children early, to give birth before marriage, and to have their own marriages break up sometime during their lives.

Single Parents in Other Countries

The growth of single-parent families is not just a United States phenomenon. Other countries, especially other developed countries, are also experiencing an increasing number of single-parent families. In many developing countries, divorce is not a common occurrence although it does happen and does create single-parent families. In many cases, developing countries do not keep accurate data concerning single-parent families, so tracking down this information can be difficult.

Policies in some countries, especially in western Europe, focus on the welfare of the child, and it does not matter whether the child has two parents or only one parent. Many western European countries have experienced a significant increase in single-mother families; they see those families as poor and vulnerable to stress, social isolation, and loneliness. In most cases, the increase is due to growing numbers of divorced and separated mothers, never-married women who are having children, and couples living together without being married. In most western European countries, as in the United States, the number of widows with young children is declining.

Government and private-sector policy makers and researchers believe many of these families will experience financial difficulties for several reasons. Lack of child support by noncustodial parents, primarily fathers, contributes to the problems facing these single-parent families. Another factor is low wages; when single mothers can find work, they often are not paid a wage adequate to support their families. In order to compensate for the financial difficulties faced by these families, many governments have set up specific programs to help mothers with young children. Financial aid to all families in need helps mothers to stay at home and raise the children. Specific aid to single mothers in some countries helps mothers to survive without having to work outside the home. Cash benefits, housing assistance, and other programs provide help in several countries.

In many western European countries, single-parent families are becoming more common. However, many of these countries have developed support systems to help single parents, who are primarily mothers. The Nordic countries in particular, including Norway, Sweden, Denmark, Finland, and Iceland, are ahead of the United States in caring for single mothers and their children. These countries have all established some type of guaranteed child-support payment system. The services include health insurance, child-care services, maternity and parenting benefits, and housing subsidies. The national governments pay for these services when noncustodial parents fail to support their children (Schlesinger and Schlesinger 1994). Many of these mothers are expected to work, but at least the governments have set up some support systems to help these parents survive.

In Sweden most single mothers are economically active. However, Sweden also has one of the best support systems for single parents. Benefits have been geared to supplement earnings rather than replace earnings. Common benefits include a universal child allowance, a parental allowance, housing allowance, and an advanced maintenance allowance that ensures child support payments to single mothers when the father does not support his children. Child care charges are usually based on the ability to pay (Sainsbury 1996).

In France, one-parent families are generally worse off than two-parent families, especially with respect to economics, housing, child care, and social isolation. These families are more likely to rent than own their own homes and are more likely to have to move more than once. The children of single-parent families are more likely to repeat years in school. However, approximately 80 percent of single parents work; most of them work full-time. Combined with social security and other maintenance provisions, the French also have a well-developed system of child care and preschooling. The French family policy is popular and provides real benefits (Baker 1991).

In Japan, very few children are born to unwed mothers. Discrimination against the children of unwed mothers is still legal. The law grants illegitimate descendants only one-half of the amount of an inheritance that is granted to legitimate descendants. As a result, a Japanese teenager who becomes pregnant will most likely abort the fetus (Yoshizumi 1995). Many groups, especially women's organizations, are working to change this law and other related laws.

Many single-parent families in developing countries are created by the death of a spouse, usually the father. Widows in developing countries are generally not treated well. The death of her husband often signals major changes in a woman's social status and her lifestyle. Widows often are ostracized socially and are reminded of their inferior status. In some areas of Africa and India, the custom of *levirate* is practiced. According to this custom "the widow is remarried to her husband's brother or other male relative . . . to support the widow and to ensure that any future children she has are conceived in the name of the dead man" (Owen 1996, 15). Women are often considered the property of the husband and his family and, especially if a brideprice has been paid by the husband's family, will continue to be the family's property. Expanding knowledge and an increased awareness of women's rights are helping many women to resist this custom.

In many areas of the Third World widows are not allowed to inherit property owned by their husbands. They can lose their homes, their possessions, and the land they have worked. In some cases a widow's children are also taken from her, to be raised by her dead husband's family. Local custom, traditional laws, and religious laws frequently discriminate against widows and often take precedence over statutory laws. In some cases widows are thrown off their husband's property and are left with no place to live and no way to support the children. Most developing countries do not have any established system of social support for these families (Owen 1996).

Under Muslim law a woman must always be protected by a male—usually a father, husband, brother, or other male relative. In the case of a widow the most prevalent practice is to find her another husband. The woman usually has no control over her marriage to someone else. If, for some strange reason, she fights remarriage she is open to seclusion and many indignities. Either way the woman has no choice; she usually has no means of financially supporting herself and her children.

Refugee women are frequently single parents. Their husbands have died or been killed, imprisoned, or are missing, or have deliberately deserted them. These women have a particularly difficult time trying to reestablish a life for themselves and their children. They encounter huge social, economic, and psychological challenges. According to Owen,

> Some react with incredible resilience, taking on responsibilities they would never have dreamed of in their previous life, courageously challenging old taboos and customs in order to ensure the survival of their depen-

dents. Through sheer necessity they confront unimaginable vicissitudes and become strong, independent and creative, and leaders of other women. Others, alienated and marginalized, having suffered some of the especially terrible experiences that men have devised to subdue women—for example, of rape and torture or watching loved ones being tortured—never recover from their ordeals and may remain in a traumatized state indefinitely. (Owen 1996, 167)

In Korea, most families comprise the traditional mother, father, and children, along with extended family members. However, some nontraditional families can be found. The country's laws now allow a single person to adopt a child, but not many of these families exist, and the few that do are considered strange (Rosenheim and Testa 1992). Divorce is not common, so very few single-parent families are created through divorce. Special considerations are made for young widows with children; they receive some financial assistance and housing at special homes set up specifically for widows and children.

Several organizations have been formed in developing countries to help women, especially widows, cope with the discrimination that they often face. In Uganda the AIDS Support Organization (TASO) was started in 1987 by a Ugandan widow whose husband died of AIDS. The organization provides care to over 8,000 Ugandans with HIV/AIDS. Members help other women, provide shelter, help raise money for projects and school fees, support each other in their decisions to live without men, and teach their children about safe sex. TASO has done more than any other program in Africa to support women, confront prejudices, and reduce the stigma associated with being a widow and having AIDS.

A grassroots organization in Bangladesh is helping landless divorced and widowed women and their children. Dwip Unnayam Sangstha was formed in 1985 and is financed primarily by Oxfam, an international partnership of non-governmental organizations (NGOs) working to end poverty, primarily through local organizations in more than 100 countries. By 1992 it included over 200 women's groups that started out as savings groups and developed into self-help and development groups to help these women develop their own businesses.

In India, SEWA, the Self-Employed Women's Association, has continued to empower women. While the organization does not focus on single mothers, they have helped to reduce discrimination against single mothers and have helped these women establish small businesses and survive the trauma of widowhood. Staff members can also help advise women on legal problems. In 1995 SEWA developed a plan to help women insure their husbands and therefore help them survive should their husbands die first. The economic support and resources SEWA provides have helped many widows support their children.

The Widows and Orphans Society in Kenya was established in 1991 in response to the many women who were becoming widows as a result of AIDS. Village-to-village widows groups are established in many villages, with over 100,000 members nationwide. The group provides loans to help establish income-generating projects, as well as counseling, continuing education, legal advice and representation, and help with complaints concerning rape, sexual abuse, and violence (Owen 1996).

For the single parent in developing countries, life can be harsh and survival can be a daily struggle. Developed countries have done much more to help single parents and their children. However, the stigma of being a single parent is still strong in most countries, creating additional problems for these families. Single parents who can afford to support their children are much better off, but fewer in number, than those who have a difficult time financially.

Sources of Research Data

Many of the studies cited in this section relied on data collected from a variety of national samples collected from the 1970s on. A brief description of these samples is provided below.

Panel Study of Income Dynamics (PSID)

Started in 1968 the PSID is a nationally representative longitudinal survey that includes approximately 5,000 families in the United States. These families have been interviewed every year since 1968. Poor families are overrepresented; the sample includes a relatively large number of African-American and single-parent families. The PSID collects annual information on parents' marital status, family income, welfare participation, fertility history, community resources, and other valuable information concerning family life, residential mobility, family disruption, and child well-being.

National Longitudinal Survey of Young Men and Women (NLSY)

The NLSY is a nationally representative sample of approximately 14,000 young men and women who were born between 1958 and 1965. Among the respondents were a large number of minorities, including Hispanics and African-Americans. Respondents were first interviewed in 1979 when they were between the ages of 14 and 21; they have been interviewed every year since 1979. Information is collected on a variety of topics, including child well-being, family disruption, education, and parental and community resources.

High School and Beyond Study (HSB)

The purpose of the HSB was to collect information on school characteristics, curriculum, and student performance and includes approximately 50,000 high school seniors and sophomores attending 1,000 high schools throughout the United States. These students were interviewed in 1980, and then a smaller group of the same students were reinterviewed in 1982, 1984, and 1986. Students attending Catholic schools as well as Hispanics are overrepresented in the sample.

National Survey of Families and Households (NSFH)

As a nationally representative sample of adults, the NSFH collected information on family history retrospectively. Survey respondents were asked to recall their experiences growing up and to report past achievements, including education level, marriage, children, and other past experiences.

References

Abramovitz, Mimi. 1996. *Regulating the Lives of Women: Social Welfare Policy from Colonial Times to the Present.* Rev. ed. Boston: South End Press.

Acock, Alan C., and K. J. Kiecolt. 1989. "Is It Family Structure or Socioeconomic Status? Family Structure During Adolescence and Adult Adjustment." *Social Forces* 68:553–571.

Amato, Paul R. 1987. "Family Processes in One-Parent, Stepparent, and Intact Families: The Child's Point of View." *Journal of Marriage and the Family* 49:327–337.

Amato, Paul R., and B. Keith. 1991a. "Parental Divorce and the Well-Being of Children: A Meta-Analysis." *Psychological Bulletin* 110:26–46.

———. 1991b. "Separation from a Parent During Childhood and Adult Socioeconomic Attainment." *Social Forces* 70:187–206.

Anderson, Paul, and Devin Davey. 1995. "Commutarianism." *New Statesman and Society* (March 3):2.

Angel, Ronald J., and Jacqueline L. Angel. 1993. *Painful Inheritance: Health and the New Generation of Fatherless Families.* Madison: University of Wisconsin Press.

Astone, Nan Marie, and Sara S. McLanahan. 1991. "Family Structure, Parental Practices, and High School Completion." *American Sociological Review* 56:309–320.

Baker, John. 1991. "Family Policy as an Anti-Poverty Measure." in *Lone Parenthood: Coping with Constraints and Making Opportunities in Single-Parent Families,* ed. Michael Hardey and Graham Crow. Toronto: University of Toronto Press.

Bane, Mary Jo. 1985. "Household Composition and Poverty: Which Comes First?" Albany: New York State Department of Social Services.

———. 1986. "Household Composition and Poverty." In *Fighting Poverty: What Works and What Doesn't,* ed. Sheldon H. Danziger and Daniel H. Weinberg. Cambridge: Harvard University Press.

Bane, Mary Jo, and David T. Ellwood. 1983. "The Dynamics of Dependence: The Routes to Self-Sufficiency." Report prepared for Assistant Secretary for Planning and Evaluation, Office of Evaluation and Technical Analysis, Office of Income Security Policy, U.S. Department of Health and Human Services, Washington, DC.

———. 1994. *Welfare Realities: From Rhetoric to Reform.* Cambridge: Harvard University Press.

Bassi, L. 1987. "Family Structure and Poverty Among Women and Children: What Accounts for Change?" Report. Washington, DC: Georgetown University.

Bassuk, E. L. 1991. "Homeless Families." *Scientific American* 265:66–72, 74.

Becker, Gary S. 1981. *A Treatise on the Family.* Cambridge, MA: Harvard University Press.

Benkov, Laura. 1994. *Reinventing the Family: The Emerging Story of Lesbian and Gay Parents.* New York: Crown Publishers.

Berry, Dawn Bradley. 1995. *The Domestic Violence Sourcebook: Everything You Need to Know.* Los Angeles: Lowell House.

Billy, John, and David Moore. 1992. "A Multilevel Analysis of Marital and Nonmarital Fertility in the U.S." *Social Forces* 70:977–1011.

Blank, Rebecca M. 1989. "Analyzing the Length of Welfare Spells." *Journal of Public Economics* 39:245–273.

Blankenhorn, David. 1995. *Fatherless America: Confronting Our Most Urgent Social Problem.* New York: Basic Books.

Boumil, Marcia Mobilia, and Joel Friedman. 1996. *Deadbeat Dads: A National Child Support Scandal.* Westport, CT: Praeger.

Boyd, D. A., and T. S. Parish. 1985. "An Examination of Academic Achievement in Light of Familial Configuration." *Education* 108:228–230.

Brewer, Rose M. 1988. "Black Women in Poverty: Some Comments of Female-Headed Families." *Signs* 13(2):331–339.

Buehler, C. 1988. "The Social and Emotional Well-Being of Divorced Residential Parents." *Sex Roles* 18(5–6):247–257.

Burns, Ailsa, and Cath Scott. 1994. *Mother-Headed Families and Why They Have Increased.* Hillsdale, NJ: Lawrence Erlbaum Associates.

Burtless, Gary. 1994. "Public Spending on the Poor: Historical Trends and Economic Limits." In *Confronting Poverty: Prescriptions for Change,* ed. Sheldon H. Danziger, Gary D. Sandefur, and Daniel H. Weinberg. Cambridge: Harvard University Press.

Center for the Study of Social Policy. 1986. "The 'Flip-Side' of Black Families Headed by Women: The Economic Status of Black Men." In *The Black Family: Essays and Studies,* ed. Robert Staples. 3d ed. Belmont, CA: Wadsworth Publishing.

Chambers, Diane. 1997. *Solo Parenting: Raising Strong and Happy Families.* Minneapolis: Fairview Press.

Chesler, P. 1986. *Mothers on Trial: The Battle for Children and Custody.* Seattle: Seal Press.

Children's Defense Fund. 1990. *S.O.S. America! A Children's Defense Budget.* Washington, DC: Children Defense Fund.

———. 1991. *The State of America's Children: 1991.* Washington, DC: Children's Defense Fund.

Chilton, Roland A. 1968. *Consequences of a State Suitable Home Law for ADC Families in Florida.* Tallahassee: Florida State University (Institute for Social Research).

Coontz, Stephanie. 1997. *The Way We Really Are: Coming to Terms with America's Changing Families*. New York: Basic Books.

Corcoran, Mary E., and James P. Kunz. 1997. "Do Unmarried Births among African-American Teens Lead to Adult Poverty?" *Social Service Review* 71 (2):274–287.

Czapanskiy, Karen. 1989. "Child Support and Visitation: Rethinking the Connections." *Rutgers Law Journal* 20:619.

Danziger, Sheldon H., and Daniel H. Weinberg. 1994. "The Historical Record: Trends in Family Income, Inequality, and Poverty." In *Confronting Poverty: Prescriptions for Change,* ed. Sheldon H. Danziger, Gary D. Sandefur, and Daniel H. Weinberg. Cambridge: Harvard University Press.

DeFrancis, Vincent. 1976. *Protecting the Child Victims of Sex Crimes Committed by Adults*. Denver: American Humane Society, Children's Division.

Dornbusch, Sanford M., J. Merrill Carlsmith, Steven J. Bushwall, Philip L. Ritter, Herbert Leiderman, Albert H. Hastorf, and Ruth T. Gross. 1985. "Single Parents, Extended Households, and the Control of Adolescents." *Child Development* 56:326–341.

Dowd, Nancy E. 1997. *In Defense of Single-Parent Families*. New York: New York University Press.

Dreier, Peter, and Richard Applebaum. 1992. "The Housing Crisis Enters the 1990's." *New England Journal of Public Policy* 8(1):155–167.

Duncan, Greg J. 1984. *Years of Poverty, Years of Plenty*. Ann Arbor, MI: Institute for Social Research.

Duncan, Greg J., and Saul D. Hoffman. 1990. "Teenage Welfare Receipt and Subsequent Dependence among Black Adolescent Mothers." *Family Planning Perspectives* 22:16–20.

Edin, Kathryn. 1991. "Surviving the Welfare System: How AFDC Recipients Make Ends Meet in Chicago." *Social Problems* 38(4):462–474.

Edin, Kathryn, and Laura Lein. 1997. *Making Ends Meet: How Single Mothers Survive Welfare and Low-Wage Work*. New York: Russell Sage Foundation.

Ellwood, David T. 1986. *Targeting "Would Be" Long-Term Recipients of AFDC*. Princeton: Mathematica Policy Research.

———. 1988. *Poor Support: Poverty in the American Family*. New York: Basic Books.

Ellwood, David T., and Mary Jo Bane. 1985. "The Impact of AFDC on Family Structure and Living Arrangements." *Research in Labor Economics* 7:137–297.

Emery, R. E. 1988. *Marriage, Divorce, and Children's Adjustment*. Beverly Hills, CA: Sage.

Engelstein, P., M. Antell-Buckley, and P. Urman-Klein. 1980. "Single Women Who Elect to Bear a Child." In *Psychological Aspects of Pregnancy, Birthing, and Bonding,* ed. B. L. Blum, 103–119. New York: Human Sciences Press.

Ercole, A. 1988. "Single Mothers: Stress, Coping, and Social Support." *Journal of Community Psychology* 16:41–54.

Etzioni, Amitai. 1993. *The Spirit of Community: Rights, Responsibilities, and the Commutarian Agenda.* Southbridge, MA: Crown Publishing.

Fitzgerald, John. 1991. "Welfare Durations and the Marriage Market: Evidence from the Survey of Income and Program Participation." *Journal of Human Resources* 26:545–561.

Franklin, D. L. 1988. "Race, Class and Adolescent Pregnancy: An Ecological Analysis." *American Journal of Orthopsychiatry* 58:339–354.

Furstenberg, Frank F., Jr., and Andrew J. Cherlin. 1991. *Divided Families: What Happens to Children When Parents Part.* Cambridge: Harvard University Press.

Garfinkel, Irwin. 1992. *Assuring Child Support.* New York: Russell Sage.

Garfinkel, Irwin, and Sara S. McLanahan. 1986. *Single Mothers and Their Children: A New American Dilemma.* Washington, DC: Urban Institute Press.

Gay and Lesbian Parents Coalition International. 1997. "In the News." *Gay and Lesbian Parents Coalition International Network Newsletter* (Spring): 3.

Geiser, R. L. 1979. *Hidden Victims: The Sexual Abuse of Children.* Boston: Beacon Press.

Geronimus, Arline T. 1991. "Teenage Childbearing and Social and Reproductive Disadvantage: The Evolution of Complex Questions and the Demise of Simple Answers." *Family Relations* 40:463–471.

Geronimus, Arline T., and Sanders D. Korenman. 1992. "The Socioeconomic Consequences of Teen Childbearing Reconsidered." *Quarterly Journal of Economics* 107:1187–1214.

Glenn, N. D., and K. B. Kramer. 1985. "The Psychological Well-Being of Adult Children of Divorce." *Journal of Marriage and the Family* 47:905–912.

Glenwick, D. S., and J. D. Mowrey. 1986. "When Parent Becomes Peer: Loss of Intergenerational Boundaries in Single Parent Families." *Family Relations* 35:57–62.

Gowan, Gary, Laura Desimore, and Jennifer McKay. 1995. "Poverty and the Single Mother Family: A Macroeconomic Perspective." *Marriage and Family Review* 20:115–142.

Green, R. 1978. "Sexual Identity of 37 Children Raised by Homosexual or Transsexual Parents." *American Journal of Psychiatry* 135:692–697.

Greif, Geoffrey L. 1985. *Single Fathers.* Lexington, MA: Lexington Books.

Gringlas, Marcy, and Marsha Weinraub. 1995. "The More Things Change . . . Single Parenting Revisited." *Journal of Family Issues* 16(1):29–52.

Hanson, S. 1986. "Healthy Single Parent Families." Special Issue: The Single Parent Family. *Family Relations* 35:125–132.

Hao, Lingxin. 1995. "How Does a Single Mother Choose Kin and Welfare Support?" *Social Science Research* 24:1–27.

Harris, Kathleen Mullan. 1991. "Teenage Mothers and Welfare Dependency: Working Off Welfare." *Journal of Family Issues* 12:492–518.

———. 1993. "Work and Welfare among Single Mothers in Poverty." *American Journal of Sociology* 99:317–352.

———. 1996. "Life After Welfare: Women, Work, and Repeat Dependency." *American Sociological Review* 61:407–426.

———. 1997. *Teen Mothers and the Revolving Welfare Door.* Philadelphia: Temple University Press.

Harrison, P. 1983. *Inside the Inner City: Life Under the Cutting Edge.* Harmondsworth, England: Penguin.

Hetherington, E. Mavis. 1972. "Effects of Father Absence on Personality Development in Adolescent Daughters." *Developmental Psychology* 7: 313–326.

Hetherington, E. Mavis, and W. G. Clingempeel. 1992. "Coping with Marital Transitions." *Monographs of the Society for Research in Child Development* 57(227):2–3.

Hetherington, E. Mavis, Martha Cox, and Roger Cox. 1985. "Long-Term Effects of Divorce and Remarriage on the Adjustment of Children." *Journal of the American Academy of Child Psychiatry* 24(5):518–530.

Hill, Martha S., Sue Augustyniak, and Michael Ponza. 1985. "The Impact of Parental Marital Disruption on the Socioeconomic Attainments of Children as Adults." Ann Arbor: University of Michigan, Survey Research Center, Institute for Social Research.

———. 1987. "Effects of Parent Divorce on Children's Attainments: An Empirical Comparison of Five Hypotheses." Unpublished manuscript, Survey Research Institute, University of Michigan, Ann Arbor.

Hogan, Dennis P., and Evelyn M. Kitagawa. 1985. "The Impact of Social Status, Family Structure and Neighborhood on the Fertility of Black Adolescents." *American Journal of Sociology* 90:825–855.

Holme, A. 1985. *Housing and Young Families in East London.* London: Routledge and Kegan Paul.

Kamarck, Elain Ciulla, and William A. Galston. 1990. *Putting Children First: A Progressive Family Policy for the 1990s.* Washington, DC: Progressive Policy Institute (September).

Kamerman, Sheila B., and Alfred J. Kahn. 1988. *Mothers Alone: Strategies for a Time of Change.* Dover, MA: Auburn House.

Keith, V. M., and B. Finlay. 1988. "The Impact of Parental Divorce on Children's Educational Attainment, Marital Timing, and Likelihood of Divorce." *Journal of Marriage and the Family* 50:797–809.

Krein, Sheila Fitzgerald, and Andrea H. Beller. 1986. "Family Structure and Educational Attainment of Children; Differences by Duration, Age and Gender." Paper presented at the annual meeting of the Population Association of America, San Francisco, April.

———. 1988. "Educational Attainment of Children from Single-Parent Families: Differences by Exposure, Gender, and Race." *Demography* 25:221–234.

Kurdek, L. A. 1988. "Social Support of Divorced Single Mothers and Their Children." *Journal of Divorce* 11:167–188.

Leonard, D., and M. Speakman. 1986. "Women in the Family: Companions or Caretakers?" In *Women in Britain Today,* ed. V. Beechey and E. Whitelegg. Philadelphia, PA: Open University Press.

Letiecq, Bethany L., Elaine A. Anderson, and Sally A. Koblinsky. 1996. "Social Support of Homeless and Permanently Housed Low-Income Mothers with Young Children." *Family Relations* 45:265–272.

Lewis, W. 1986. "Strategic Interventions with Children of Single Parent Families." *School Counselor* 33:375–376.

Lichter, Daniel T., and David J. Eggebeen. 1994. "The Effect of Parental Employment on Child Poverty." *Journal of Marriage and the Family* 56:633–645.

Lichter, Daniel T., Diane K. McLaughlin, George Kephard, and David J. Landry. 1992. "Race and the Retreat from Marriage: A Shortage of Marriageable Men?" *American Sociological Review* 57:781–799.

London, Rebecca A. 1996. "The Difference Between Divorced and Never-Married Mothers' Participation in the Aid to Families With Dependent Children Program." *Journal of Family Issues* 17(2):170–185.

Lopata, Helena Znaniecka. 1996. *Current Widowhood: Myths and Realities.* Thousand Oaks, CA: Sage Publications.

Ludtke, Melissa. 1997. *On Our Own: Unmarried Motherhood in America.* New York: Random House.

Lundberg, Shelly, and Robert D. Plotnick. 1990. "Effects of State Welfare, Abortion and Family Planning Policies on Premarital Childbearing among White Adolescents." *Family Planning Perspectives* 22:246–251.

Mack, Dana. 1997. *The Assault on Parenthood: How Our Culture Undermines the Family.* New York: Simon and Schuster.

Matsueda, Ross L., and Karen Heimer. 1987. "Race, Family Structure, and Delinquency: A Test of Differential Association and Social Control Theories." *American Sociological Review* 52:826–840.

McChesney, K. Y. 1990. "Family Homelessness: A Systemic Problem." *Journal of Social Issues* 46(4):191–205.

McCrate, Elaine. 1992. "Expectations of Adult Wages and Teenage Childbearing." *International Review of Applied Economics* 6:309–328.

McDonald, P., ed. 1986. *Settling Up: Property and Income Distribution in Divorce in Australia.* Sydney: Prentice-Hall.

McLanahan, Sara S. 1988. "Family Structure and Dependency: Early Transitions to Female Household Headship." *Demography* 25:1–15.

———. 1985. "Family Structure and the Reproduction of Poverty." *American Journal of Sociology* 90:873–901.

McLanahan, Sara S., Nan M. Astone, and Nadine Marks. 1988. "The Role of Mother-Only Families in Reproducing Poverty." Paper presented to the Conference on Poverty and Children, Lawrence, Kansas (June):20–22.

McLanahan, Sara S., and Karen Booth. 1989. "Mother-Only Families: Problems, Prospects, and Politics." *Journal of Marriage and the Family* 51:557–580.

McLanahan, Sara S., and Larry Bumpass. 1988. "Intergenerational Consequences of Family Disruption." *American Journal of Sociology* 94:130–152.

McLanahan, Sara S., and Irwin Garfinkel. 1989. "Single Mothers, the Underclass, and Social Policy." *Annals of the American Academy of Political and Social Science* 501:92–104.

McLanahan, Sara S., and Gary Sandefur. 1994. *Growing Up with a Single Parent: What Hurts, What Helps.* Cambridge, MA: Harvard University Press.

Mednick, M. 1987. "Single Mothers: A Review and Critique of Current Research." *Applied Social Psychology Annual* 7:184–201.

Merritt, S., and L. Steiner. 1984. *And Baby Makes Two: Motherhood Without Marriage.* New York: Franklin Watts.

Michael Robert T., and Nancy B. Tuma. 1985. "Entry into Marriage and Parenthood by Young Men and Women: The Influence of Family Background." *Demography* 22:515–544.

Millar, J. 1987. "Lone Mothers." In *Women and Poverty in Britain,* ed. C. Glendinning and J. Millar. Hemel Hempstead, England: Harvester Wheatsheaf.

Miller, B. 1979. "Gay Fathers and Their Children." *The Family Coordinator* 28:544–551.

Miller, Naomi. 1992. *Single Parents by Choice: A Growing Trend in Family Life*. New York: Plenum Press.

Mnookin, Robert H., Eleanor E. Maccoby, Catherine R. Albiston, and Charlene E. Depner. 1990. "Private Ordering Revisited: What Custodial Arrangements Are Parents Negotiating?" In *Divorce Reform at the Crossroads*, ed. Stephen D. Sugarman and Herma H. Kay. New Haven: Yale University Press.

Moffitt, Robert. 1992. "Incentive Effects of the U.S. Welfare System: A Review." *Journal of Economic Literature* 30:1–61.

Moore, Kristin A., Dee Ann L. Wenk, Sandra L. Hofferth, and Cheryl D. Hayes. 1987. "Statistical Appendix: Trends in Adolescent Sexual and Fertility Behavior." In *Risking the Future: Adolescent Sexuality, Pregnancy, and Childbearing*. Vol. 2. *Working Papers and Statistical Appendixes*, ed. Sandra L. Hofferth and Cheryl D. Hayes. A-1353–1–168/520. Washington, DC: National Academy Press.

Mueller, D. P., and P. W. Cooper. 1986. "Children of Single Parent Families: How They Fare as Young Adults." *Family Relations* 35:169–176.

Mulroy, Elizabeth A. 1995. *The New Uprooted: Single Mothers in Urban Life*. Westport, CT: Auburn House.

Mulroy, Elizabeth A., ed. 1988. *Women as Single Parents: Confronting Institutional Barriers in the Courts, the Workplace, and the Housing Market*. Dover, MA: Auburn House Publishing Co.

Nathanson, Constance A. 1991. *Dangerous Passage: The Social Control of Women's Sexuality in Adolescence*. Philadelphia: Temple University Press.

National Adoption Information Clearinghouse. 1990. "Single Parent Adoption: What You Need to Know." Washington, DC: National Adoption Information Clearinghouse.

National Center for Health Statistics. 1995. "Births to Unmarried Mothers: United States, 1980–1994." *Vital and Health Statistics*, series 21, no. 53. Hyattsville, MD: US Public Health Service (June).

National Coalition for the Homeless. 1997. "Domestic Violence and Homelessness." Washington, DC: National Coalition for the Homeless.

Nichols-Casebolt, Ann, and Irwin Garfinkel. 1991. "Trends in Paternity Adjudications and Child Support Awards." *Social Science Quarterly* 72(1):83–97.

Nieto, D.S. 1983. "Hispanic Fathers: The Growing Phenomenon of Single Fathers Keeping Their Children." *National Hispanic Journal* 1:15–19.

O'Neill, June A., Laurie J. Bassi, and Douglas A. Wolf. 1987. "The Duration of Welfare Spells." *Review of Economics and Statistics* 69:241–249.

Owen, Margaret. 1996. *A World of Widows.* Atlantic Highlands, NJ: Zed Books.

Pascall, G. 1986. *Social Policy: A Feminist Analysis.* London: Tavistock.

Pearson, Jessica, and Nancy Thoennes. 1988. "Supporting Children after Divorce: The Influence of Custody on Support Levels and Payments." *Family Law Quarterly* 22:319.

Pillay, A. L. 1987. "Psychological Disturbances in Children of Single Parents." *Psychological Reports* 61:803–806.

Piven, Frances Fox, and Richard A. Cloward. 1993. *Regulating the Poor: The Functions of Public Welfare.* Updated ed. New York: Vintage Books.

Plotnick, Robert D. 1990. "Welfare and Out-of-Wedlock Childbearing: Evidence from the 1980s." *Journal of Marriage and the Family* 52:735–746.

Polikoff, Nancy. 1982. "Why Mothers Are Losing: A Brief Analysis of Criteria Used in Child Custody Determinations." *Women's Rights Law Reporter* 7(3):235–243.

Rank, Mark R. 1987. "The Formation and Dissolution of Marriages in the Welfare Population." *Journal of Marriage and the Family* 49:15–20.

————. 1994. *Living on the Edge: The Realities of Welfare in America.* New York: Columbia University Press.

Rector, Robert. 1992. *Making Government Work: A Conservative Agenda for the States.* San Antonio: Texas Public Policy Foundation.

Reischauer, Robert D. 1989. "The Welfare Reform Legislation: Directions for the Future." In *Welfare Policy for the 1990s,* ed. Phoebe H. Cottingham and David T. Ellwood. Cambridge, MA: Harvard University Press.

Richards, Leslie N., and Cynthia J. Schmiege. 1993. "Problems and Strengths of Single-Parent Families: Implications for Practice and Policy." *Family Relations* 42:277–285.

Richardson, D. 1981. "Lesbian Mothers." In *The Theory and Practice of Homosexuality,* ed. J. Hart and D. Richardson. London: Routledge and Kegan Paul.

Robinson, Bryan E., and Robert L. Barret. 1986. *The Developing Father: Emergent Roles in Contemporary Society.* New York: Guilford.

Rodgers, Harrell R. 1996. *Poor Women, Poor Children: American Poverty in the 1990s.* Armonk, NY: M. E. Sharpe.

Rosenheim, Margaret K., and Mark F. Testa, eds. 1992. *Early Parenthood and Coming of Age in the 1990s.* New Brunswick, NJ: Rutgers University Press.

Sainsbury, Diane. 1996. *Gender, Equality, and Welfare States.* Cambridge, England: Cambridge University Press.

Saluter, Arlene F. 1994. "Marital Status and Living Arrangements: March 1993." *Current Population Reports*, Series P20–478. Washington, DC: Bureau of the Census, Economics and Statistics Administration.

Schein, Virginia. 1995. *Working from the Margins: Voices of Mothers in Poverty*. Ithaca, NY: ILR Press (Cornell University Press).

Schlesinger, Ben, and Rachel Aber Schlesinger. 1994. "One-Parent Families in Europe: A Review." *International Journal of Sociology* 24(2):15–24.

Schoeni, R. F. 1994. "Does Aid to Families with Dependent Children Displace Family Assistance?" Manuscript. Rand Corporation.

Shaw, Lois B. 1982. "High School Completion for Young Women: Effects of Low Income and Living with a Single Parent." *Journal of Family Issues* 3:147–163.

Shinn, Marybeth, and Beth Weitzman. 1996. "Homeless Families Are Different." In *Homelessness in America*. Washington, DC: National Coalition for the Homeless.

Shireman, Joan F., and Penny R. Johnson. 1985. "Single Parent Adoptions: A Longitudinal Study." *Children and Youth Services Review* 7:332.

Siegel, Judith M. 1995. "Looking for Mr. Right? Older Single Women Who Become Mothers." *Journal of Family Issues* 16(2):194–211.

Singh, S. 1986. "Adolescent Pregnancy in the United States: An Interstate Analysis." *Family Planning Perspectives* 18:210–220.

Skolnick, Arlene S., and Jerome H. Skolnick, eds. 1971. *Family in Transition*. Boston: Little, Brown.

Spencer, Rich. 1989. "Child Support Collections Jump in '88." *The Washington Post*, 8 December, 13.

Stefancic, Jean, and Richard Delgado. 1996. *No Mercy: How Conservative Think Tanks and Foundations Changed America's Social Agenda*. Philadelphia: Temple University Press.

Steinberg, Laurence. 1987. "Single Parent, Stepparents, and the Susceptibility of Adolescents to Antisocial Peer Pressure." *Child Development* 58:269–275.

Steinbock, Marcia R. 1995. "Homeless Female-Headed Families: Relationships at Risk." *Marriage and Family Review* 20(1/2):143–159.

Terdal, Leif, and Patricia Kennedy. 1996. *Raising Sons Without Fathers: A Woman's Guide to Parenting Strong, Successful Boys*. Secaucus, NJ: Carol Publishing Group.

Thompson, M. S., and Ensminger, M. E. 1989. "Psychological Well-Being Among Mothers with School Age Children: Evolving Family Structures." *Social Forces* 67:715–730.

Tillitski, C. 1992. "Fathers and Child Custody: Issues, Trends, and Implications for Counseling." *Journal of Mental Health Counseling* 14(3):351–361.

Turner, P. H., L. Scadden, and M. B. Harris. 1990. "Parenting in Gay and Lesbian Families." *Journal of Gay and Lesbian Psychotherapy* 1(3):55–66.

Uehara, E. 1990. "Dual Exchange Theory, Social Networks, and Informal Social Support." *American Journal of Sociology* 96:521–557.

Uhlenberg, Peter. 1978. "Changing Configurations of the Life Course." In *Transitions: The Family and the Life Course in Historical Perspective*, ed. Tamara K. Hareven. New York: Academic Press.

U.S. Bureau of the Census. 1991. "Housing Characteristics of Selected Races and Hispanic-origin Households in the United States: 1987," Series H121–87–1. Washington, DC: Low Income Housing Information Service.

———. 1988. *Survey of Income and Program Participation, 1986 and 1987.* Ann Arbor: Inter-University Consortium for Political and Social Research.

U.S. General Accounting Office. 1991. *Mother-Only Families: Low Earnings Will Keep Many Children in Poverty.* April. GAO/HRD, 91–62.

U.S. House of Representatives. 1994. *1994 Green Book: Overview of Entitlement Programs.* Washington, DC: U.S. Government Printing Office. CD-ROM.

Vinovskis, Maris A. 1988. *An "Epidemic" of Adolescent Pregnancy? Some Historical and Policy Considerations.* New York: Oxford University Press.

Vissing, Yvonne. 1996. *Out of Sight, Out of Mind: Homeless Children and Families in Small Town America.* Lexington: University Press of Kentucky.

Wacquant, Loic J. D., and William Julius Wilson. 1989. "Poverty, Joblessness, and the Social Transformation of the Inner City." In *Welfare Policy for the 1990s*, ed. Phoebe H. Cottingham and David T. Ellwood. Cambridge, MA: Harvard University Press.

Walker, R. 1988. "The Costs of Household Formation." In *Money Matters: Money, Wealth and Financial Welfare*, ed. R. Walker and G. Parker. London: Sage.

Wallerstein, Judith S. 1985. "The Overburdened Child: Some Long-term Consequences of Divorce," *Social Work* 30:116–123.

———. 1987. "Children of Divorce: A Ten-Year Study." In *The Impact of Divorce, Single Parenting and Stepparenting on Children*, ed. E. Mavis Hetherington and J. D. Arasteh. Hillsdale, NJ: Lawrence Erlbaum.

Wallerstein, Judith S., and Sandra Blakeslee. 1989. *Second Chances: Men, Women, and Children a Decade After Divorce.* New York: Ticknor & Fields.

Wallerstein, Judith S., and Joan B. Kelly. 1980. *Surviving the Breakup: How Children and Parents Cope with Divorce.* New York: Basic Books.

Weinreb, L. W., and J. C. Buckner. 1993. "Homeless Families: Program Responses and Public Policies." *American Journal of Orthopsychiatry* 63:400–409.

Weitzman, L. 1985. *The Divorce Revolution: The Unexpected Social and Economic Consequences for Women and Children in America.* New York: Free Press.

White House Working Group on the Family. 1986. *The Family: Preserving America's Future* (November 13). Washington, DC: U.S. Government Printing Office.

Whitehead, Barbara Dafoe. 1993. "Dan Quayle Was Right." *Atlantic Monthly* (April):47–84.

Wilson, William Julius. 1987. *The Truly Disadvantaged: The Inner City, the Underclass, and Public Policy.* Chicago: University of Chicago Press.

———. 1991. "Studying Inner-City Social Dislocations: The Challenge of Public Agenda Research. 1990 Presidential Address." *American Sociological Review* 56:1–14.

Wilson, William J., and Kathryn Neckerman. 1986. "Poverty and Family Structure: The Widening Gap Between Evidence and Public Policy Issues." In *Fighting Poverty: What Works and What Doesn't,* ed. S. Danziger and D. Weinberg. Cambridge, MA: Harvard University Press.

Woods, L., V. Been, and J. Schulman. 1982. "The Use of Sex and Economic Discriminatory Criteria in Child Custody Awards." Paper published by the National Center on Women and Family Law.

Yoshizumi, Kyoko. 1995. "Marriage and Family: Past and Present." In *Japanese Women: New Feminist Perspectives on the Past, Present, and Future,* ed. Fujimura-Fanselow and Atsuko Kameda. New York: Feminist Press.

Zill, Nicholas, Kristin A. Moore, Christine W. Nord, and Thumar Stief. 1991. "Welfare Mothers as Potential Employees: A Statistical Profile Based on National Survey Data." Washington, DC: Child Trends.

Zorza, Joan. 1991. "Woman Battering: A Major Cause of Homelessness," *Clearinghouse Review* 25(4). Chicago: National Clearinghouse for Legal Services.

Chronology 2

This chapter provides a chronology of the major events, including passage of federal laws, that are relevant to the study of single parents. A significant number of organizations have been established and laws have been passed to help single parents, primarily in the area of financial assistance, housing, and child care/child custody.

Our current social policies concerning welfare are based on laws, especially the Poor Law, passed in England during the seventeenth century. The purpose of the Poor Law was to provide for people who could not provide for themselves. People served included the aged, the ill, the handicapped, and the widowed. Local jurisdictions were allowed to levy taxes to provide help; local parishes were responsible for guaranteeing either "outdoor relief" or "indoor relief." "Outdoor relief" provided help for needy people who were able to remain in the community, while "indoor relief" provided care to people who needed to be institutionalized.

Widowed mothers and their children were considered virtuous and worthy of help; they were seen as one of the most privileged groups needing help and were usually treated accordingly. However, even when women did not normally work outside the home, mothers and children were required to seek work to help themselves. The local authorities would help them find jobs, but if no job could be found, indenture was the only alternative. Families were split up and the children were indentured.

In the late 1700s and early 1800s in the United States, Societies for the Prevention of Pauperism were organized to support and protect the family. Several religious organizations started to place orphans in institutions, protecting them from the dangers of life on the streets. During the mid-1800s states urged the removal of children from almshouses (poorhouses) and started state schools and orphan asylums. Associations for Improving the Conditions of the Poor (AICPs) appeared in many states. These organizations were staffed by volunteers and supported by cities and provided help to the urban poor. In the 1890s the AICPs were replaced by the Charity Organization Societies (COSs), which mobilized community resources to help families.

Unwed mothers did not usually receive the same treatment as widows. Unwed mothers, when they could, chose to live in boardinghouses and find work to support themselves and their children. Young Women's Christian Associations (YWCAs) were established to protect young women and were used by some unwed mothers. When this was not possible, they, too, found themselves in poorhouses. Maternity homes did not appear until the twentieth century, and by the 1960s were considered obsolete by many people (Kamerman and Kahn 1988).

Specific events, legislation, and other actions that may be relevant to the study of single parents are described below.

1797 The New York Society for the Relief of Poor Widows with Small Children is founded. The organization helps women who have lost their husbands and who have young children to raise. In order to receive help, a woman must prove that her husband has died or that he has been absent from the home for at least 12 months. In order to continue receiving help a woman must not be found drinking, acting promiscuously, dancing, or living in a disreputable neighborhood. If she does any of these things, she may be refused further assistance.

1865 William Booth, a Wesleyan preacher, leaves the church and founds the Salvation Army in England.

The Salvation Army will build the second largest network of homes for unwed mothers.

1880   George Railton helps to establish the Salvation Army in the United States.

1882   The largest organization of maternity homes for unwed mothers, the Florence Crittenton Homes, is established. Charles Crittenton, known as the millionaire evangelist, established the home following the death of his daughter Florence. The first home is the Florence Night Mission in New York City. This home rescues young girls and women who are victimized by a range of circumstances, and includes prostitutes and wayward girls as well as unwed mothers.

1890   The National Conference of Charities and Corrections, a national organization for social workers, discusses the possibility of providing public aid to families without male breadwinners (i.e., single mothers). Following discussion, the group decides that their help is not required.

1897   New York State nearly passes a Destitute Mothers' Bill, calling for aid to single mothers and their children. Many private charities help defeat the measure because they believe that it could threaten their existence. They believe that if the bill passes, single mothers will no longer need their help.

1900   In Australia, the 1900 Marriage Act Amendment Act gives women the right to "claim confinement expenses as well as maintenance from the father of their child" (Swain and Howe 1995, 71).

In the United States, three out of four single parents become single parents as a result of the death of a spouse. Almost one in three of these single parents is a father. Only 5 percent of children living in single-parent families have a parent who is divorced or has never been married (Gordon and McLanahan 1991).

1909   The first White House Conference on Children is held. Focusing on the removal of children from homes of the poor, participants tell President Theodore Roosevelt that "except in unusual circumstances, the home should not be broken up for reasons of poverty, but only for considerations of inefficiency or immorality" (Bremner 1971, 365). Private relief organizations are encouraged, because they do not believe that all children should be taken from their mothers just because their mothers are unmarried.

1910   Shelters that have been established to help prostitutes begin to shift their focus to provide maternity care for unmarried mothers.

1911   A Mother's Pension Law is enacted in Missouri, followed quickly by a similar law in Illinois. According to this law, states are required to provide money to single mothers to help them maintain a suitable home as long as the mothers prove that they are competent and proper custodians. Most women who are covered are widowed, deserted by their husbands, or divorced. Unwed mothers are usually not covered by this law.

1912   The U.S. Children's Bureau is established. One of the agency's major goals is to protect children and help those living in poverty and in single-parent families.

1913   The Massachusetts Commission on the Support of Dependent Minor Children of Widowed Mothers establishes a Mothers' Pension program. The program is set up to serve only women who officials believe are deserving of help, meaning mothers who provide a suitable home for their children. In Massachusetts, as in many other states, fit mothers are usually white and widowed, and most likely to follow the prevailing family ethic and social norms.

1914   The New York State Commission on Relief for Widowed Mothers issues a report claiming that women cannot be both homemakers and breadwinners. They believe that widowed mothers deprive their children of emotional support and education in order to support them financially. These mothers are distracted at work because they worry about their children and they are distracted at home because they are worried about providing for their children. The Commission suggests that the government should become involved in helping these families, because private charities do not have the funds to support them.

1915   Twenty-nine states have established mothers' pension programs to help provide support for women, primarily widows, with young children. Other single mothers with children are not generally covered by these laws; states do not want to encourage fathers to desert their families, which they believe would happen if these women are also covered.

1918   The U.S. Women's Bureau is established.

There are 78 homes within the Florence Crittenton Homes organization. These homes are now incorporated into the National Florence Crittenton Mission. A special act of Congress provides them with a national charter.

1920   Liberal divorce legislation is introduced and passed in Sweden. This legislation leads to an increase in the number of single-parent families.

The Katy Ferguson Home is founded in New York City. This home focuses on helping black single mothers and is one of the first to help black women and their children.

1921   Forty states now have established some type of mothers' pension program. Only six of these states limit aid to widows. Other states also assist children of divorced mothers and mothers whose husbands have deserted them. Even so, the overwhelming ma-

1921
(cont.)

jority of women supported by these pension programs are widows.

1931

Forty-six states now have established mothers' aid programs. However, only 17 programs receive state funds. Most programs are administered on the county or municipal level (Gordon 1994).

A survey conducted by the Children's Bureau finds that only 55 out of more than 60,000 mothers' pension recipients have been families of unwed mothers (Bremner 1971).

1932

Recognizing the problems faced by poor single mothers, social workers call on the federal government to provide welfare relief to these women and their children.

It is estimated that almost 360,000 female-headed families are receiving some type of relief assistance from the federal government (Gordon 1994).

1935

The Social Security Act is enacted. Although it focuses on unemployment insurance and old age pensions, one category, Aid to Dependent Children (ADC), is directed at single parents and their children. Most of the single parents that the program is set up to help are widows with young children. Eligible mothers are still expected to work and help support their families.

1939

Young widows with children are brought under the coverage of Old Age Insurance. This effectively removes them from the ADC program and leaves women who are generally considered less deserving of aid (single mothers) dependent on the more stigmatized public assistance program.

1947

States begin to pass "surveillance" laws, which establish special investigative units to find unwed mothers who are involved in sexual relations with men. Women who are found with men lose their ADC eligibility.

1950   The Uniform Reciprocal Enforcement of Support Act
            (URESA) is passed by the U.S. Congress. The Act
            helps custodial parents enforce child support awards
            across state lines.

1951   Georgia becomes the first state to outlaw ADC bene-
            fits to more than one illegitimate child of an unwed
            mother. The state law is an attempt to prevent single
            women from having more than one child.

            Only seven maternity homes for unwed mothers in
            the United States provide services primarily to black
            women. Several other homes will accept a few black
            girls and women.

1959   Ursula Gallagher, in charge of programs and services
            for unmarried mothers at the U.S. Children's Bureau,
            observes that in "some courts it is almost impossible
            for a Negro unmarried mother to give up her baby
            for adoption. The general interpretation of this is that
            the courts believe the girl should be made to support
            her children and should be punished by keeping
            them" (quoted in Solinger 1992, 27). The situation for
            white unwed mothers is quite different. Most states
            have improved their adoption services for white
            unwed mothers.

            In a number of states, public housing authorities do
            not allow single women who are pregnant or unmar-
            ried mothers to live in publicly subsidized facilities.
            For example, the Chicago Committee on Services to
            Unmarried Parents finds that one publicly subsi-
            dized facility has sent a letter to all their tenants who
            have an illegitimate child. The letter warns them that
            if they have another child they will be evicted
            (Solinger 1992).

1960   The Louisiana state legislature denies public assis-
            tance to illegitimate children of unwed mothers. It
            also continues to target black unmarried mothers by
            passing a bill making it a crime to have more than
            one illegitimate child. Eighteen other states attempt

1960
(cont.)

to pass similar laws, including legislation that requires imprisonment or sterilization of women who
have more than one illegitimate child (Solinger 1992).

Twenty-three states pass "suitable home" legislation
that eliminates some single mothers from receiving
ADC benefits. The legislation is aimed primarily at
black women. Unwed mothers are considered to be
immoral and state officials believe that this is reason
enough to prohibit them from receiving ADC benefits.

1961

Many states start rejecting claims for benefits from
families in which the children are illegitimate or in
which a man resides. The policy requires that children be removed from these homes or benefits dis-
continued. However, the secretary of the U.S. Department of Health, Education and Welfare, Arthur
Fleming, decrees that states cannot claim that homes
are unsuitable in order to deny ADC benefits.

The U.S. Congress passes legislation that extends
ADC program coverage (ADC-UP) to two-parent
families in which both parents are unemployed. It is
adopted by only 22 states.

1962

The Illinois State Public Aid Commission passes a
resolution that mandates ADC officials to warn
mothers who receive ADC that they face a jail term if
they give birth to an illegitimate child.

The ADC program is renamed Aid to Families with
Dependent Children (AFDC), which attempts to prevent family breakup by covering two-parent as well
as one-parent families living in poverty.

1963

The first welfare rights group, the Aid to Needy Children's Mothers' Organization, is formed in Los Angeles. The group protests midnight raids (in which
welfare officials enter the homes of single mothers to
make sure that a man is not present) and develops
into an organization that helps AFDC mothers win
their rights from the welfare system.

1965   Two Harvard University psychiatrists, Solomon and
        Kilgore (1965), postulate that unwed mothers have at
        least a mild psychiatric disorder that allows them to
        give birth to illegitimate children. The authors claim
        that every unwed mother is "the victim of mild,
        moderate or severe emotional or mental distur-
        bance" (quoted in Solinger 1992, 87).

        Daniel Patrick Moynihan publishes his *The Negro
        Family: The Case for National Action*, which soon be-
        comes known as the Moynihan Report. In this re-
        port he cites increasing rates of divorce, female-
        headed families, out-of-wedlock births, and
        welfare dependency among urban blacks. He be-
        lieves that the deterioration of the black family is
        responsible for their limited economic opportuni-
        ties. He sees a "web of pathology" that holds blacks
        back from advancement. This report generates a
        great deal of criticism; many people believe that
        Moynihan does not understand the culture of the
        black family.

1966   A march on the state capital of Ohio (Columbus) is
        the first major welfare rights action to receive na-
        tional attention. Sympathizers demonstrate in 16
        other cities. The groups want increased welfare bene-
        fits to help women and their children.

1967   The Social Security Act amendments authorize a
        new program that focuses on training and job
        searching. Known as WIN, the Work Incentives
        Now program adds a strong requirement that recipi-
        ents work for their benefits. Mothers with children
        under the age of six years are exempt from this re-
        quirement. This legislation is later repealed during
        the Nixon administration.

        The Great Society and the War on Poverty programs
        of the Johnson Administration have some impact on
        single parents. Advocates believe that poor single
        mothers should be allowed to stay at home with their
        young children. The caseload for AFDC increases

1967
(cont.)

dramatically—from 1.3 million in 1967 to 2.5 million cases in 1970.

The National Welfare Rights Organization is established. It is composed of local welfare rights groups, with thousands of dues-paying members. Their purpose is to bring together diverse groups to help welfare families, and especially single mothers, gain AFDC and other benefits to which they are entitled under the Social Security Act.

The U.S. Supreme Court declares that midnight raids on the homes of single mothers receiving welfare benefits are unconstitutional. These raids have been conducted to find homes that are considered unsuitable for children because the mother is spending time with a man who is not her husband. The discovery of a man in the house had been enough to deny a woman welfare benefits.

1970

California becomes the first state to allow no-fault divorce.

The federal Title X Family Planning Services and Population Research Act of 1970 is passed. The Act provides substantial funds for reducing unintended pregnancies among poor women. One-third of the funding is spent on the provision of contraceptives to unmarried teenagers.

1971

The U.S. Congress passes the Comprehensive Child Development Act of 1971. However, President Nixon vetoes the legislation, which would have authorized the provision of child care for all children. Nixon does not want to encourage women, especially mothers, to go to work. He believes that the family as an institution is in danger of disappearing, leading to the moral decline of society if the government becomes involved in encouraging women to work.

The AFDC regulations now require that women receiving AFDC benefits who have children over the age of six years must look for employment. This is the first time that AFDC recipients are required to look for work.

1972   Title IX of the Education Amendments requires that schools provide education to pregnant teenagers and teenage mothers.

1973   A study by Herzog and Sudia (1973) changes the thinking about children growing up in single-mother families. The authors review the research on this topic and argue that earlier interpretations of statistics contain serious flaws in their methodology. They believe that many of the differences between mother-only and two-parent families can be explained by differences in the socioeconomic status of these families. The article, as well as an improving political climate, encourages researchers to conduct new studies that focus on the strengths of single-mother families.

1974   The Finer Committee, set up by the British government in the early 1970s to study single-parent families, especially those headed by women, delivers its final report. The report focuses on the economic circumstances and problems faced by single parents, but does include thoughts and recommendations on the problems they face in other areas, such as housing. The problems that children face by being on welfare are discussed. The report's goal is to assure that single mothers and their children will have an adequate standard of living without requiring that the mothers go to work. While the report stimulates discussion concerning single parents, nothing comes of it, primarily due to arguments about the cost involved in helping single parents and the objections of two-parent families who believe single parents would receive preferential treatment.

1975   The Australian Family Law Bill is passed by 56 percent of the members of Parliament. This comprehensive legislation covers many aspects of family life, including mediation and counseling services to help

1975
(cont.)

families, dispute resolution, reconciliation, duties and responsibilities of the Family Court of Australia, dissolution of marriages, services and programs for children, parental responsibility, parenting plans, child abuse, family violence, spousal support, and other administrative matters. One section focuses on the conditions under which courts will grant no-fault divorces.

Title IV-D of the Social Security Act becomes law and focuses on child support. It requires states to do a number of things, including covering part of the cost of establishing paternity, providing help in locating absent fathers, and collecting child support payments. States are allowed to use Internal Revenue Service data to help locate absent fathers.

The Uniform Parentage Act (UPA) is drafted by a national commission of experts and enacted by several states. The parent-child relationship is extended to every parent and every child, regardless of the parents' marital status. Other states have enacted similar statutes. As a result in most states children born out of wedlock have most of the same rights as those born to married parents. For example, if a biological connection is established, an absent parent has a legal responsibility to support the child. The UPA and other state statutes also address questions about donor insemination and paternity.

The U.S. Congress passes the Child Support Enforcement Amendments and establishes a federal Office of Child Support Enforcement. The federal government is finally beginning to help in enforcing private child support efforts.

1976

The National Survey of Children is conducted for the first time by Frank Furstenberg, Nicholas Zill, and their colleagues. Using a nationally representative sample of approximately 2,000 children, this survey confirms earlier findings that children of divorce do less well in school and have lower levels of social adjustment.

1978   Diana Pearce is among the first to examine and document the growing number of poor families that are headed by women. She refers to this process as the "feminization of poverty."

1979   The U.S. Bureau of the Census begins to collect national data on the payment of child support by nonresident fathers.

1980   The Adoption Assistance and Child Welfare Act is passed by the U.S. Congress. This Act creates a program that subsidizes adoption, provides incentives to move children quickly out of foster care, and encourages and strengthens natural families in order to avoid child placement.

1981   The Omnibus Budget Reconciliation Act (OBRA) of 1981 decreases the work incentives provided by the 1967 Social Security Act and limits work expense and child care allowances. It also changes the eligibility requirements for participating in AFDC. The U.S. Department of Health and Human Services estimates that nearly 700,000 families lose eligibility or benefits as a result of these changes, a net savings of $1.1 billion in 1983 (U.S. Congress 1986).

     Reagan administration staffers start campaigning for "workfare," which suggests that people on welfare should work for part of their benefits. The U.S. Congress does not pass this requirement.

1982   The Sperm Bank of California in Oakland is established by the Oakland Feminist Women's Health Center to provide advice and services to all women who want to become pregnant. It is established in response to the problems that many unmarried women face in finding a doctor who is willing to inseminate an unmarried woman.

1983   The U.S. Congress restores some of the benefits lost following the passage of the Omnibus Budget Reconciliation Act, because they believe that these changes unfairly penalize low-income families.

1984   Both houses of Congress unanimously pass additional child support legislation, expanding the role of the Child Support Enforcement Amendments, originally passed in 1975. This legislation requires all states to establish enforcement procedures for withholding wages to gather child support payments, expedites legal processes, extends deadlines for establishing paternity, expands systems for enforcing support orders, and improves enforcement of interstate cases. If a parent owes back child support payments, states are required to deduct the outstanding balance from that parent's income tax refunds or through other legitimate means, such as garnishing wages.

1986   For the first time in the history of the United States, a majority of all poor families are single-mother families (U.S. Bureau of the Census 1993).

1988   The Family Support Act (FSA) is enacted. Based on the assumption that both parents should be responsible for caring for their children, the FSA is phased in over five years. It has five major provisions. Title I, Child Support and Paternity, requires all states to provide services to withhold wages of the noncustodial parent to help support his or her children. Title II, Job Opportunities and Basic Skills Training Program (JOBS), requires all states to set up job training programs for recipients of welfare. Title III, Supportive Services, requires states to provide child care to participants in school, job training, or at work. Title IV, AFDC Amendments, requires states to allow two-parent families to receive AFDC benefits. Title V, Demonstration Projects, provides funding for a variety of innovative programs in order to determine the most effective programs that alleviate problems and create viable solutions. The Act basically transforms AFDC from a program to help single mothers stay at home with their children to a mandatory work program.

The Hague Convention on the Civil Aspects of International Child Abduction is passed, ratified originally by 10 countries, including the United States. The Convention helps to resolve the problems associated with international child abduction. Foreign courts do not recognize custody orders that are issued by courts in the United States. The convention declares that a child who has been wrongfully removed from or retained in a ratifying country should be returned to his or her country of habitual residence.

1989   At the International Economic Consequences of Divorce Conference, speakers from several countries are concerned about the growing number of women who are raising their children alone and in poverty. The speakers believe that this large underclass will threaten national solidarity (Funder 1989).

1992   CBS airs the season premiere of the television show *Murphy Brown*. This episode takes on the "status of a national event" according to the *New York Times*. In an earlier episode Murphy Brown chooses to become a single mother when she decides not to marry the father of her child. Former U.S. Vice President Dan Quayle denounces this show, claiming that it mocks the importance of fathers. A national controversy, with many people criticizing Quayle, erupts. In this episode, Murphy Brown rebukes the Vice President for his unfair remarks about the necessity of fathers and reminds viewers that "families come in all shapes and sizes" ("Place Where 'Reality Ends, Fiction Begins,'" *USA Today*, 22 September 1992, 1).

In New Jersey, the Family Development Program takes effect. The best-known component of this legislation is the child exclusion law, also known as the "family cap" law. This section bars additional cash

1992
(cont.)

assistance for children born to AFDC families more than 10 months after the mother's application for AFDC. "In other words, any child conceived after the mother has applied for AFDC will not be given cash assistance. There are no exceptions for cases of documented rape, incest, or contraceptive failure. Although the infant's eligibility for Medicaid and food stamps is not affected, the monetary loss is significant since the increase to the monthly AFDC grant would be between $64 and $102, depending on the size of the family" (Sidel 1996, 96).

Following riots in Los Angeles, U.S. Vice President Dan Quayle comments that "the anarchy and lack of structure in our inner cities are testament to how quickly civilization falls apart when the family foundation cracks" (Yang 1992, 1). He believes the growth of single-parent families has contributed greatly to the breakdown of society.

The Child Support Recovery Act of 1992 is passed by the U.S. Congress. The Act makes it a federal crime for a noncustodial parent living in one state to fail to pay child support to dependent children living in another state.

1993

The state of Wisconsin obtains federal approval for its "Work Not Welfare" waiver proposal. The program, which goes into effect in January 1995, is implemented in two pilot counties. The new program requires a family seeking assistance to participate in a four-year benefit period. During this time, the family may be eligible for a total of up to 24 months of assistance. Eligibility for up to 12 months is determined by participating in an education and training program. Eligibility for the remaining 12 months can be earned through work. Families entering the system while pregnant or with a baby under one year of age are exempt from the required work time. If the mother has another baby, a six-month leave from participation is required. The additional child will not be covered by additional assistance. Once a family has exhausted its 24 months of eligibility, it will be ineligible for cash assistance for three years unless it qualifies for an exception.

The Omnibus Budget Reconciliation Act is passed by the U.S. Congress. One of the provisions requires states to establish streamlined procedures to determine paternity. If states do not comply, they will no longer receive federal funding.

1995   The National Center for Missing and Exploited Children, in cooperation with the U.S. State Department, becomes increasingly involved in international cases of child abduction. Many single parents who receive custody of their children following divorce find that the foreign spouse (often the husband) abducts the child to the father's country of origin and the parent with custody has a difficult time regaining custody.

1996   The Personal Responsibility and Work Opportunity Reconciliation Act (PRWORA) of 1996 is passed. This legislation focuses on ways that single mothers can be helped to become self-sufficient. Aid to Families with Dependent Children (AFDC), the Job Opportunities and Basic Skills (JOBS) program, and the Emergency Assistance programs are replaced by Temporary Assistance to Needy Families (TANF). Most program and rule-making authority is transferred from the federal government to the states. The legislation requires states to deny benefits to single mothers who are under the age of 18 unless they are living with their parents or other adult relatives.

1997   The Welfare to Work Partnership is formed. The Partnership is a national, independent, nonpartisan effort, encompassing over 2,000 small and large businesses, which maintains a list of companies that are committed to hiring individuals who receive public assistance. Another list contains information on organizations that provide job training, child care, and other related services. The Partnership has a toll-free hotline, a Web site (www.welfaretowork.org), pub-

1997
(cont.)
lishes "A Blueprint for Business" manual to help companies hire people on welfare, and a challenge to 12 cities with high levels of poverty to help promote innovative and effective welfare-to-work initiatives.

The Balanced Budget Act of 1997 modifies the PRWORA, authorizing the U.S. Department of Labor to provide $3 billion in welfare-to-work grants to states and local communities for activities such as on-the-job training, job placement and retention services, and for creating jobs for the hardest-to-employ TANF recipients.

President Clinton directs all heads of federal agencies or departments to develop a plan to hire welfare recipients. The U.S. Department of Transportation provides grants to 24 states to develop welfare-to-work transportation strategies.

Senator Dodd introduces two bills in the U.S. Senate to help custodial parents obtain child support payments from noncustodial parents. Senate Bill 1074, the Child Support Reform Act of 1997, will create a new child support enforcement division within the IRS. Senate Bill 1075, the Child Support Assurance Act of 1997, will create incentives for states to improve enforcement for noncustodial parents to comply with their obligations. Both of these bills have been referred to the Committee on Finance for further action.

Howard Hinman, a custodial father of five children, wins a major appellate decision in a child support case in California. The California Court of Appeals denies the appeal of Aisha Hinman (Howard's ex-wife) to reduce the amount of child support she is required to pay to her ex-husband. Mr. Hinman is a member of Sole Mothers International and acted as his own attorney in this case due to his limited financial resources.

1998
Several child support provisions in the PRWORA of 1996 become effective this year. These provisions

include the following requirements: states must conduct automated matches of social security numbers in case registry and new hire registry; the U.S. Department of Health and Human Services is required to operate a federal case registry; and states must be able to provide for operation of a centralized collection and disbursement unit for child support payments.

In their annual Kids Count study, the Annie E. Casey Foundation reports that finding safe and reliable day care is preventing many welfare recipients from moving off welfare into the workforce.

References

Bremner, Robert H., ed. 1971. *Children and Youth in America: A Documentary History*, Vol. II. Cambridge, MA: Harvard University Press.

Funder, K. 1989. "International Perspectives on the Economics of Divorce." *Family Matters* 24:18–22.

Gordon, Linda. 1994. *Pitied but Not Entitled: Single Mothers and the History of Welfare 1890–1935*. New York: Free Press.

Gordon, Linda, and Sara S. McLanahan. 1991. "Single Parenthood in 1900." *Journal of Family History* 16(2):97–101.

Herzog, Elizabeth, and Cecelia E. Sudia. 1973. "Children in Fatherless Families." In *Review of Child Development Research*, vol. 3, ed. B. Caldwell and H. N. Ricciuti, 141–232. Chicago: University of Chicago Press.

Kamerman, Sheila B., and Alfred J. Kahn. 1988. *Mothers Alone: Strategies for a Time of Change*. Dover, MA: Auburn House.

Moynihan, Daniel Patrick. 1967. "The Negro Family: The Case for National Action." In *The Moynihan Report and the Politics of Controversy: A Trans-actional Social Sciences and Public Policy Report*, ed. Lee Rainwater and William L. Yancey, 39–124. Cambridge, MA: MIT Press.

"Place Where 'Reality Ends, Fiction Begins,'" 1992. *USA Today*, 22 September.

Sidel, Ruth. 1996. *Keeping Women and Children Last: America's War on the Poor*. New York: Penguin Books.

Solinger, Rickie. 1992. *Wake Up Little Susie: Single Parenting and Race Before Roe v. Wade*. New York: Routledge.

Solomon, Philip, and Morris Ward Kilgore. 1965. "The Psychiatric Case Conference in a Maternity Home Setting." American Protestant Hospital Association Conference, *Salvation Army Session Papers*, No. 82-1, Salvation Army Archives.

Swain, Shurlee, and Renate Howe. 1995. *Single Mothers and Their Children: Disposal, Punishment and Survival in Australia.* Cambridge: Cambridge University Press.

U.S. Bureau of the Census. 1993. "Poverty in the United States: 1992." *Current Population Reports,* series P-60, no. 185. Washington, DC: Government Printing Office (September).

Yang, J. E. 1992. "Clinton Finds New Voice of Emotion: Quayle Decries 'Poverty of Values.'" *Washington Post,* 20 May.

Biographical Sketches 3

This chapter provides brief biographical sketches of people who have been or currently are playing key roles in activities involving single parents, legislation affecting single parents, or are otherwise involved in the field.

Jane Addams (1860–1935)

Born to a wealthy and prominent family in Cedarville, Illinois, Jane Addams was raised by her father and stepmother following her mother's death when Jane was two years old. As a child, Jane was often sick and suffered a bout of tuberculosis that left her spine somewhat deformed. She was always encouraged by one of her stepbrothers and her father, who recognized that education was not only for boys.

She attended Rockford Seminary, a Presbyterian finishing school, as a member of the class of 1881. Along with many of her classmates she began to rebel against the strict religious discipline and conservatism of the school and its administration. The college magazine became a forum for debate about social reform, which was a topic of intense interest at the time; Addams was one of the contributors. Members of her generation were among the first women who were allowed to attend institutions of higher learning, and she learned quickly about the role expected of women in society, but also what that role potentially could be.

Backaches and little energy prevented her from continuing her education at Smith College. Instead she recuperated at home and, following her father's death, decided to go to Philadelphia with her stepmother, who suggested that Jane attend medical school there. However, Jane became depressed and gave up the idea of going to medical school. She traveled to Europe in hopes of overcoming her depression.

While touring the English slums she realized the many ways that workers were being exploited and the negative aspects of industrialization. On her return from Europe she moved to Chicago and worked with Ellen Starr to establish Hull House, which provided welfare services to those in need. She set up programs to help feed, house, and care for the sick and impoverished among the working class. Eventually, Hull House grew into a complex of 13 buildings offering services such as nursery care, physical education, recreational activities for children and adults, adult education classes, theater arts workshops, a music school, and a social service center.

Addams spent many years writing, lecturing, and presenting her views concerning ways to improve social and economic conditions for many people, including single mothers and their children. Her book, *Twenty Years at Hull House,* was published in 1910, and describes her experiences in establishing and expanding the services at Hull House. Other books written by Addams include *Democracy and Social Ethics* (1902) and *The Spirit of Youth and the City Streets* (1909). She became a role model for young women during her lifetime.

Maya Angelou (1928–)

Born Marguerite Johnson in St. Louis, Maya Angelou was three years old when she and her brother were sent to live with their paternal grandmother following their parents' divorce. Her grandmother was one of many strong women who provided Maya with a strong role model. At the age of seven and a half Maya was raped by her mother's boyfriend during a visit to her mother's home. The boyfriend was tried, found guilty, and died while in prison. Confused by everything concerning this attack and feeling responsible for the boyfriend's death, Maya withdrew into herself. She did not speak for five years. Her mother sent her back to stay with her grandmother, who helped her regain her desire to talk. By the end of her eighth-grade school year, Maya was at the top of her class.

Angelou spent time with her mother in California, as well as with her father, and then lived for a month with other runaway children in an abandoned van. She managed to graduate from school when she was 16 years old and gave birth to a son a short time later. The pregnancy was not planned, and Angelou became a single mother. She supported herself and her son as a cook, nightclub waitress, and then as a professional dancer. In 1954 she toured Europe and Africa in a production of *Porgy and Bess.* On her return to New York, she settled in Harlem and became a member of the Writers' Guild. She became a nightclub singer and actress. She also wrote short stories, poetry, and songs.

Angelou and her son traveled to Africa with Vusumzi Make, a South African freedom fighter, and spent some time living in Cairo, Egypt. When Angelou applied for a job as an editor for the *Arab Observer*, Make was not happy, and the couple broke up. Angelou and her son lived in Ghana for several years and returned to the United States in 1966. In 1970 Angelou's book, *I Know Why the Caged Bird Sings*, was published and became a bestseller. The book was part of her autobiography, and was followed by other segments, including *Gather Together in My Name, Singin' and Swingin' and Gettin' Merry Like Christmas, The Heart of a Woman*, and *All God's Children Need Traveling Shoes.*

Angelou has inspired many people by her writings and by her success as a single parent. Many people, including single mothers, continue to receive comfort and insight through her writing. She moved back to the American South in 1981 and accepted a lifetime appointment as Reynolds Professor of American Studies at Wake Forest University.

Diane Chambers (1960–)

Diane Chambers started the on-line organization Sole Mothers International to help single mothers cope with the problems and challenges of being a single mother. She is also the author of a syndicated column, "Successful Single Parenting," which appears monthly in several regional parenting magazines. Her book, *Solo Parenting: Raising Strong and Happy Families*, is a valuable resource for single parents. Topics range from finances, child care, and discipline to dating and acquiring new job skills. The book and the organization grew out of her frustrations and experiences as a single mother. At first overwhelmed by her new responsibilities, Chambers was forced to prioritize the tasks ahead of her and break them into manageable parts. In a press release from the publisher of her book, she explains what she went through: "There were a number of issues I had to resolve in a very short period of time: overcoming the pain and trauma of divorce, re-budgeting my financial picture, redirecting my career, becoming a part-time lawyer, a full-time father-figure, and finding time somewhere in between to pay attention to what my kids were doing and thinking" (Fairview Press 1997, 1).

David Ellwood

David Ellwood is currently chief academic dean at the JFK School of Government at Harvard University. He is known for his experience and opinions concerning welfare and its effect on society. Ellwood has spent most of his career in academics and in the government. He came to Washington, D.C., in 1993 as assistant secretary for planning and evaluation in the Department of Health and Human Services (DHHS). He has written several books and articles, primarily on poverty and welfare.

With Lawrence Summers, Ellwood (1986) wrote an article for inclusion in the book *Fighting Poverty: What Works and What Doesn't*. The authors questioned whether welfare causes poverty or whether welfare helped people escape from poverty. They studied government benefits and found that disability payments did not decrease recipients' attempts to work; another finding was that public assistance was not a major cause of family breakup.

In the mid-1980s, as now, the subject of welfare was the topic of many discussions throughout government and the private sector. Some people believed that the only way to get people off of welfare was to end their welfare benefits. Some suggested that specific time limits be placed on receipt of welfare benefits. In *Poor Support: Poverty in the American Family* (1988), Ellwood, then an economist at Harvard University, agreed that time limits could be imposed but believed that more spending and support would be required to help welfare recipients get off welfare within a certain amount of time.

When Ellwood first wrote of time limits on welfare, he believed that a large increase in federal outlays was the only way for this program to succeed. As assistant secretary for planning and evaluation at DHHS, Ellwood argued, along with Mary Jo Bane, that some restrictions could be placed on welfare benefits, but he still believed that more money was required to develop job training and child care programs to help those on welfare, especially single mothers trying to go to school or work while worrying about how and who would care for their children. Ellwood and Bane suggested that single mothers would spend more time on welfare than most people believed. Both Bane and Ellwood fought hard for additional help for single parents on welfare, but would see new welfare legislation passed that did not provide that support. Ellwood left the government and returned to academia.

Andrea Engber (1949–)

The author of *The Complete Single Mother* (1995) (along with Leah Klungness), Andrea Engber is the founder and director of the National Organization of Single Mothers (NOSM). She is the editor of *SingleMOTHER,* the newsletter of NOSM, which provides a variety of information concerning single mothers, and has been referred to as one of the best sources of information for single mothers. As one of the leading sources of statistics and other information concerning single mothers, Engber writes for and acts as an adviser for several magazines, including *Redbook, Working Mother, New Woman, Woman's Own, Parenting, American Woman, American Baby,* and *Parent's Magazine.*

Engber writes a column on single parenting for *Working Mother* magazine; she also writes a nationally syndicated weekly column called *Single . . . With Children* that is distributed by Universal Press Syndicate. The No-Nonsense American Woman Award was given to her in 1995 for her efforts toward helping single mothers and their families.

Engber became a single mother in 1986 after her live-in partner left her when she was four months pregnant. She gave birth to her son in the hospital, unmarried, uninsured, and unprepared to care for a baby. She found herself fired from her job as art director of an advertising agency after her boss decided that having a single mother on the staff was not a good idea. In 1990 she founded NOSM when she realized that there were other single mothers who were running into the same problems she was encountering.

Frank Furstenberg

As a professor in the department of sociology at the University of Pennsylvania, Frank Furstenberg has studied single parents and the effects of divorce on parents. With Andrew Cherlin, he wrote *Divided Families: What Happens to Children When Parents Part* in 1991. The authors examined the problems faced by these suddenly single parents and the effects on the children. He has conducted extensive research on adolescent parents, and has concluded that "clearly, marriage is not always in a woman's best interest or the best interest of the child" (quoted in Ludtke, p. 424). He believes that unstable marriages increase the chances that a child will not have a good relationship with his or her father outside the home. He believes that a poor relationship with a father is worse than no such relationship. In other words, promoting marriage as a good idea for young parents may not be in the best interest of the child; it may also be bad for the parents themselves.

Geoffrey L. Greif (1949–)

A noted researcher and writer concerning issues of importance to single fathers, Geoffrey Greif received his master's degree in social work from the University of Pennsylvania in 1974 and his doctorate from the Columbia University School of Social Work in 1983. He has written more than 30 articles on single parents and is the author of *Single Fathers* and *The Daddy Track and the Single Father* and is the coauthor of *Mothers without Custody* (with Mary S. Pabst). His work has been widely cited in professional literature, newspapers, and magazines, and he has appeared on television and radio.

Greif has been a social worker in New Jersey, Pennsylvania, and Maryland; a clinical supervisor in Baltimore; a trainer and clinician for a drug dependency program; a family therapy consultant; and a coleader of divorce support groups. He founded the Baltimore area parent support group known as Help! My Kids are Driving Me Crazy! He is a consultant to several organizations, including the National Victims Center and the Juvenile Justice Resource Center. Organizations for which he is a board member include Parents Without Partners, Parents Anonymous, and the Maryland Committee for Children.

Greif has been interested in men's issues for quite a while. His master's thesis focused on men's consciousness-raising groups. His current interest in single fathers grew out of his interest in men's roles and his experiences with his wife in raising their daughter. He believes that single fathers, as well as single mothers, do not have to be superparents in order to be successful parents. Greif, along with his teaching and research duties, counsels single fathers. He is contributing editor to *The Single Parent* magazine. He is currently an associate professor at the University of Maryland at Baltimore School of Social Work.

Kathleen Mullan Harris

Kathleen Mullan Harris is an assistant professor of sociology at the University of North Carolina at Chapel Hill and a faculty fellow at the Carolina Population Center. Her research interests are in the area of family, poverty, and social policy. She recently completed a book on the welfare experiences of teenage mothers (1997). She is currently studying the impact of maternal employment and welfare receipt on outcomes for children in poor families. She is also conducting a study of family processes and adolescent risk behaviors as an investigator in the Adolescent Health Study for the Carolina Population Center.

In her study on teenage mothers she investigated long-term patterns of urban black teenage mothers in Baltimore and their experiences with welfare over 20 years. She found that most teenage mothers use public assistance as an aid to get an education and find a job. Occasionally they return to welfare for a short period of time but this is usually caused by the uncertainty of the escape routes off of welfare.

Julia Lathrop (1858–1932)

Born in Rockford, Illinois, Julia Lathrop was the daughter of a lawyer and a strong suffragist. She attended Rockford Seminary and then graduated from Vassar College in 1880. Following graduation, she returned home, unsure of what to do with her life. She found work as a secretary in her father's law office and at other local businesses and participated with her father in several local Republican party activities. In 1890 her life changed when she joined Jane Addams at Hull House. This move marked the beginning of her career in social reform.

Lathrop stayed at Hull House for 20 years. She was appointed to the Illinois Board of Charities in 1893 and she lobbied for many reforms, including the separation of relief programs for children and for the insane. She visited Europe to study mental health care programs and became a member of the National Committee for Mental Hygiene in 1909. She helped found the Illinois Immigrants' Protective League, which focused on helping poor immigrants adjust to life in America; she also worked to defend their interests.

Many of Lathrop's activities centered on children's issues. She lobbied for the establishment of a juvenile court and probation system. In 1912 she became the first head of the U.S. Children's Bureau in Washington, D.C., becoming the highest female official in the federal government. Starting with a staff of 15 members and a $25,000 budget, she headed the Bureau until 1921. She focused her efforts on welfare, infant mortality, child care, and child labor laws. Along with Grace Abbott, Lathrop was largely responsible for seeing that the mothers' pension programs were included in the Social Security Act. Her activities concerning infant mortality led directly to the passage of the Sheppard-Tower Act of 1921, the first welfare program at the federal level. She retired in 1921, returned to Rockford, and remained active in national and international women's reform activities.

Jane Mattes

Choosing to become a mother without the benefit of the child's father in the home is a difficult decision. Jane Mattes, as a single mother, faced this decision and many other challenges in becoming a single mother.

Mattes has been a psychotherapist with her own practice in New York City for over 20 years. Her initial meetings with other single mothers grew into the national organization Single Mothers by Choice, which was founded in 1981. The organization currently has over 20 chapters throughout the country. In writing a book about her experiences, also titled *Single Mothers by Choice* (1994), she drew on her extensive professional counseling experience, her close contact with hundreds of members of the Single Mothers by Choice organization, and her personal experience as the single mother of a teenage son.

Since 1990 Mattes has participated as a coresearcher on a 10-year longitudinal study of single mothers and the impact that their decision to parent on their own has had on their children's well-being. She also edits a newsletter for the organization.

Sara S. McLanahan

Sara McLanahan is currently professor of sociology and public affairs at Princeton University. She has written extensively on the topic of single parents, which she has been studying since the early 1980s. She has examined family structure and its effects on poverty and on children. Based on her studies, McLanahan believes that children who grow up with a single parent are worse off in general than children who grow up in a two-parent family. This finding remains strong even when looking at the parent's race, educational background, and marital status when the children are born.

McLanahan is arguably the nation's leading expert on single-parent families and the effects of this family structure on the children. She has studied the effect of childhood family instability on later childhood development and behavior, the effect of growing up in a single-parent family on the likelihood of children's becoming single parents themselves, and the effect that lack of parental and community resources has on children growing up in single-parent families and in poverty.

Carol Moseley-Braun (1947–)

Born in Chicago, Carol Moseley-Braun attended the University of Illinois at Chicago and received her law degree from the University of Chicago. She was elected to the Illinois General Assembly in 1978 and served for 10 years. Upon her election as Cook County recorder of deeds in 1987 she became the first African-American woman ever to hold executive office in the Cook County government. Elected to the United States Senate in 1992, she is the first African-American woman to hold a Senate seat.

Moseley-Braun's interests include education, health care, the political empowerment of women and minorities, and family-centered issues. As a single parent herself she understands the problems of single parenthood and many of the issues that affect families. She believes that the government should develop a family agenda as a priority, providing concrete and specific responses to many issues that affect families. Although she believes that children are better off with two parents, she knows that it is not always possible to have two parents and that the government must be as supportive of the single parent as it is of the traditional two-parent family.

Moseley-Braun believes the government must realize that affordable child care is necessary for the health of the nation; that it is unconscionable that women make 76 cents to a man's dollar; that companies need to consider alternative work schedules, flexible scheduling, part-time positions, and job sharing; that a system must be developed to establish paternity as well as one to enforce collection of child support; and that "personal economic issues, while critical, are not the only determinant in the revitalization of American family life" (Moseley-Braun 1994, 242).

Daniel Patrick Moynihan (1927–)

Daniel Patrick Moynihan is an outspoken supporter of helping the poor in the United States. He received his master's degree (1949) and doctorate degree (1961) from the Fletcher School of Law and Diplomacy and continued his graduate study at the London School of Economics and Political Science. Before joining the federal government in 1961 Moynihan was a director of public relations for the International Rescue Committee, a special assistant and then acting secretary to the governor of New York, director of the New York State Government Research Project, and assistant professor of political science at the Maxwell School of Citizenship and Public Affairs at Syracuse University.

As an urban affairs specialist, Moynihan was active in the 1960 presidential campaign of John F. Kennedy. Following Kennedy's election, in 1961 he joined the U.S. Department of Labor, first as a special assistant to the secretary of labor, then an executive assistant to the secretary of labor and assistant secretary of labor for policy planning and research. He returned to New York in 1965 and ran for president of the New York City Council. Unsuccessful in this bid, he became codirector of policy and planning for the mayoral campaign of Abraham Beame in New York City. He became the director, then senior member, of the Joint Center for Urban Studies at Harvard University and the Massachusetts Institute of Technology. He has been a professor of government at the Kennedy School of Government and professor of education and urban politics in the Graduate School of Education at Harvard University. He returned to government in 1969 as an assistant for urban affairs to President Nixon, counselor to the president, and executive secretary of the Urban Affairs Council. In 1973 Moynihan was named ambassador to India and in 1975 became the U.S. ambassador to the United Nations.

Moynihan was a member of the committee that designed the War on Poverty during the Lyndon Johnson Administration. In a white paper on the black family submitted to President Johnson, Moynihan suggested that the instability of the black family was responsible for causing poverty and its related problems. Critics attacked Moynihan for blaming the victim instead of suggesting that changes in the social and economic system should be made. Known as the Moynihan Report, this white paper brought the young Moynihan to the attention of many people.

Moynihan is probably best known as the U.S. Senator from New York State, first winning his seat in 1977, and for some of his writings, including *Beyond the Melting Pot; The Negroes, Puerto Ricans, Jews, Italians, and Irish of New York City* (with Nathan Glazer) and *The Negro Family: The Case for National Action*. Because of his background as a social scientist, he has been able to understand the forces that propel people into poverty and the problems that many families—but primarily single-parent families—face in trying to support their children and improve their life situation. He believes that the two-parent family is being destroyed, especially in inner cities, and has examined the effects of the many problems single parents face, including school failure, drug addiction, and crime. According to Moynihan, the basic goal of all social policy should be to help people participate fully in society. He worked hard to defeat the 1996 welfare reform law, The Personal Responsibility and Work Opportunity Reconciliation Act of 1996, understanding the problems that many families face as single parents and while living in poverty.

One researcher on single-parent families comments as follows on Moynihan and his experience:

> Being a contrarian on the issue of unmarried motherhood—and what social institutions can do about it—is not a new role for this senator [Moynihan]. This is, after all, a subject he has studied with professional acuity for more than half of his seventy years. His views are shaped more by scholarly judgment than by the shifting winds of popular opinion. These days, as escalating anger at mothers who rely on government assistance for their family's support propels policy changes, the senator rarely allows an opportunity slip by to remind folks that children are the ones the welfare program was designed to protect. (Ludtke 1997, 409)

Elizabeth A. Mulroy

Elizabeth Mulroy is a social worker and urban planner. She has taught social policy, planning, and management at Boston University School of Social Work, has directed the Human Services Management Program at Boston University, and is currently an associate professor at the School of Social Work at the University of Hawaii at Manoa. She completed her undergraduate work at Simmons College, and received her master's and doctorate degrees in social work from the University of Southern California. She has been an administrative assistant to former U.S. Congresswoman Margaret Heckler (R-Mass.), and has served as a consultant in housing management, planning, and human services for families and children. Mulroy has lectured extensively on urban planning and the changing family.

Her most recent research is on single mothers and housing, management of social programs, and organizational change. Her previous books have focused on the many pressures felt by single mothers and their experiences in trying to support their families. In *Women as Single Parents* (1988) Mulroy approaches the single-parent family phenomenon from an interdisciplinary perspective, drawing on the expertise of academics and practitioners in fields of law, social work, urban planning, housing, economics, and public policy.

In her more recent book, *The New Uprooted: Single Mothers in Urban Life* (1995), Mulroy provides a new approach to the study of single parents. She examines how single mothers from a variety of backgrounds experience their two roles as sole family breadwinners and sole resident parents. Mulroy examines the failure of many fathers to support their children, the violence that many women have experienced in their homes, the limited employment options that are available to single mothers, and the problems they face in finding adequate safe housing for themselves and their children.

Charles Murray (1943–)

Charles Murray is well known for his articles on poverty, welfare, and other social problems. He is currently a resident scholar at the American Enterprise Institute (AEI) in Washington, D.C. Murray received his B.A. degree from Harvard University in 1965 and his Ph.D. degree from Massachusetts Institute of Technology in 1974. He was a Peace Corps volunteer in Thailand, a program evaluator for the American Institutes for Research, and a Bradley Fellow at the Manhattan Institute for Policy Research before he joined AEI in 1990.

As a social scientist, Murray is probably best known for his criticism of the modern welfare state. His first book, *Losing Ground: American Social Policy, 1950–1980,* published in 1984, created quite a bit of controversy. In it he wrote that social spending should be cut drastically in order to help people end their dependency on welfare. He thought that welfare created more problems than it solved. He believed that during the 1960s a major change in the popular view on poverty occurred, in which it was no longer believed that individuals were responsible for their own well-being. The new theory suggested that poverty "was produced by conditions that had nothing to do with individual virtue or effort. Poverty was not the fault of the individual but of the system" (Murray 1984, 29). Even though the government spent millions of dollars on poverty programs during the 1960s poverty did not go away; people did not get off welfare in the large numbers that were expected. Murray suggested that returning to equal opportunity was the best action the government could take. If the government eliminated many federal programs that provide help to the working-age population, such as AFDC, Food Stamps, Medicaid, Unemployment Insurance, Workers' Compensation, subsidized housing, disability insurance, and other similar programs, those in need would learn to stand on their own and support themselves. For those who couldn't do so, private charities and other family members could provide help. As a result of this book and his research on poverty Murray became one of the most influential scholars concerning poverty and welfare during the Reagan administration.

His next book, *In Pursuit: Of Happiness and Good Government* (1988), took a more philosophical approach to welfare. He suggested that by providing welfare benefits to those living in poverty, the government was denying them the pleasure of being able to provide for their own living. Government assistance was damaging to the self-respect of poor people by not allowing them to accomplish success on their own. His more recent book, written with Richard J. Herrstein in 1994, was *The Bell Curve: Intelligence and Class Structure in American Life.* This book created great controversy by suggesting that intelligence is genetically based, that Asian-Americans and Caucasians are generally more intelligent than African-Americans. The authors argued that standardized intelligence tests are not racially biased, that they reflected reality.

An article Murray wrote that appeared in the *Wall Street Journal* in 1993 brought the term "illegitimacy" back into the vocabulary of many people. Murray suggested in "The Coming of the White Underclass" that the single most important current social problem was illegitimacy. Illegitimate children contributed to the problems created by poverty, crime, and ignorance. Murray was particularly concerned about single white women, who are among the growing number of women having children out of wedlock. He could find no value in these births; they contributed to the breakdown of society. Others, especially other conservatives, quickly agreed with Murray, and most of his critics could not accuse him of racist attitudes in this case because he focused on white women.

Lynn Woolsey (1937–)

Lynn Woolsey is a U.S. congresswoman from California. She received her B.A. degree in 1980 from the University of San Francisco. She has served on the Petaluma City Council and as the vice mayor for the city of Petaluma. She has represented her district in California since 1993. In Congress she is a member of the Economic and Educational Opportunity Committee and the House Budget Committee. She also cochaired the Democratic Party's task force on welfare reform, and opposed the 1996 welfare reform act. She believes that the current child support computer systems are ineffective and wants the Internal Revenue Service to help enforce child support decisions. She believes that mothers should be able to stay home with their children until they reach the age of 11 years.

Woolsey grew up in the Pacific Northwest and moved to Marin County, California, approximately 30 years ago. In 1968 she was a housewife with three children under the age of six years when her marriage ended. She applied for and received welfare benefits because her husband did not pay her any alimony or child support. Finding a low-paying job, she struggled to support her family. A job with a high-tech company helped save her; over time she became a top executive. A second marriage and a move to Petaluma helped because her mother could live with her and help take care of the children. Putting herself through business school at night, Woolsey earned a degree in human resources and established her own personnel service.

While on the Petaluma Council she worked to limit growth and set up affirmative action programs and a Women of Color Task Force. Because of her earlier experiences, she helped implement requirements that 15 percent of new housing should be set aside for low-income buyers as well as a voucher system for child care for low-income families.

Woolsey is a member of the Sonoma County National Women's Political Caucus, the Sierra Club, and the League of Women Voters. Awards she has won include designation as Woman of the Year by the Petaluma Business and Professional Women in 1983, and as one of the Women of Power named by the National Organization for Women in 1993.

Leontine Young (1910–1988)

Leontine Young was a social worker and a prominent authority on social casework theory in the area of unwed mothers. She was frequently hired as a consultant by federal, state, and local governments concerned about illegitimacy. She served on national boards of organizations involved with the problems of unmarried motherhood. She received her master's degree (1944) and her degree as doctor of social welfare (1963) from Columbia University. She was a caseworker or consultant for federal, state, and private agencies in Nebraska, Hawaii, and New York. As supervisor of a treatment center for adolescent girls in the early 1940s and at the Inwood House for Unmarried Mothers in New York, she saw many of the problems that these young girls faced in their daily lives.

She returned to academia and became an assistant professor in the School of Social Work at Columbia University in 1945 and then in 1952 moved to Ohio State University where she was a professor in casework in the School of Social Administration. She published several books including *The Treatment of Adolescent Girls in an Institution, Out of Wedlock, Life Among the Giants*, and *Wednesday's Children: A Study of Child Neglect and Abuse*. At the time she wrote *Out of Wedlock* in 1954, she believed, along with many other mental health and social work professionals, that the fact that a young, pregnant girl hadn't prevented or terminated her pregnancy proved she was psychologically disturbed. According to Young (1954) "we know that pregnancy is purposive because the girl doesn't consider contraception and doesn't want an abortion" (page 31).

Young believed that many young girls became pregnant to rebel against their mothers, and that most girls did not feel a strong attachment to their babies. She cautioned, in 1954, "the caseworker has to clarify for herself the differences between the feelings of the normal [married] woman for her baby and the fantasy use of the child by the neurotic unmarried mother" (Young 1954, 216). Most professionals belittled the importance of the relationship of these young mothers to their infants.

Young was one of many social workers at the time who did not consider the problems of black single mothers. She believed that these girls were "socially disorganized girls who have no standards of their own and little control over their impulses. . . . Becoming an unmarried mother is only one incident in a life history that is largely chaotic. . . . [These girls] grew up in homes characterized by the same lack of social and moral standards as they suffer from" (Young 1954, 87–88).

Young returned to the world of social work in 1960 as executive director of the Child Service Association in Newark, New Jersey. She also kept her hand in academia, as a visiting professor of social work at Rutgers.

References

"Author Instructs Moms and Dads About the Rules of 'Flying Solo,'" press release. Minneapolis: Fairview Press.

Ellwood, David T., and Lawrence H. Summers. 1986. "Poverty in America: Is Welfare the Answer or the Problem?" In *Fighting Poverty: What Works and What Doesn't*, ed. Sheldon H. Danziger and Daniel H. Weinberg, 78–105. Cambridge, MA: Harvard University Press.

Harris, Kathleen Mullan. 1997. *Teen Mothers and the Revolving Welfare Door*. Philadelphia: Temple University Press.

Ludtke, Melissa. 1997. *On Our Own: Unmarried Motherhood in America*. New York: Random House.

Mattes, Jane. 1994. *Single Mothers by Choice: A Guidebook for Single Women Who Are Considering or Have Chosen Motherhood*. New York: Times Books.

Moseley-Braun, Carol. 1994. "The Silent Constituency." In *The Single Mother's Companion: Essays and Stories by Women*, ed. Marsha R. Leslie. Seattle: Seal Press.

Mulroy, Elizabeth A. 1995. *The New Uprooted: Single Mothers in Urban Life.* Westport, CT: Auburn House.

Murray, Charles. 1984. *Losing Ground: American Social Policy, 1950–1980.* New York: Basic Books.

Young, Leontine. 1954. *Out of Wedlock.* New York: McGraw Hill.

Facts and Statistics 4

This chapter presents facts and statistics concerning single-parent families. Statistics about the number of single parents, the number of children living in single-parent families, the number of unmarried mothers, divorces, and other aspects of single parenthood are provided. The role of the federal government in the lives of single-parent families, primarily through public laws that focus on helping single mothers living in poverty, is discussed. The impact of the legal system on single parents in the areas of paternity, child custody, and adoption is examined. The experiences of single-parent families in other countries are described. Cases decided by the United States Supreme Court that have had an impact on the lives of single parents are presented. Citations locating state statutes concerning child custody and adoption are included. Finally, the future of single-parent families is discussed.

Increasing Numbers of Single-Parent Families

The number of single-parent families has varied over the years, but has increased since statistics were first collected. This increase can be attributed to many factors, including the growing number of divorces in the United States, the desire by single women and men to have children, and the growing number of teenagers participating in sexual activity, often without the benefits of contraception or without any intention of becoming pregnant. According to the U.S. Department of Labor, Women's Bureau (1993), the number of single-mother families has grown from 8.8 million in 1980 to 11.7 million in 1992. The percentage has grown from 14.8 percent in 1980 to 17.6 percent in 1992.

Table 1 shows the growth from 1970 to 1995 in the number of one- and two-parent family groups, according to the U.S. Bureau of the Census (1996a). These numbers are based on the Census of 1980 and 1990, as well as estimates based on representative samples and projections based on established trends.

During the 1970s the increasing number of single parents was noticed by many experts. Another report from the U.S. Bureau of the Census (1995a) estimated that the number of single parents grew from 3.8 million in 1970 to 6.9 million in 1980. By 1990 there were an estimated 9.7 million single parents and 11.4 million single parents in 1994. These estimates differ from the numbers in the table; this difference may be due to differing bases of estimating the number of single parents as well as differing definitions of a single-parent family. Single parents refer to family groups comprised of parents with one or more children under the age of 18 years living with them. The Bureau of the Census defines family group as including family households, related subfamilies, and unrelated subfamilies. They believe that sometimes single parents live with their children alone, sometimes they move in with other family members, and sometimes they share housing with other, unrelated persons, such as other

TABLE 1
Number of Two-Parent and One-Parent Families, 1970 and 1995

	1970	1995
Two-parent families	25,961,000	25,241,000
One-parent families	6,061,000	9,055,000
Female heads	5,445,000	7,615,000
Male heads	616,000	1,440,000

Source: Based on data from the U.S. Bureau of the Census (1996a).

single parents and their children, combining to create one single household.

Approximately 64.2 percent of all single-parent family groups in 1994 were white, 31.2 percent were black, and 13.9 percent were Hispanic (the total percent is more than 100 due to Hispanics sometimes being counted with whites and sometimes with Hispanics). Within each racial and ethnic category the number of single parents as a proportion of all parent groups varies significantly. Table 2 demonstrates the variety across racial and ethnic groups in 1994.

The percentage of single-parent families varies from 24.7 percent of all white family groups to 36.2 percent of all Hispanic family groups to 64.8 percent of all black family groups.

Children Living in Single-Parent Families

Estimates vary widely on the number of children in America who will at some time during their childhood live in a single-parent family. Chambers (1997) estimates that 25 percent of all American children will live with just one parent at some point during their childhood. Garfinkel and McLanahan (1986) estimate that almost one-half of all children born today will spend part of their childhood in a single-parent family. Dowd (1997) believes that the figure is closer to 70 percent.

In 1960 only 8 percent of all children lived in a single-mother family. By 1993 almost 25 percent of all children lived with a single mother (Rodgers 1996). According to statistics compiled by the Federal Interagency Forum on Child and Family Sta-

TABLE 2
Composition of Family Groups with Children by Racial and Ethnic Groups, 1994
(percentage)

	White	Black	Hispanic
Two-parent family group	75.3	35.2	63.8
One-parent family group	24.7	64.8	36.2
Mother-only	20.7	59.7	31.2
Father-only	4.0	5.1	5.0

Source: Based on data from the U.S. Bureau of the Census (1995a).

tistics (1997), in 1996, 28 percent of all children lived with only one of their parents—24 percent with their mothers and 4 percent with their fathers.

The percentage of children living with both of their natural parents has been declining among all major racial and ethnic groups. In 1996, 75 percent of all white children, 33 percent of all black children, and 62 percent of all Hispanic children lived with two parents. Table 3 presents statistics on the number and percentage of children living in various family configurations.

Based on the same data used in Table 3, Table 4 provides information concerning the number and percent of children living with their mothers and the marital status of the mother for the years 1970 and 1995.

TABLE 3
Number of Children and Their Living Arrangement, 1970 and 1995

	1970		1995	
	Number	Percent	Number	Percent
Living with both parents	58,787,700	85	48,475,260	69
Living with mother only	7,607,820	11	16,158,420	23
Living with father only	691,620	1	2,810,160	4
Living with neither parent	2,074,860	3	2,810,160	4

Source: Based on data from the U.S. Bureau of the Census (1996a).

TABLE 4
Number and Percentage of Children Living with Single Mother,
by Marital Status of Mother

	1970		1995	
	Number	Percent	Number	Percent
Never married	691,620	1	5,620,320	8
Married, spouse absent	3,458,100	5	4,215,240	6
Divorced	2,074,000	3	6,322,860	9
Widowed	1,383,240	2	702,540	1

Source: Based on data from the U.S. Bureau of the Census (1996a).

Becoming a Single Parent

In the early years of the twentieth century, the majority of single mothers achieved that status as a result of the death of their husbands. By 1960, however, only 24 percent of all single mothers were widowed, while 48 percent of all single mothers were separated from their husbands, 24 percent were divorced, and 4 percent were never married (Blankenhorn 1995). By the early 1970s more marriages ended in divorce than in death.

Over time the reasons why women become single mothers have changed. By 1992 only about 5 percent of all single-mother families had experienced the death of the father. Approximately 37 percent had experienced parental divorce; and in 36 percent of these families the parents had never married. The remaining 22 percent of these single-mother families are classified by the U.S. Census Bureau as "married, spouse absent" (Rawlings 1993). Today more fathers are avoiding the responsibilities of fatherhood, according to many researchers (Blankenhorn 1995; Quayle and Medved 1996).

Unmarried Mothers

The number of unmarried women who are having children is growing. Between 1960 and 1990 the ratio of births to unmarried women as a percentage of births to all women increased from 5.3 percent to 28 percent, an increase of over 500 percent (Coontz 1997). By 1995 the percentage had increased to 32 percent. The number of births to unmarried women increased as the number of births to married women fell. Between 1980 and 1994 birthrates for unmarried women increased from 29 to 47 per 1,000. In 1994 one out of every three births was to an unmarried woman. These increases were across all age groups; for unmarried women between the ages of 15 and 17 years the rate increased from 21 to 32 per 1,000; for unmarried women between the ages of 20 and 24 years the rate increased from 41 to 72 per 1,000 (Federal Interagency Forum 1997).

The Children's Defense Fund (1994) reported that "if the proportion of births to unmarried women continues to climb over the next seven years as it has in the past seven years, more than 40 percent of all babies born in 2001 will go home from the hospital to a single parent family" (Children's Defense Fund

1994). Merritt and Steiner (1984) suggest that the number of unmarried women deciding to have children has grown, becoming a new and significant social phenomenon. Over 40,000 babies were born to single women who were in their 30s in 1978; by 1980 the number of births to single women in their 30s and older had increased to 59,000, and by 1984 the number was 84,000.

Contrary to popular opinion the majority of out-of-wedlock births do not occur among black women and teenagers. The majority of these births are to white women; this group is the fastest growing category of unwed mothers (National Center for Health Statistics 1989). While the absolute number of single white women bearing children is higher than single black women, the proportion of single women with children is higher for blacks than for whites. In 1984, 45,000 single white women and 35,000 single black women bore children; these numbers represent 8 percent of white women and 34 percent of black women (Kamerman and Kahn 1988). As Coontz (1997) explains, "the probability that an unmarried African-American woman would have a child actually fell from 9.8 to 9.0 percent between 1960 and 1990, for example; but because married couple childbearing decreased among African-Americans even more sharply, the proportion of black children born to unwed mothers rose" (p. 29).

Divorce

By 1985 all states had some version of no-fault divorce available. As states began enacting no-fault divorce statutes in the 1970s (California was the first to do so in 1970), the divorce rate started increasing. Between the early 1960s and the mid-1970s the rate more than doubled. Some people predict that three out of five first marriages will end in divorce. The rate for second marriages is predicted to be higher. Table 5 shows the number of people who were never married, married, widowed, and divorced in 1970 and in 1995.

Single Fathers

The number of single-father families is also growing. In 1983 almost 600,000 single fathers were raising their children (close to one million children) alone as the result of separation or divorce. This number represents a 180 percent increase since 1970, com-

TABLE 5
Marital Status of Persons over the Age of 18 Years, 1970 and 1995 (in millions)

	1970	1995
Never married	21.4	43.9
Married	95.0	116.7
Divorced	4.3	17.6
Widowed	11.8	13.4

Source: Based on data from the U.S. Bureau of the Census (1996a).

pared with an increase of 105 percent in single-mother families (U.S. Department of Commerce 1984).

According to the U.S. Bureau of the Census (1996a) single-father family groups grew from 393,000 in 1970 to 616,000 in 1980, and to 1,440,000 in 1995. The number of children living in single-father family groups increased from 692,000 in 1970 to 2,810,000 in 1995. While the number of children living in single-mother family groups is considerably larger than these numbers for single-father families, these numbers nevertheless represent a significant number of fathers and their children. As these numbers continue to grow additional studies will begin to examine the characteristics of single-father families and more will be known about them.

Single Parents and Poverty

In 1959 approximately 60 percent of all single-mother families were poor. Over the years the actual rate has dropped; for example, in 1993 the rate was 46 percent. However, the absolute number has grown: single-mother families are the major poverty group in the United States. The number of poor white and black single-mother families more than doubled between the early 1970s and 1993.

The number of children living in single-parent families has also steadily increased, especially in families living in poverty. Between 1959 and 1993 the number of poor black children in single-mother families increased from 1.5 million to 4.1 million (180 percent). During the same period the number of poor white children in single-mother families increased from 2.4 million to 4.1 million. Although separate statistics on Hispanic children were not available until 1974, the number of poor Hispanic children in single-mother families has also increased, from 600,000 in 1974 to 1.7 million in 1993 (Rodgers 1996).

In 1995, 10 percent of children in two-parent families were living in poverty, while 50 percent of children living in single-mother families were living in poverty. When examined by racial and ethnic group the differences are even more pronounced. In 1995, for example, 13 percent of black children in two-parent families lived in poverty, while 62 percent of all children in single-mother families lived in poverty. For Hispanics 28 percent of children in two-parent and 66 percent of children in single-mother families were living in poverty (Federal Interagency Forum 1997).

Even children in single-father families are not exempt from poverty. In 1993, 20 percent of white, 32 percent of black, and 28 percent of Hispanic father-only families lived in poverty in the United States (U.S. Bureau of the Census 1995a).

Table 6 presents statistics from the U.S. Bureau of the Census (1996b) concerning two-parent and single-parent family groups and poverty. Statistics are based on data for 1994.

Economic Status

The economic status of families varies according to family structure. According to the Women's Bureau in the U.S. Department of Labor (1993), 12 million women maintained families in 1992; only 5.6 million women maintained families in 1972. Single-mother families often have the lowest median income of all family types. For example, their median income in 1991 was $14,560 (compared with $27,046 for single-father families, and $39,152 for two-parent families). Broken down by race or ethnicity, white single-mother families had a median income of $19,547; for similar black families it was $11,414; and for Hispanic single-mother families it was $12,132 (U.S. Bureau of the Census 1992). By 1993 the median household income of single-parent families was $38,935, which was 18 percent lower than for two-parent families. The number of single-parent families living below the poverty line was twice as high (17 percent) as for two-parent families (8 percent). For single-parent families headed by women, the percentages are even higher: the median family income was $15,837, meaning that 42 percent of single-mother families lived below the poverty line (Ozer et al. 1998).

TABLE 6
Poverty Status of Families with Children under the Age of 18 Years,
by Marital Status for 1994

Family Groups	Total Number (1,000s)	Total Percent	White Number (1,000s)	White Percent	Black Number (1,000s)	Black Percent
Two-parent						
Total	26,367		22,839		2,147	
Below poverty line	2,197	8.3	1,708	7.5	245	11.4
One-parent						
All one-parent groups						
Total	10,415		6,709		3,292	
Below poverty line	4,211	40.4	2,287	34.1	1,709	51.9
Mother-only						
Total	8,665		5,390		2,951	
Below poverty line	3,816	44.0	2,034	38.3	1,591	53.9
Father-only						
Total	1,750		1,319		341	
Below poverty line	395	22.6	253	19.2	118	34.6

Source: Based on data from the U.S. Bureau of the Census (1996b).

In 1995 the median family income for various family configurations had not changed much since 1991. For single-mother families the median income was $16,235; for single-father families it was $26,990; and for two-parent families the median income was $40,016 (U.S. Bureau of the Census 1996a).

Employment

In 1995, 88 percent of two-parent families included at least one parent who worked full time year-round. This number compares with 70 percent of families headed by single fathers and 45 percent of families headed by single mothers. Single parents with children under the age of six years were less likely to be working full time than single parents with children between the ages of 6 and 17 years. Broken down by sex of the parent, data indicate that 61 percent of single fathers with children six years old and younger and 75 percent of fathers with older children worked full time. For single mothers 33 percent with children aged six years and younger worked full time compared with 54 percent of mothers with older children (Federal Interagency Forum 1997).

Some researchers suggest that when young men cannot find jobs that pay enough to support a family, they tend to avoid getting married. In some cases they may be rejected by women who don't want to marry a man who cannot support them (Wilson and Neckerman 1986, Rodgers 1996). A study conducted by the Casey Foundation (1995) found that 77 percent of young women admitted that one essential requirement for a husband was that he have a well-paying job. The same study reported that in 1993 almost 50 percent of all black and Hispanic men who were between 25 and 34 years old did not make enough money to support a family (with two children) above the poverty level. The problem for these young men is that there is a shortage of jobs that pay workers with few skills. Few entry-level jobs are available that will lead to a middle-income opportunity (Rodgers 1996).

Father Absence

According to statistics, the average father will spend only seven years in the same household as his children, half of noncustodial fathers see their children less than once a year, and many of these fathers do not see their children at all (Furstenberg 1988). Greif and Pabst (1988) found that two-thirds of noncustodial fathers see their children less than once every month. Cherlin (1988) found that over half of fathers do not pay their court-ordered child support.

Teenage Pregnancy

In the United States today approximately 4 in 10 (or 40 percent) of girls become pregnant at least once before they reach the age of 20 years. The great majority of these births (76 percent) are out of wedlock (National Campaign to Prevent Teen Pregnancy 1997). The percentage of births to unwed teenage mothers in 1960 was 15 percent (National Center for Health Statistics 1967), by 1993 the percentage had reached 72 percent (Ventura et al. 1995), and today the percentage has grown to 76 percent (National Campaign to Prevent Teen Pregnancy 1997).

Most pregnant teenagers are 18 or 19 years old, although 40 percent are 17 years or younger. One-half are white and most are unmarried. The fathers of the children born to teenage mothers are usually older than the mothers: 39 percent are 20 years old or over, 35 percent are 18 or 19 years old, and 26 percent are under 18 years (National Campaign to Prevent Teen Pregnancy 1997).

According to research conducted by the Alan Guttmacher Institute (1994) most teenage pregnancies are unplanned (85 percent). Limited knowledge about or access to birth control may be one reason for this high number of unintended pregnancies. Teenager confusion over preventing pregnancy and their failure to make decisions concerning abstinence and birth control are other reasons. These unplanned pregnancies often lead to abortion (32 percent), while 14 percent result in miscarriages and 54 percent result in birth. Most teenage mothers decide to keep their children.

The rates for teenage pregnancy and births dropped in the early 1990s. Between 1955 and 1986 the rate dropped 45 percent and then started growing again in 1987. In 1991 the rate of teenage births was 62 per 1,000 women who were between 15 and 19 years old. However, by 1995 the rate had fallen to 57 births per 1,000 women (Ventura et al. 1996). Part of this decline can be traced to increased use of contraceptives.

Although the rate of teenage births has declined, the rate of all out-of-wedlock births in the United States has increased. In 1960 only 15 percent of teenage births were to unmarried teenagers; in 1995 the rate was 75 percent (Ventura at al. 1996). These rates reflect trends in the larger society. Births to unmarried women are losing the stigma they once had. Births to unmarried women have become more acceptable; in fact, only 30 percent of all births to unmarried women were to teenagers in 1994 (U.S. Department of Health and Human Services 1995).

Teenagers are more sexually active today than they were years ago. For example, in 1970 only 35 percent of teenage girls and 55 percent of teenage boys reported having had sex by the time they were 18 years old. By 1988 these figures had grown to 56 percent for girls and 73 percent for boys (Alan Guttmacher Institute 1994). Teenagers are increasingly using contraceptives to prevent pregnancy. Approximately 67 percent of teenagers use some type of contraception the first time they have sex (National Campaign to Prevent Teen Pregnancy 1997).

Teenage pregnancy can have serious consequences. Many researchers suggest that for many teenage girls from disadvantaged backgrounds, having a baby makes their situation worse.

Teenage mothers are less likely to complete high school (only 32 percent get a high school diploma), they are more likely to be single mothers, they are more likely to have additional children than women who delay childbearing, and they are more likely to end up on welfare as young mothers. According to research, over 75 percent of unmarried teenage mothers began receiving AFDC payments within five years of the birth of their first child (U.S. Congressional Budget Office 1990). In fact 52 percent of all mothers who receive AFDC benefits had their first child when they were teenagers (Moore et al. 1993).

Welfare

In 1992 all families who received some type of government support collected $594 billion in public transfers, including cash programs, tax incentives, subsidies, and welfare, while single-parent families received $198 billion. Single-parent families received $70 billion in universal transfers, including social security, unemployment, workers compensation, and Medicare; $14 billion in tax expenditures, which included the earned income tax credit, child care tax credit, personal exemptions, and homeowner deductions; $18 billion in third-party health care and private child support; and $96 billion in welfare payments, which included cash payments such as Aid to Families with Dependent Children and SSI, as well as in-kind contributions such as Medicaid, food stamps, nutrition, housing, Head Start educational benefits, child care, employment, and foster care (Garfinkel 1996).

Statistics from the Department of Health and Human Services reported that the new welfare law, the Personal Responsibility and Work Opportunity Reconciliation Act of 1996, has resulted in the largest caseload decline in history. From January 1993 to May 1997 the welfare caseload fell by 3.4 million recipients, from 14.1 million to 10.7 million—a drop of 24 percent. Only two states have not reported a decline in their caseloads and 10 states have reduced the number of people on welfare by 40 percent or more in the last four years. According to the Council of Economic Advisors, the strong economic growth in recent years, the waivers granted to states to test innovative strategies to move people from welfare to work, and other factors such as strengthened child support enforcement and increased funding for child care are the reasons for the reduction in welfare rolls (DHHS Fact Sheet 1997).

Some sources suggest that the large number of people removed from the welfare rolls were the easiest ones to move off of welfare. They were the most employable, had the most education, and had previous work experience. Many believe that those who are left are the harder ones to place in employment. The government wants companies in the private sector to help out by hiring people who are receiving welfare benefits.

The government also collected $12 billion in child support from noncustodial parents in 1996, a 50 percent increase since 1992. The establishment of paternity also almost doubled to nearly 1 million cases in fiscal year 1996 (from 516,000 in 1992). The number of families actually receiving child support rose to 4 million cases, up from 2.8 million cases in 1992.

Homelessness among Single-Parent Families

Two major social trends have contributed to the growing number of homeless in our society. One is the shortage of affordable rental housing and the other is the increase in poverty. Changes in welfare programs and low wages for many unskilled workers have pushed more people into poverty. According to Kaufman (1997) a worker who earns the minimum wage would have to work 83 hours each week in order to be able to afford a two-bedroom apartment at 30 percent of his income, which is the federal government's definition of affordable housing. In 49 states and 357 metropolitan areas, the maximum grant amount under the new welfare law does not fully cover the fair market rent for a two-bedroom apartment (Kaufman 1997). The U.S. Department of Housing and Urban Development (HUD) determines the fair market rent for all areas; it is the monthly amount necessary "to rent privately owned, decent, safe, and sanitary rental housing of a modest (nonluxury) nature with suitable amenities" (National Coalition for the Homeless 1998, 2).

Although the majority of homeless people are single men, the number of families experiencing homelessness is growing. According to Levitan, Mangum, and Mangum (1998), only about 10 percent of all homeless are families. However, among these families, the vast majority of them are single-mother families. According to Steinbock (1995) between 70 and 90 percent of all homeless families are single-mother families; this number is increasing, as more single mothers and their children lose their welfare benefits and their homes.

Among the homeless single mothers and their families are women who have left abusive husbands. Some of these women find that shelters for abused women are full. Waxman and Trupin (1997) found that 32 percent of requests for shelter by homeless women and their children were denied in 1997 because there were no resources available.

According to Douglass (1995) a survey of homeless adults in Michigan found that the most frequently cited reason for being homeless was domestic violence or physical abuse. In Virginia 35 percent of people in homeless shelters are there because of family violence and in 1994 over 2,000 women were turned away from battered women's shelters because there was no space available (Virginia Coalition for the Homeless 1995). Other states report similar statistics. Twenty-five percent of homeless women in Minnesota had left abusive homes (Owen et al. 1995). In Nebraska 25 percent of those who are homeless are victims of domestic violence (Hanna Keelan Associates 1995) and in Missouri, 24 percent of the homeless are victims of domestic violence (De Simone et al. 1995).

The Federal Government and Single Parents

The federal government, together with state governments, has been involved with helping to support single parents and their children since the early 1900s. The first programs were developed by the states, and were known as mothers' pension programs. The federal government later took over with several types of programs to help these families. These programs included Aid to Dependent Children, then Aid to Families with Dependent Children, and the fairly recent Personal Responsibility and Work Opportunity Reconciliation Act of 1996, specifically the Temporary Assistance to Needy Families (TANF) program. These programs started off primarily helping widows with young children to stay at home and raise them, then later included single mothers and their families, added families with dependent children, and then cut back to focus on moving single parents, primarily mothers, off of welfare and into the work force.

Most of the early mothers' pension programs were originally set up to help young widows and their children. Some states expanded their programs to cover divorced women with children and women with children whose husbands had deserted them. For example, by 1921, 40 states had mothers' pension programs; 6 of these states restricted support to widows, 17 states helped deserted mothers, and 6 assisted divorced mothers with children (Abramovitz 1996). Most states did not provide any type of assistance to unmarried mothers. Many of these states also removed women and their children from their lists if they found that the women engaged in activities that were contrary to the family ethic. Such activities included using alcohol or tobacco, failing to attend church, housing a male boarder, having extramarital relations, neglecting a child, and having a delinquent child (Leff 1973).

At least in theory these programs discouraged mothers from working while trying to raise their children. Many states required that the children live with the mother and that she not work outside of the house. Some states allowed mothers to work on a limited basis, such as one day each week. Many mothers performed work at home.

Most states' programs also primarily served white women. In 1931 of the more than 46,000 families receiving help who reported their race, 96 percent were white. One-half of the black families being helped lived in either Ohio or Pennsylvania. Many states did not have any black families being helped (Abramovitz 1996). Other minorities did not fare well either. The Children's Bureau issued a study in 1922 that found 11 out of 45 agencies studied gave smaller amounts of money to Mexican, Italian, and Czechoslovakian families than to white (Anglo-Saxon) families (Abramovitz 1996).

Through the end of World War II participants in the ADC program were generally those judged to be deserving of aid. During and following World War II the number of women being helped by ADC had grown steadily, from 372,0000 in 1940 to 803,000 in 1960 (U.S. Congress 1974). During this time the government found it more difficult to restrict aid to deserving women and their children; the composition of the caseload changed from white widows to unwed mothers and women of color. According to Abramovitz (1996) the "natural growth of the population along with rising rates of divorce, desertion, fertility, and births outside of marriage enlarged the pool of women eligible for ADC from all demographic groups" (p. 320).

The number of black women and their families participating in the ADC program grew over the years. Because of racial discrimination black women were less likely than white women to benefit from expanding employment opportunities during World War II. Even after the war black women had a difficult time finding any work other than as domestic servants. For example, from 1955 to 1968 the jobless rate of black women ranged from 7.3 percent to 11.8 percent (U.S. Women's Bureau 1969).

The growing participation in ADC by divorced, separated, or deserted wives led to a shrinking percentage of widows. Between 1948 and 1953 the number of widowed mothers declined by 25 percent. By 1961 the percent of widowed families on the ADC caseload was down to 7.7 (in 1937 it had been 43 percent). The number of unwed mothers on ADC grew by 58 percent, divorced mothers rose by 9 percent, and deserted or separated mothers with children increased by 28 percent (Abramovitz 1996).

In 1950 Congress passed the Notification of Law Enforcement Officers (NOLEO) amendment to the Social Security Act. This amendment required welfare agencies to notify law enforcement officials when they provided assistance to children whose fathers had abandoned or deserted them. In essence this amendment reflected public disapproval of irresponsible fathers who did not want to support their families. Public opinion also suggested that the ADC program itself encouraged the breakup of families by supporting them, giving the fathers an "excuse" not to support their own families. The mothers receiving ADC were the ones who bore the brunt of this criticism; mothers were required to cooperate with law enforcement officials in finding the fathers of their children in order to continue to receive help (Abramovitz 1996). The Jenner Amendment, passed in 1951, allowed welfare rolls to be made public in order to combat welfare fraud. Mothers and their children were no longer protected from the embarrassment of taking public welfare. Public perceptions of women on welfare who did not deserve help were growing.

The application of moral standards to participation in the ADC program continued to grow. Following World War II, 15 states abolished their suitable home requirements, although many other states did not. In fact many states began passing laws that disqualified many unwed mothers and women of color from ADC benefits. These rules included suitable home, man-in-the-house, and substitute father rules. Child care, guidance, and home management standards were enacted and enforced by welfare workers. In many cases state welfare agencies denied help to women who were unwed mothers, refused to identify the fathers of their children, took in male boarders, or lived with men out of wedlock, as well as for any other reason the welfare worker deemed appropriate (Abramovitz 1996).

The AFDC program was enacted in 1962 to encourage and support families, primarily single-parent families. President Kennedy believed that the poor needed financial assistance as well as services to help them escape poverty. His administration established the Food Stamp program, Job Corps, and Neighborhood Youth Corps to help families and changed Aid to Dependent Children (ADC) to Aid to Families with Dependent Children (AFDC) in order to include married couples in which the head of household was unemployed. This change encouraged families to stay together.

The Economic Opportunity Act was passed in 1964 and focused on programs that emphasized jobs, job training, and work for mothers receiving AFDC benefits. Medicaid also came into existence at this time to provide health care for those who could not afford regular medical care.

Following Lyndon Johnson's presidency and efforts to help those in poverty, especially single mothers, other presidents attempted to alter the welfare system. Many of these attempts failed. President Nixon supported the Family Assistance Plan, which would have provided a basic guaranteed income through several income, work, and training provisions for all people living below the poverty line. This plan was defeated in the Senate. President Carter supported the Program for Better Jobs, which was similar to the Family Assistance Plan. This program also failed to gain enough support for passage. During the presidency of Ronald Reagan, the Family Support Act was passed (1988). This Act provided more than $3.3 billion over five years to help welfare recipients find jobs. Single parents receiving welfare who had children over the age of three years were required to participate in job training programs. States were required to increase collection of child support from noncustodial parents and to adopt consistent standards for setting child support awards. Fathers' employers were required to start withholding child support from their paychecks. According to several researchers, however, these measures did not improve the financial status of most single mothers living in poverty (Edin and Lein 1997; Edin 1995; Sorenson and Turner 1996).

The administration of President George Bush continued the policies of the Reagan era, believing that individuals can escape poverty on their own, with the help of a strong economy. Bush encouraged volunteerism and programs that empowered the poor through a variety of policies such as school vouchers and enterprise zones. Bush believed that the best way to help empower Americans living in poverty was through education. His school voucher program would have allowed parents to choose the best schools available for their children; parents in poor neighborhoods could choose to send their children to schools outside their neighborhoods that would provide them with better educational opportunities than available in their neighborhood school. In much the same way, Bush believed that enterprise zones would help revitalize inner cities by encouraging business investment and job creation. Enterprise zones were defined as specific geographic areas within cities that needed commercial revitalization and investment. By providing a combination of incentives, such as tax credits, business deductions, low-interest financing, and job training programs, these areas could provide job training and employment opportunities for local residents and improve living conditions for the residents.

The Clinton Administration has changed welfare policies to place more responsibility on individuals to take control of their lives. Prior to passage of welfare reform legislation in 1996 the Clinton Administration waived certain provisions in federal statutes and allowed 43 states to require people receiving financial assistance from the government to work, to limit assistance to a certain amount of time, and to improve child support enforcement and encourage personal responsibility.

The Personal Responsibility and Work Opportunity Reconciliation Act was passed in 1996. On 1 July 1997 this new law went into effect and welfare plans have been certified in all states. This legislation focuses on ways that parents living in poverty, especially single mothers, can be helped to become self-sufficient. Aid to Families with Dependent Children (AFDC), the Job Opportunities and Basic Skills (JOBS) program, and the Emergency Assistance programs were replaced by Temporary Assistance to Needy Families (TANF). Most program and rule-making authority was transferred from the federal government to the states. The legislation has several parts that directly impact single parents, including:

- States can decide whether to increase assistance to a recipient family when additional children are born or conceived while the parent is receiving support.
- Recipients must work after receiving benefits for two years. Mothers who have not completed high school or its equivalent are required to attend school or an approved training program once their child is 12 weeks old.
- The Maternal and Child Health Block Grant includes $50 million each year for states to develop abstinence-only programs.
- Families are limited to five years of benefits over their lifetimes. States are allowed to set shorter time limits. The length of time that a parent is under the age of 21 will not be counted against the five-year limit unless the parent marries or is declared the head of the household.
- Many options for child care are eliminated, although the child care and development block grant provides capped entitlement and discretionary funds. Child care programs may be developed that are located in or near schools for teenage parents. Child care funding increased by nearly $4 billion over six years, providing child care assistance to low-income working families and parents. In October 1996 the child care block grant funds for fiscal years 1997 were released by DHHS, providing up to $1.92 billion to states.
- States are allowed to collect child support from the grandparents when a custodial teenage parent receives TANF assistance and both of the parents are minors.
- The Department of Transportation has awarded grants to 24 states to develop welfare-to-work transportation strategies.
- The secretary of the Department of Health and Human Services is required to develop and implement a strategy for preventing out-of-wedlock births to teenage parents. At least 25 percent of all communities in the United States are required to set up teenage pregnancy prevention programs. No federal funds are allocated for this purpose.

The Legal System and Single Parents

The legal system has had a major impact on the lives of single parents, especially in the areas of paternity, child support, and adoption. This section provides information concerning these three areas.

Paternity

In the past illegitimate children had few if any rights. According to the Law of Bastardy from the old English common law, the illegitimate child was the child of no one and therefore was denied the rights provided to children born to a married couple. The illegitimate child could not inherit from his or her father, use his or her father's name, and had no legal connection to his mother. In the United States the treatment of legitimate and illegitimate children varied from state to state. In 1921 Arizona passed a law declaring all children to be legitimate children of their natural parents, but many states at that time did not give illegitimate children any rights. Even as late as 1973 illegitimate children in Texas were denied the right to claim support from their natural fathers.

The Supreme Court entered into the area of illegitimacy and rights in 1968 in the case of *Levy v. Louisiana* (see summary later in this chapter), by overturning a Louisiana statute that denied illegitimate children the right to recover for the wrongful death of their mothers, holding that the state's statute denied the children equal protection under the Fourteenth Amendment to the U.S. Constitution. In another case, *Trimble v. Gordon* (1977), the Supreme Court ruled invalid an Illinois statute that prohibited illegitimate children from inheriting from their fathers if the children were not specifically mentioned in their fathers' wills. Most states now view a child as legitimate even if the parents are not married, if the father acknowledges the child as his (known as *legitimation* of a child). Most states require the father to file a statement, given under oath, with a court or the bureau of vital statistics (Dowd 1997).

In the past a father had no responsibilities toward his illegitimate child, and he often had no rights either. By acknowledging paternity a father now has a number of legal rights, including custody rights. However, the rate for establishing paternity for children born to unmarried mothers is not very high, averaging only approximately 30 percent of all out-of-wedlock births. According to Wattenberg (1993) the rates by state vary tremendously, from a low of 14 percent in Louisiana to a high of 67 percent in Michigan. According to Dowd (1997) over two-thirds of children born to unmarried mothers have no legally recognized fathers.

Under the new welfare law states are required to develop procedures under which the name of the father is included on the birth certificate only if the mother and father have signed an acknowledgment of paternity voluntarily or following a judicial or administrative order. States are also required to determine whether a program recipient is cooperating in good faith with the state's efforts to establish paternity and collect child support.

According to the U.S. Bureau of the Census (1995b) there were 11.5 million custodial parents in 1992; 6.2 million of these parents (or over one-half) were awarded child support. Broken down by sex, 56 percent of custodial mothers and 41 percent of custodial fathers were awarded support. Mothers who received child support payments had lower incomes than fathers who received child support ($18,144 versus $33,579). Custodial parents who received no child support had even lower incomes (see Table 7).

Child Support

Single parents may have trouble collecting child support payments from their former spouses. The federal government over the years has enacted several laws to help these parents; many of these laws have encouraged the states to help find the former spouses and require them to provide the child support mandated by the courts.

In 1950 passage of the model Uniform Reciprocal Enforcement of Support Act (URESA) was designed to help custodial parents in enforcing child support awards across state lines. The Act required support payments for dependent children from the

TABLE 7
Average Income for Custodial Parents, 1991

	Custodial Mothers	Custodial Fathers
Received support	$18,144	$33,579
Did not receive support	$14,602	$25,184
Was not awarded support	$10,226	$27,578

Source: Based on data from the U.S. Bureau of the Census (1995b).

responsible noncustodial parents even though these parents had moved to another state. The Act further required that the support award was to be enforced in the noncustodial parent's state exactly as it was in the state in which the award was made. The Act was revised in 1952, 1958, and 1968. As a model law, the act was developed by legal experts and introduced into the legislature of all states. Although the law was not adopted by all states at the same time, it was eventually adopted by all states. URESA was revised (the Revised Uniform Reciprocal Family Support Act [RURESA]) and was ultimately replaced by the Uniform Interstate Family Support Act (UIFSA). By 1994, 21 states had passed the UIFSA. As of 1998, 47 states have adopted it.

In 1965 the Social Security Act was passed. In this Act, state or local welfare agencies were allowed to obtain information from the secretary of Health, Education, and Welfare concerning the addresses and places of employment of absent parents.

Changes to the Social Security Act were passed in 1967 and required people who received AFDC benefits to assign their child support benefits to the state.

In 1975 the U.S. Congress passed Title IV-D of the Social Security Act. A federal agency, the Office of Child Support Enforcement, was established and all states were required to set up similar local agencies. Services to be provided by the new agency and its state satellites included help in locating absent parents (parent locator services), an improved system to establish the identity of responsible parents, and a process to ensure that child support awards were appropriate to the needs of the children and the ability of the parent to pay.

The passage of the Child Support Enforcement Amendments of 1984 attempted to resolve some of the problems created by passage of Title IV-D. States were required to establish mechanisms to enforce child support and to set quantitative guidelines for levels of child support. If states did not establish these guidelines, they would lose federal funding for the AFDC program. The New York State Child Support Commission was set up to investigate the state child support collection system according to the 1984 Amendments. The Commission, in a 1985 study, reported that most complaints about the system revolved around the unwillingness of judges to demand compliance or to impose penalties for noncompliance (Mulroy 1988).

The Family Support Act was passed in 1988 and continued to improve the services provided for child support enforcement and to help families collect child support payments. Each state was required to develop specific statutory guidelines to determine child support awards. Specific mechanisms were to be developed to collect child support. Specific formulas were also to be developed in order to ensure awards were consistent and uniform. Legislators hoped that this law would improve the collection of child support. Following passage of this Act, in fiscal 1988 the child support enforcement system collected $4.6 billion, a large increase over the past few years (Spencer 1989).

The Child Support Recovery Act of 1992 makes it a federal crime for a noncustodial parent living in one state to fail to pay child support to dependent children living in another state. According to Boumil and Friedman (1996) an estimated 500,000 cases of willfully failing to pay child support could be prosecuted based on this law. However, lack of judicial resources makes it difficult to prosecute guilty parents. In some cases, however, the threat of criminal prosecution may be more effective in getting the parent to pay child support than any other method.

The Omnibus Budget Reconciliation Act was passed in 1993 and provided additional help to states in dealing with child support collection problems still faced by many custodial parents. The Act required that states, in order to continue to receive federal funding, establish expedited or streamlined procedures for determining paternity.

The Personal Responsibility and Work Opportunity Reconciliation Act of 1996 also addresses child support. States are required to provide certain services related to enforcement of child support obligations, develop privacy safeguards concerning child support cases, and maintain automated data systems that include information on all support orders issued after a certain date. State statutes must be enacted to establish procedures for mandatory income withholding for support payments. The Federal Parent Locator Service was revised to provide additional information to help in establishing, setting the amount of, modifying, or enforcing child support obligations.

Adoption

Single people are allowed to adopt a child in every state, although many agencies prefer to place children in two-parent homes. Single people are more likely to adopt children with special needs, that is, children who are older, physically challenged, of mixed or minority ethnicity, siblings, and children with emotional and/or behavioral problems.

Statistics on adoption by single parents are often difficult to find. Shireman (1995) estimates that between 12 and 15 percent of all nonrelative adoptions are to single parents. She believes that people who are single and want to adopt are still considered marginal by most adoption agencies and usually are approved only for older or special needs children. Few studies have been conducted on single-parent adoption, including single parents adopting children from foreign countries, single men who adopt, and lesbians and gay men who adopt (Groze 1991).

Findings from the few studies that have been conducted concerning single-parent adoption have shown that single adoptive parents tend to be primarily women, emotionally secure with a high tolerance for frustration, and have lower incomes than two-parent families who adopt. The children that single parents adopt tend to be older and usually of the same sex as the adoptive parent (Groze 1991).

International Experiences of Single-Parent Families

Many western European countries have experienced a significant increase in single-mother families. In most cases, the increase is due to growing numbers of divorced and separated mothers, never-married women who are having children, and couples living together without being married. The percentage of single-parent families during the 1980s varied from 6 percent in Italy to 32 percent in Sweden. In between were France (10 percent), Austria and Germany (13 percent), Britain (14 percent), Finland (15 percent), Norway (19 percent), Hungary (20 percent), and Denmark (26 percent). At the same time in the United States 26 percent of all families were single-parent families; 23 percent of these families were headed by mothers, 3 percent by fathers (Kamerman and Kahn 1988).

In Great Britain the number of single-parent families has increased over the years, from approximately 600,000 in 1971 to over 1,000,000 in 1986 (Haskey 1991). In 1971 approximately 8 percent of all families with dependent children were single-parent families; this number rose to 15 percent in 1987. The majority of these families were headed by women; only 1 percent of all families with dependent children were headed by men. Single mothers are provided with a means-tested financial grant until the children reach the age of 16 years. Mothers are not pressured to find work outside the home, and child allowances, national health services, and access to public housing are provided. A Family Credit Program is offered for mothers who work at least 24 hours each week and earn low wages; the program is similar to the Earned Income Tax Credit in the United States (Kamerman and Kahn 1988),

Single parents in Norway face many of the same problems as single parents in the United States. Most single parent-families are headed by women, and many have little earned income. However, the goal of Norway's government policy is to keep mothers at home if they wish. Benefits provided by the government include a child allowance, child care cash benefit, education benefit, a transitional benefit that supports single parents who are temporarily unable to support themselves and their children, advanced maintenance payments, and a housing allowance. Even with this help, most single-parent families (90 percent) have incomes of less than half the median family income. However, only 8.6 percent of all children in single-parent families fall below the poverty line (Kamerman and Kahn 1988).

The French government also provides many benefits to single parents. While the government policy favors young families, poor families, and large families, single parents also benefit because many are young and poor. A universal family allowance is provided to all families beginning with the second child, a family allowance supplement is based on income level, and a young child allowance is offered, as well as paid maternity leave, parenting leave, and a housing allowance (Kamerman and Kahn 1988). However, after children reach the age of three years, all parents, including single parents, are expected to work if they are in financial need.

In Austria, in addition to paid maternity leave (eight weeks before and eight weeks after birth) and 10 months of job-protected leave for working mothers, single mothers who have a prior work history can qualify for paid leave until the child reaches the age of three years. This leave is paid for through the unemployment insurance system, is equal to 80 percent of the unemployment benefit, is tax free, and provides full health care coverage. Most mothers return to work following this paid leave;

only 25 percent of single mothers receive some type of social as-sistance (Kamerman and Kahn 1988).

Finland's government policy focuses on all families with children and provides a universal child allowance, an income-based housing allowance, job-protected maternity leave for working mothers (one year), a taxable cash benefit, a child-rearing allowance, and an advanced maintenance benefit that is provided to single mothers when the noncustodial parent fails to make support payments.

Less than 70 percent of all families with children in Sweden are in traditional two-parent, married families. Similar to other countries, single-parent families in Sweden are financially vul-nerable. Government policy provides some supplemental bene-fits, but certainly not enough for a single-parent family to survive on with no additional source of income. Benefits include a child allowance, child support or maintenance, a housing allowance, and parental benefits (Kamerman and Kahn 1988).

In Sweden, unlike most other countries, the number of mar-riages is going down and the number of births to unmarried par-ents is up. The rate of out-of-wedlock births (52 percent in 1989) is the highest of all the European countries. However, many of these births are to two parents who are living together but are not married. Marriage became less popular in the mid-1960s; at least 25 percent of all couples are currently unmarried. Living together and having a child outside of marriage has become more popu-lar—so too have breakups among nonmarried couples, which is one reason for the relatively high number of single-mother fami-lies (Burns and Scott 1994). The Swedish government has devel-oped an extensive social security system that guarantees a home and financial support to children of single parents. Unmarried and divorced mothers are expected to continue to work or go to school, and the extensive program of social support helps them do so. Fathers are expected by the state to continue to help sup-port the children; the state decrees the amount to be paid and col-lects it, making up shortages when necessary (Burns and Scott 1994).

Several Central American countries have high rates of out-of-wedlock births. Hartley's (1975) survey in the early 1970s found that the rate in Panama was 70 percent, in Guatemala it was 67 percent, in El Salvador 67 percent, in Honduras 66 per-cent, in the Dominican Republic 62 percent, and in Nicaragua it was 53 percent. This trend has not changed much over time.

In Nicaragua, four factors generally explain the high rate of births to unmarried women. These factors include male migration, male mortality, *machismo,* and attitudes toward motherhood. First, many unemployed men find that they must migrate to other areas to find work; sometimes they fail to return. Second, men are more likely than women to die young, either through war or other causes. Third, *machismo,* or the male's attitude that demands that men conquer women, leads many men to have sex with women and then walk away. Finally, the culture's stress on motherhood, in which a woman is not truly considered a woman until she has a child, and the widespread following of the Catholic religion encourage women to have children. A lack of birth control supplies and a lack of education contribute to high fertility rates (Burns and Scott 1994).

During the 1970s and 1980s the leaders in Nicaragua made several legislative changes that raised the status of women in that country. The Sandinista government decided that paternity should be the basis for determining a man's legal responsibility to his children. The war provided women with the opportunity to enlist and fight; they proved that they could be good soldiers. Wider job opportunities were available to them and they proved themselves professionally capable of handling responsibility. Finally, by 1983, 70 percent of all students at the Central American University were women (Burns and Scott 1994).

A recent report by the Alan Guttmacher Institute (1998) examined young women's sexuality in 53 countries. Researchers found that adolescent girls give birth to over 14 million children worldwide; percentages range from only 1 percent of adolescent girls in Japan giving birth before age 18 to 53 percent in Niger.

In the United States 70 percent of the births to adolescents were unplanned. In Latin America and the Caribbean between 25 and 50 percent of all births to adolescents were unplanned; in North Africa and the Middle East between 15 and 30 percent were unplanned, and in Asia and sub-Saharan Africa between 40 and 60 percent were unplanned.

Teenage mothers in Great Britain have the highest percentage of out-of-wedlock births—87 percent of girls who gave birth between the ages of 15 and 19 years old were unmarried. In the United States the number is 62 percent, while only 10 percent of the births to adolescent girls in Japan were to unmarried girls (Alan Guttmacher Institute 1998).

Female-headed families are a topic of increasing interest throughout the world, and especially in Third World countries. Concern over female-headed households in these countries is sparked by the lack of social welfare systems that could support these families, as well as the growing numbers of these families.

Widowhood still remains the major cause of female-headed families in Third World countries, although the growing acceptance of separation and divorce may contribute to the increase in the number of these families. Traditional family norms of the extended family have been weakened in many countries. In the past, many unmarried women (never married, separated, divorced, or widowed) were cared for by the extended family system. Rapid urbanization in many areas has led to the breakdown of the family. Economic pressures have increased for many families, leading to a lessened sense of obligation to help support other family members.

The prevalence of female-headed households varies greatly from country to country. From a low of less than 5 percent in Kuwait to a high of over 40 percent in Botswana and Barbados, women often have a difficult time as heads of their household. Women living in Islamic countries tend to be less likely to head a household than in many other countries. For example, less than 10 percent of all households in Kuwait, Pakistan, and Iran are headed by women. Only Thailand, among all Asian countries, reports a rate of more than 20 percent (United Nations 1995).

Female-headed families are more likely to be found in Latin America, the Caribbean, and many African countries. More than 25 percent of all households are headed by females in countries such as Botswana, Ghana, Kenya, Rwanda, Zambia, Barbados, Cuba, Dominican Republic, Guadeloupe, Martinique, Puerto Rico, and Trinidad and Tobago (United Nations 1995).

According to Ghorayshi and Bélanger (1996) more than 30 percent of the households in Kenya are headed by women. These women are either the sole or the primary providers for their families. The majority of these women live in poverty with little chance for any improvement in their status. Widowhood, male migration for job opportunities, increasing numbers of divorces, other forms of marital instability, and sometimes a choice not to marry the father of the child have all contributed to the increasing numbers of single women with children living in poverty.

Supreme Court Decisions

The Supreme Court has faced many decisions regarding issues of importance to families. The decisions have usually reflected the attitudes of the larger society at the time the decisions were written. This section includes several Supreme Court cases and decisions that are of importance or relevance to single-parent families. These decisions are organized by date, in order to see the changes in Court thinking over time.

Glona v. American Guarantee and Liability Insurance Company, 391 U.S. 73 (1968)

A Louisiana law authorized lawsuits by mothers of legitimate children, but not by mothers of illegitimate children, to recover compensation for the wrongful deaths of their children. In this case a mother attempted to recover for the wrongful death of her illegitimate child in an automobile accident. The trial court held that, under the Louisiana wrongful death statute, the mother had no right to sue for the death of her illegitimate son. The court of appeals agreed. The U.S. Supreme Court reversed the lower court's ruling, stating that "we see no possible rational basis for assuming that if the natural mother is allowed recovery for the wrongful death of her illegitimate child, the cause of illegitimacy will be served. It would, indeed, be farfetched to assume that women have illegitimate children so that they can be compensated in damages for their death" (p. 76).

King v. Smith, 392 U.S. 309 (1968)

The Alabama State Department of Pensions and Security issued a regulation known as the substitute father regulation that denied AFDC payments to a child if the child's mother was found to be cohabiting with a man, single or married, either in her own home or somewhere else. This man was then declared to be a substitute father and payment of benefits to the child was denied. This case was a class action suit against the Department of Pensions and Security asking that this regulation be overturned. A three-judge panel in federal district court found that the regulation was inconsistent with the Social Security Act and the equal protection clause of the Fourteenth Amendment. The Supreme Court justices heard the case and agreed with the district court. The justices held that the regulation was invalid because it was in conflict with the AFDC provisions of the Social Security Act. It also was in conflict with federal policy because it was based on the state's interest in discouraging improper sexual behavior and illegitimacy and because it included in its definition of "father" a person who was not legally obligated to support the child.

Levy v. Louisiana, 391 U.S. 68 (1968)

Louise Levy had five illegitimate children who lived with her; she took them to church, enrolled them in a private school, and worked hard to try to support them. Following her death, a suit was filed on behalf of the children attempting to recover damages for her wrongful death. A Louisiana district court found for the children, but was reversed on the ground that, while the Louisiana wrongful death statute did authorize actions on behalf of legitimate children, it did not authorize any actions on behalf of illegitimate children. The United States Supreme Court reversed this decision, and reinstated the original ruling in favor of allowing the lawsuit on behalf of Levy's children to go forward. Writing for the majority, Justice Douglas said that

> legitimacy or illegitimacy of birth has no relation to the nature of the wrong allegedly inflicted on the mother. These children, though illegitimate, were dependent on her; she cared for them and nurtured them; they were indeed hers in the biological and in the spiritual sense; in her death they suffered wrong in the sense that any dependent would. We conclude that it is invidious to discriminate against them when no action, conduct, or demeanor of theirs is possibly relevant to the harm that was done the mother. (p. 73)

In a dissenting opinion, Justice Harlan (with Justices Black and Stewart) suggested that the "rights created by wrongful death statutes stemmed from the existence of a family relationship, and that it was reasonable for the state not to recognize the family relationship unless the formalities of marriage, or of the acknowledgment of children by their natural parents, were complied with" (p. 77).

Shapiro v. Thompson, 394 U.S. 618 (1969)

This case involved consolidated appeals from decisions in federal district courts holding invalid state statutes (including one in the District of Columbia) that denied welfare assistance to residents of the state or District who had not resided within their jurisdictions for at least one year immediately preceding their application for such assistance. In one case the Connecticut Welfare Department had denied the application for welfare assistance of Vivian Thompson because she had not lived in the state for one year. A federal district court ruled that this regulation was unconstitutional because it violated the equal protection clause of the Fourteenth Amendment to the United States Constitution and because it had "a chilling effect on the right to travel." States could not set time-limited residency requirements that denied benefits to families with dependent children, said the court. The United States Supreme Court affirmed the judgments of the district court in all three cases.

Dandridge v. Williams, 397 U.S. 471 (1970)

The state of Maryland imposed a maximum limit on the total amount of AFDC benefits a family could receive. Several AFDC recipients believed that this regulation was in conflict with the federal Social Security Act and the equal protection clause of the Fourteenth Amendment. A federal district court agreed with them. However, the Supreme Court reversed the decision by the district court and held that the maximum grants regulation was not inconsistent with the Social Security Act and did not violate the equal protection clause. In essence the Court allowed states to place a cap on the amount of support payments to AFDC recipients, in effect penalizing those families who have more children than the state deems proper for poor families. Justice Stewart, in writing the opinion of the Court, stated that the Court did

> not decide today that the Maryland regulation is wise, that it best fulfills the relevant social and economic objectives that Maryland might ideally espouse, or that a more just and humane system could not be devised. Conflicting claims of morality and intelligence are raised by opponents and proponents of almost every measure, certainly including the one before us. But the intractable economic, social, and even philosophical

problems presented by public welfare assistance programs are not the business of this Court. (p. 487)

Wyman v. James, 400 U.S. 309 (1971)

In this case a beneficiary of the AFDC program refused to allow her caseworker to visit her home, although she agreed to provide relevant information to the caseworker. Based on New York statutory and administrative regulations, the woman's AFDC benefits were terminated as a result of this refusal. The district court agreed that the home visit, in the absence of a warrant or voluntary acquiescence, would have been an unconstitutional search and the woman's refusal did not justify termination of her benefits. However, the Supreme Court justices reversed that decision, declaring that the home visit was not a "search" within the meaning of the Fourth Amendment of the Constitution, and even if it were a "search," it was not unreasonable because it was not an unwarranted invasion of personal privacy and it did not violate any rights guaranteed by the Fourth Amendment. Justice Blackmun, in writing the opinion of the Court, stated that "we therefore conclude that the home visitation as structured by the New York statutes and regulations is a reasonable administrative tool; that it serves a valid and proper administrative purpose for the dispensation of the AFDC program; that it is not an unwarranted invasion of personal privacy; and that it violates no right guaranteed by the Fourth Amendment" (p. 327). Justice Douglas dissented, and quoted Judge Skelly Wright in the *Wyman* opinion (1970), saying that

> welfare has long been considered the equivalent of charity and its recipients have been subjected to all kinds of dehumanizing experiences in the government's effort to police its welfare payments. In fact, over half a billion dollars are expended annually for administration and policing in connection with the . . . [AFDC] program. Why such large sums are necessary for administration and policing has never been adequately explained. No such sums are spent policing the government subsidies granted to farmers, airlines, steamship companies, and junk mail dealers, to name but a few. The truth is that in this subsidy area society has simply adopted a double standard, one for aid to

business and the farmer and a different one for welfare. (400 U.S. at 332)

Stanley v. Illinois, 405 U.S. 645 (1972)

Joan Stanley lived with Peter Stanley off and on for 18 years. During this time they had three children. When Joan died Peter lost custody of his children, who were declared wards of the state. Under Illinois law an unwed father was not included in the statutory definition of "parent," and therefore could be deprived of custody of his illegitimate children following dependency proceedings. He was not entitled to a hearing concerning his fitness as a parent because he was presumed to be unfit. Stanley appealed the decision declaring his children wards of the state, but the Illinois Supreme Court rejected his claim that he had been deprived of equal protection of the law guaranteed by the Fourteenth Amendment. The U.S. Supreme Court reversed the lower court's decision, stating that the state of Illinois could not take custody of the children of an unwed father without a finding that he was indeed an unfit parent. Justice White, writing for the Court, held that an unwed father, like other parents, is entitled to a hearing on his fitness before his children may be taken from him and that the equal protection clause was violated in Stanley's case. White stated that all parents have a constitutional right to a hearing, which conforms to due process requirements, on their fitness before children may be removed from their custody.

Gomez v. Perez, 409 U.S. 535 (1973)

The issue in this case was whether the laws of Texas could constitutionally grant legitimate children a right to support from their natural fathers while denying that right to illegitimate children. The mother of an illegitimate child sought financial support for the child from the child's natural father. Support was denied on the basis that under Texas law a father had no legal obligation to provide support to an illegitimate child. The Texas Court of Appeals agreed, as did the Texas Supreme Court. The U.S. Supreme Court reversed the decision, saying that the denial of an illegitimate child's right to support from the child's natural father violated the equal protection clause of the Fourteenth Amendment. The justices stated that "we therefore hold that once a State posits a judicially enforceable right on behalf of children to needed support from their natural fathers there is no constitutionally sufficient justification for denying such an essential right to a child simply because its natural father has not married its mother" (p. 539).

Carey v. Population Services International, 431 U.S. 678 (1977)

In this case the issue was the constitutionality of a New York statute that made it a crime for anyone to sell or distribute contraceptives to minors under the age of 16 years, for anyone other than a licensed pharmacist to distribute contraceptives to persons over the age of 15 years, and for anyone to advertise or display contraceptives. A three-judge panel in federal district court decreed the statute unconstitutional and a majority of the U.S. Supreme Court justices, although divided, agreed. Four justices suggested that New York's prohibition on the distribution of contraceptives to anyone under the age of 16 years was not allowable as a way to regulate morality in pursuit of the state's interest in discouraging promiscuous sexual intercourse among minors. Justice Rehnquist, in his dissent, believed that a state should be allowed to properly use its police power to legislate public morality by trying to discourage teenagers from having sex. Justice Stevens believed that the state did have an interest in the sexual activity of teenagers, but that common sense would indicate that teenagers are going to have sex, and they should be able to be protected when they did have sex. As he suggested, prohibiting contraceptive sales is primarily a symbolic act but the results are counterproductive. "It is as though a state decided to dramatize its disapproval of motorcycles by forbidding the use of safety helmets" (p. 704).

Quilloin v. Walcott, 434 U.S. 246 (1978), 54 L Ed 2d 511

Under Georgia law the adoption of a child born in wedlock can take place only with the consent of each living parent. Consent need not be obtained from a parent who has previously voluntarily surrendered his or her parental rights or who has been judged to be an unfit parent. However, for children born out of wedlock, only the mother's consent to adoption is required, unless the father has legitimated the child. In this case a husband petitioned to adopt his wife's illegitimate son, who had been in her custody for 11 years. The child's natural father filed a petition for legitimation and objected to the adoption. The lower court granted the adoption, ruling that it was in the best interests of the child. Even though the natural father was not found to be an unfit parent, he had never sought actual or legal custody of the child. The equal protection rights of the father

> were not violated by application of the Georgia statutes, since the state could properly give the illegitimate child's father less adoption veto authority than it provided to a married father, even one who was separated or divorced, in view of the difference in the extent of commitment to the child between (a) the illegitimate child's father, who never had nor sought custody of his child and thus never assumed any significant responsibility with respect to the rearing of his child, and (b) married fathers, legal custody of children being a central aspect of the marital relationship, and even a father whose marriage had failed having borne full responsibility for the rearing of his children during the period of the marriage. (p. 511)

Married and unmarried fathers were treated differently by Georgia's law. The Supreme Court ruled that the best interests of the child would be served by allowing it to be adopted and the objections of the natural father could be ignored without infringing on his parental rights.

Caban v. Mohammed, 441 U.S. 380 (1979)

A New York statute provided an unwed mother with the authority to block the adoption of her child simply by withholding her consent; the statute did not give the unwed father the same right. Following the granting of a petition from a stepfather to adopt his two stepchildren, the natural father of the children challenged the constitutionality of this statute on the grounds that it violated the equal protection clause of the Fourteenth Amendment. The natural father had resided with the mother for several years, was identified as the father on the children's birth certificates, and contributed to their support. He had continued contact with the children after he left their mother. The New York Supreme Court affirmed the granting of the adoption. The United States Supreme

Court reversed, holding that the statute did indeed violate the equal protection clause, that maternal and paternal roles were not invariably different in importance, and that the statute was not substantially related to the state's interest in promoting the adoption of illegitimate children. The majority of the Court agreed that even if unwed mothers as a class were closer than unwed fathers to their newborns, the generalization concerning parent-child relations would become less acceptable to support legislative distinctions as the children's age increased. Unwed fathers are no more likely to oppose adoption of their children than are unwed mothers, said the Court.

Califano v. Westcott, 443 U.S. 76 (1979), 61 L Ed 2d 383

Two married couples brought a suit challenging the constitutionality of a section of the Social Security Act governing an AFDC program, the AFDC Unemployed Father (or AFDC-UF) program. This section provided benefits to families with dependent children when the children are deprived of parental support because the father is unemployed. No benefits were provided when the mother is the unemployed parent. A federal district court ruled that the gender-based classification did violate the due process clause of the Fourteenth Amendment and ordered that benefits be paid to families deprived of support because of the mother's unemployment to the same extent that they are paid when the father is unemployed. The U.S. Supreme Court affirmed this decision, agreeing that the section in question "cannot be constitutionally justified either on the ground that it does not discriminate against women as a class because the impact of the gender qualification is felt by family units rather than individuals, or on the ground that the distinction is substantially related to the important governmental objective of deterring real or pretended desertions by fathers in order to make families eligible for benefits" (61 L Ed 2d 393).

Parham v. Hughes, 441 U.S. 347 (1979), 60 L Ed 2d 269

A Georgia man sued to recover for the wrongful death of his biological child in an automobile accident, despite a Georgia state statute that denied fathers the right to sue for wrongful deaths of their illegitimate children. The father in this case had signed the dead child's birth certificate and contributed to his support, but he had never legitimated the child by the formal acknowledgment procedure prescribed by law. The trial court held that the statute violated both the due process and equal protection clauses of the Fourteenth Amendment. The Georgia Supreme Court, however, reversed this decision. A sharply divided U.S. Supreme Court agreed that the statute did not violate the equal protection clause of the Fourteenth Amendment. Five justices believed that the statute represented a rational method for the state to use in dealing with the problem of proving paternity. Four justices dissented from the majority opinion, believing that

> the statute discriminated on the basis of sex between unmarried mothers and unmarried fathers by requiring unmarried fathers to have pursued the statutory legitimization procedure in order to bring suit for the wrongful death of their children, and thus violated the equal protection clause of the Fourteenth Amendment since the classification could not be justified by the state's interests in (1) promoting a legitimate family unit and setting a standard of morality, (2) forestalling potential problems in proving paternity, (3) protecting wrongdoers and their insurance companies from multiple recoveries, and (4) preventing recovery by a party who suffered no real loss resulting from wrongful death. (60 L Ed 2d 270)

Many of the justices believed that people who choose not to follow the general patterns of relationships practiced by a society have no reason to object when they are treated as pariahs by the society. Laws that penalize those who ignore society's interests and morals are therefore justified.

Mills v. Habluetzel, 456 U.S. 91 (1982)

A Texas statute required a suit to identify the natural father of an illegitimate child to be brought before the child reached the age of one year. In this case the mother of an illegitimate child and the Texas Department of Human Resources brought suit against the natural father of the child, who asserted that the action was prohibited by the Texas statute because the child was one year and seven months old when the suit was filed. The trial court agreed with the father and dismissed the case; other lower courts agreed. The U.S. Supreme Court, however, reversed the decision, holding that the Texas statute denied illegitimate children the equal protection of law; the state did not allow enough time or adequate opportunity for children to obtain support; and the short time limit was unrealistic and was not related to the state's interest in avoiding the prosecution of stale or fraudulent claims. Five justices went on to suggest that reasons other than birth-related circumstances compelled the conclusion that the statutory distinction between legitimate and illegitimate children was unconstitutional; a review of the factors significant in determining that the one-year statute of limitation was invalid also suggested that longer periods of limitation could also be considered unconstitutional. The Court agreed that there is a public interest in having parents support their children, thereby reducing the number of people on welfare.

Lehr v. Robertson, 463 U.S. 248 (1983)

In this case a child was adopted by her stepfather when she was over two years old. The child's natural father had never provided support to the child and did not enter his name in a putative father registry, which would have entitled him to receive notice of the adoption proceeding. However, unaware that the adoption proceeding had been started, the natural father filed a paternity petition to have himself declared the child's father. Upon learning of the adoption proceeding several months later, he then filed a petition to vacate the adoption on the ground that it was obtained by fraud and in violation of his constitutional rights. The natural father's petition to vacate the order of adoption was denied by lower courts. The U.S. Supreme Court affirmed the lower court's ruling, agreeing that the natural father's rights under both the due process and equal protection clauses were not violated by failing to provide him notice because the father did not have any significant custodial, personal, or financial relationship with the child.

Palmore v. Sidoti, 466 U.S. 429 (1984), 80 L Ed 2d 421

Race was the issue in this case. A white couple living in Florida was divorced and the mother awarded custody of their three-year-old daughter. Later, the father sought a modification of the custody award because the child's mother was cohabiting with a black man, whom she later married. The father was awarded custody by the Florida trial court on the grounds that the mixed-race household would have a damaging effect on the child. The U.S. Supreme Court reversed this award, stating that "the effects of racial prejudice, however real, cannot justify a racial classification removing an infant child from the custody of its natural mother. The Constitution cannot control such prejudice, but neither can it tolerate it" (80 L Ed 2d 426).

Rivera v. Minnich, 483 U.S. 574 (1988)

Jean Minnich, an unmarried woman, gave birth to a child on May 28, 1983, and three weeks later filed a complaint for child support against Gregory Rivera, alleging that he was the father of her child. Before the trial Rivera requested that the court rule that the state statute that governs proceedings against a defendant to establish his paternity and that specifies that the burden of proof is by a preponderance of the evidence violated the due process clause of the Fourteenth Amendment to the Constitution. Rivera also wanted the court to instruct the jury that paternity must be established by clear and convincing evidence. The trial court denied this motion and the jury found that the defendant was the child's father. However, the trial judge reconsidered his ruling on the burden of proof issue and granted the defendant's motion for a new trial. Minnich appealed to the Pennsylvania Supreme Court, which held that the statute was constitutional and reinstated the jury's verdict. On appeal, the United States Supreme Court agreed, holding that determining paternity using a preponderance of the evidence standard complies with the due process clause of the Fourteenth Amendment.

Clark v. Jeter, 486 U.S. 456 (1988)

Cherlyn Clark, an unmarried mother, gave birth to a daughter in June 1973. Ten years later, in September 1983, Clark filed a support complaint, naming Gene Jeter as the girl's father. The court ordered Jeter to take a blood test to determine paternity, and the results showed a 99.3 percent probability that Jeter was the girl's father. However, the court ruled that a suit to establish paternity must be brought within six years of the child's birth, as required by a Pennsylvania statute. The mother argued, unsuccessfully, that the statute was unconstitutional under the equal protection and due process clauses of the Fourteenth Amendment. While Clark's appeal to the Superior Court was pending, the Pennsylvania legislature enacted an 18-year statute of limitations for actions to establish paternity, changing their six-year limit to comply with federal standards. The Superior Court ruled that the statute could not be applied retroactively and that the six-year limit was constitutional. The United States Supreme Court reversed the Superior Court's ruling, holding that the six-year limit violated the equal protection clause of the Fourteenth Amendment.

Thompson v. Thompson, 484 U.S. 174 (1988)

Susan Thompson filed for divorce from David Thompson in July 1978 and sought custody of their child. Joint custody was originally awarded; however, the mother wanted to move to Louisiana from California. The court awarded her sole custody once she left California for Louisiana, pending more study. The mother moved to Louisiana and filed a petition in that state's court to enforce the California custody determination; the Louisiana court agreed, awarding her sole custody. However, two months later the California court awarded sole custody to the father. The father then requested that the district court declare the Louisiana decree invalid, based on the Parental Kidnapping Prevention Act of 1980, which required all states to accept a custody determination from another state if the determination is in agreement with the Act's provisions. The district court dismissed the complaint, as did the United States Court of Appeals, on the grounds that the Act did not create a private right of action to determine the validity of two conflicting custody decrees. The United States Supreme Court agreed, holding that the Parental Kidnapping Prevention Act does not furnish implied action to determine which of two state custody determinations is valid.

Blessing v. Freestone, 520 U.S., 137 L Ed 2d 569 (1997)

Five women in Arizona who had custody of their children, some of whom were receiving AFDC benefits, filed suit against the director of Arizona's child support agency. They claimed that the Arizona Title IV-D program of the Social Security Act, which focuses on child support enforcement programs, violated federal law. In order to qualify for federal AFDC funds, states must certify that their child support enforcement program will conform with the requirements set forth in the Title IV-D program of the Social Security Act. States are required to establish a comprehensive system to establish paternity, locate absent parents, and help families obtain support orders; these services should be provided free to AFDC recipients and for a nominal charge to custodial parents and their children who are not receiving AFDC benefits. The mothers claimed that they had properly applied for child support services but that the agency had never taken any steps to collect child support payments from the fathers of their children; therefore, the state violated their federal rights under Title IV-D. The district court found in favor of the state, but the Ninth Circuit Court reversed. The United States Supreme Court held that Title IV-D does not give individuals a federal right to force a state agency to substantially comply with Title IV-D.

For those readers interested in exploring their state statutes regarding adoption or child custody, the section of state code where the appropriate statute can be found is listed in Table 8.

The Future of Single-Parent Families

Single-parent families will continue to exist in the United States and all other countries of the world. In many countries society supports these families in a variety of ways; in other countries these families receive less support and are stigmatized because they vary from the normal two-parent family. From the beginning of United States history, society has viewed the two-parent family as the norm. Divorce was uncommon in the early days, but many single-parent families were created by the death of one parent. In cases in which the mother was the parent who died, the father usually remarried quickly so that he would have someone to take care of his family. When the father died the mother often had a more difficult time. She was not as likely to find a new man to marry, especially if she had children. She was more likely to have to find support through her extended family members, find a job, or depend on the charity of the larger society.

TABLE 8
State Statutes

Child custody	
Alabama	§§30-3-1 to 99
Alaska	§25.24.150
Arizona	§§25-331 *et seq.*
Arkansas	§§9-13-101 *et seq.*
California	Fam. §3400
Colorado	§14-10-123
Connecticut	§§46b-56 *et seq.*
Delaware	tit. 13, §721 *et seq.*
District of Columbia	§§16-911(a)(5); 16-914
Florida	ch. 61.13
Georgia	§19-9-1
Hawaii	§571-46
Idaho	32-717
Illinois	750 ILCS 5/601
Indiana	§31-1-11.5-21
Iowa	§598.41
Kansas	§60.1610
Kentucky	§403.270
Louisiana	Civ. Code Ann. art. 131; Rev. Stat. Ann. §9:572
Maine	tit. 19, §752
Maryland	Fam. Law §5-203
Massachusetts	ch. 208 §28
Michigan	§722.21 *et seq.*
Minnesota	§518.155 *et seq.*
Mississippi	§93-5-23
Missouri	§452.375
Montana	40-4-211 *et seq.*
Nebraska	§42-364
Nevada	§125.480
New Hampshire	§458:17
New Jersey	§2A:34-23
New Mexico	§40-4-9
New York	Dom. Rel. §240
North Carolina	§50-11.2
North Dakota	§14-05-22
Ohio	§3109.03, 3105.21
Oklahoma	tit. 43, §112
Oregon	§107.105
Pennsylvania	tit. 23, §5301
Rhode Island	§15-5-16
South Carolina	§20-3-160
South Dakota	§25-4-45
Tennessee	§36-6-101, -102
Texas	Fam. §§3.55; 14.01

(continues)

TABLE 8
State Statutes (continued)

Utah	§§30-3-10, 30-3-5
Vermont	tit. 15, §665
Virginia	§§20-107.2, 20-124.1 *et seq.*
Washington	§§26.09.050; 26.27 *et seq.*
West Virginia	§48-2-15
Wisconsin	§767.24
Wyoming	§20-2-113
Adoption	
Alabama	§§26-10A-1 to 26-10A-38
Alaska	§§25.23.010 to 25.23.240
Arizona	§§8-101 to 8-145
Arkansas	§§9-9-201 to 224; 9-9-301 to 303; 9-9-402 to 412; 9-9-501 to 508
California	Fam. §§8600 *et seq.*
Colorado	§§14-1-101; 19-5-201 to 304
Connecticut	§§45a-724 to 765
Delaware	tit. 13, §§901 to 965
District of Columbia	§§16-301 to 315
Florida	ch. 63
Georgia	§§19-8-1 to -26
Hawaii	§§578-1 to -17
Idaho	§§16-1501 *et seq.*
Illinois	750 ILCS 50/1 to 50/24
Indiana	§31-3-1-1
Iowa	§§600.1 *et seq.*
Kansas	§§59-2111 *et seq.*
Kentucky	§199.470
Louisiana	Ch. C. art. 1167–1270
Maine	tit. 19, §§1101 *et seq.*
Maryland	Fam. Law §§5-301 *et seq.*
Massachusetts	ch. 210
Michigan	§§710 *et seq.*
Minnesota	§§259.21
Mississippi	§§93-17-1 *et seq.*
Missouri	§§453.010 to .170
Montana	§40-8-101
Nebraska	§43-101 to 43-160
Nevada	§§127 *et seq.*
New Hampshire	§§170-B *et seq.*
New Jersey	§§9:3 *et seq.;* 2A:22-1 *et seq.*
New Mexico	§§32A-5 *et seq.;* 40-14-1-15
New York	Dom. Rel. §§109–117
North Carolina	§48
North Dakota	ch. 14–15
Ohio	§3107
Oklahoma	tit. 10, §§60.1 *et seq.*

(continues)

TABLE 8
State Statutes (continued)

Oregon	§§109.305 *et seq.*
Pennsylvania	tit. 23, §§2101 to 2910
Rhode Island	§§15-7 *et seq.*
South Carolina	§§20-7-1646 to -1890
South Dakota	§§25-6 *et seq.*
Tennessee	§§36-1 *et seq.*
Texas	Fam. ch. 11, 16
Utah	§§78-30 *et seq.*
Vermont	tit. 15, §§431 *et seq.*
Virginia	§§63.1-220 *et seq.*
Washington	§26.33
West Virginia	§48-4
Wisconsin	§§48.81 *et seq.*
Wyoming	§1-22-101

Over time society's response to single women with children evolved into distinguishing between mothers who had been married but lost their husbands through death and mothers who had never been married or whose husbands had deserted them. Today, that distinction remains in the minds of many people. Society has more sympathy and is more willing to help support a family that has lost a parent, particularly a father, through death or divorce. We as a society are less willing to help out people (usually women) who become single parents while unmarried. Many people believe that these single parents knew what they were getting into by having a child, or at least that they knew that unprotected sex could result in a pregnancy, but they still made a conscious decision to assume that risk. They should therefore be held accountable for their actions and take full responsibility for caring for their children. Society should be willing to help those who have become single parents through no fault of their own, but should not have to help those who they believe have acted irresponsibly.

The new federal welfare law, the Personal Responsibility and Work Opportunity Reconciliation Act of 1996, is one example of society's attempt to legislate responsibility. No longer is the country willing to help support single-parent families unless they are willing to help themselves and take responsibility for their actions. This line of thought holds all single parents responsible for their dilemma, that it is their own fault. As a result, society is absolved from feeling a need to help these families. The Family Research Council (1998) believes that the welfare programs developed by the federal government in the past have "discouraged personal responsibility, encouraged family disintegration, abdicated church involvement in local outreach, and overlooked localized initiatives to uplift the poor." The Council supports the new welfare law and encourages the development of "faith-based and church-based programs."

Other groups in the United States are calling for a strengthened family. People must work harder to stay together and divorce should not be easily or readily granted. Only by strengthening the two-parent family, they reason, will the number of single-parent families decline. Single parents are blamed for a variety of society's ills, and by strengthening the traditional family, society will benefit. Alternative family forms cannot contribute positively to society, according to this line of thinking.

However, many professionals believe that society must help all families in order to strengthen the family and society. All families experience problems and challenges to their existence and well-being. Problems faced by single-parent families are exacerbated by the lack of another parent to provide income and support or backup. In any case, helping all families will benefit society.

Public policy should recognize that a variety of family forms exist and will probably continue to exist. However, according to Dowd (1997),

> these are not auspicious times to draft a policy of support for single-parent families, indeed for any family. The watchwords of current public policy about family are personal responsibility and family values. They translate into ideological support for traditional families and condemnation of unwed mothers (and by extension, all single parents). Current policy also emphasizes private support, maximizing resources for those with greater resources, and minimizing public economic support of any families, and particularly disfavored families. (p. 120)

Whether society focuses on strengthening two-parent families or looks at ways to help people become more responsible for their actions, single-parent families, as well as other family forms, will continue to be created. Many single-mother families will continue to find life difficult. The number of single-father families may continue to increase, if divorce continues to be readily obtainable and if fathers continue to take more responsibility for their actions. Attempts to deter single-parent families that are based on economically punitive policies have failed in the past, and have only hurt the children in these families.

As Senator Daniel Patrick Moynihan has emphasized over the years, the point of welfare and other public assistance programs is to help the children. According to Dowd (1997),

> society's economic and social stability and growth depends upon the strength of future generations. . . . The care of children is a fundamental ethical responsibility. Social responsibility for children arguably underlies our strong support of two-parent families. We implicitly recognize the inability of family alone to nurture two-parent families, yet even with those supports, they are struggling. Stronger collective, communal support for all families regardless of form should be our model. (p. 128)

References

Abramovitz, Mimi. 1996. *Regulating the Lives of Women: Social Welfare Policy from Colonial Times to the Present.* Rev. ed. Boston: South End Press.

Alan Guttmacher Institute. 1998. *Into a New World: Young Women's Sexual and Reproductive Lives.* New York: Alan Guttmacher Institute.

————. 1994. *Sex and America's Teenagers.* New York: Alan Guttmacher Institute.

Blankenhorn, David. 1995. *Fatherless America: Confronting Our Most Urgent Social Problem.* New York: Basic Books.

Burns, Ailsa, and Cath Scott. 1994. *Mother-Headed Families and Why They Have Increased.* Hillsdale, NJ: Lawrence Erlbaum Associates.

Casey Foundation. 1995. *Kids Count Data Book.* Baltimore, MD: Annie E. Casey Foundation.

Chambers, Diane. 1997. *Solo Parenting: Raising Strong and Happy Families.* Minneapolis: Fairview Press.

Cherlin, Andrew J., ed. 1988. *The Changing American Family and Public Policy.* Washington, DC: The Urban Institute Press.

Children's Defense Fund. 1994. *The State of America's Children, 1994.* Washington, DC: Children's Defense Fund.

Coontz, Stephanie. 1997. *The Way We Really Are: Coming to Terms with America's Changing Families.* New York: Basic Books.

DeSimone, Peter, et al. 1995. "Homelessness in Missouri: Unabated, Increasing." Jefferson City: Missouri Association for Social Welfare.

Douglass, Richard. 1995. "The State of Homelessness in Michigan: A Research Study." Lansing, MI: Michigan State Housing Development Authority.

Dowd, Nancy E. 1997. *In Defense of Single-Parent Families.* New York: New York University Press.

Edin, Kathryn. 1995. "Single Mothers and Child Support: The Possibilities and Limits of Child Support Policy." *Children and Youth Services Review* 17:203–230.

Edin, Kathryn, and Laura Lein. 1997. *Making Ends Meet: How Single Mothers Survive Welfare and Low-Wage Work.* New York: Russell Sage Foundation.

Family Research Council. 1998. "Does FRC Support Welfare Reform? Why?" *Frequently Asked Questions, #27.* Washington, DC: Family Research Council.

Federal Interagency Forum on Child and Family Statistics. 1997. *America's Children: Key National Indicators of Well-Being.* Washington, DC: Federal Interagency Forum on Child and Family Statistics.

Furstenberg, Frank F., Jr. 1988. "Good Dads–Bad Dads: Two Faces of Fatherhood." In *The Changing American Family and Public Policy,* ed. Andrew J. Cherlin. Washington, DC: The Urban Institute Press.

Garfinkel, Irwin. 1996. "Economic Security for Children." In *Social Policies for Children,* ed. Irwin Garfinkel, Jennifer L. Hochschild, and Sara S. McLanahan. Washington, DC: Brookings Institution.

Garfinkel, Irwin, and Sara McLanahan. 1986. *Single Mothers and Their Children: A New American Dilemma.* Washington, DC: The Urban Institute Press.

Ghorayshi, Parvin, and Claire Bélanger, eds. 1996. *Women, Work and Gender Relations in Developing Countries: A Global Perspective.* Westport, CT: Greenwood Press.

Greif, Geoffrey L., and Mary S. Pabst. 1988. *Mothers Without Custody.* Lexington, MA: Lexington Books.

Groze, Vic. 1991. "Adoption and Single Parents: A Review." *Child Welfare* 70(3):321–332.

Hanna Keelan Associates. 1995. "A Study of Homeless and Near-Homeless in Nebraska." Lincoln: Nebraska Department of Economic Development.

Hartley, S. F. 1975. *Illegitimacy.* Berkeley: University of California Press.

Haskey, John. 1991. "Lone Parenthood and Demographic Change." In *Lone Parenthood: Coping With Constraints and Making Opportunities in Single-Parent Families,* ed. Michael Hardey and Graham Crow. Toronto: University of Toronto Press.

Kamerman, Sheila B., and Alfred J. Kahn. 1988. *Mothers Alone: Strategies for a Time of Change.* Dover, MA: Auburn House.

Kaufman, Tracy. 1997. *Out of Reach: Rental Housing at What Cost?* Washington, DC: National Low Income Housing Coalition.

Leff, Mark H. 1973. "Consensus for Reform: The Mother's Pension Movement in the Progressive Era," *Social Service Review* 47:245–260.

Levitan, Sar A., Garth L. Mangum, and Stephen L. Mangum. 1998. *Programs in Aid of the Poor.* 7th ed. Baltimore: The Johns Hopkins University Press.

Merritt, Sharyne, and Linda Steiner. 1984. *And Baby Makes Two: Motherhood without Marriage.* New York: Franklin Watts.

Moore, K. A., D. R. Morrison, C. Blumenthal, M. L. Daly, and R. Bennett. 1993. *Data on Teenage Childbearing in the United States.* Washington, DC: Child Trends, Inc.

Mulroy, Elizabeth A., ed. 1988. *Women as Single Parents: Confronting Institutional Barriers in the Courts, the Workplace, and the Housing Market.* Dover, MA: Auburn House.

National Campaign to Prevent Teen Pregnancy. 1997. *Whatever Happened to Childhood? The Problem of Teen Pregnancy in the United States.* Washington, DC: National Campaign to Prevent Teen Pregnancy.

National Center for Health Statistics, Division of Vital Statistics. 1967. *Vital Statistics of the United States 1965.* Vol. 1. *Natality.* Washington, DC: Public Health Service, U.S. Department of Health, Education, and Welfare.

———. 1989. Monthly Vital Statistics Report, 38(3). *Advance Report of Final Natality Statistics, 1987.* Washington, DC: U.S. Government Printing Office.

National Coalition for the Homeless. 1998. "Homeless Families with Children." *Fact Sheet #12.* Washington, DC: National Coalition for the Homeless.

Owen, Greg, et al. 1995. *Minnesota Statewide Survey of Persons Without Permanent Shelter.* Vol. 1: *Adults and their Children.* St. Paul: Wilder Research Center.

Ozer, Elizabeth M., Claire D. Brindis, Susan G. Millstein, David K. Knopf, and Charles E. Irwin. 1998. *America's Adolescents: Are They Healthy?* San Francisco: University of California, San Francisco, National Adolescent Health Information Center.

Quayle, Dan, and Diane Medved. 1996. *The American Family: Discovering the Values That Make Us Strong.* New York: HarperCollins.

Rawlings, Steve W. 1993. "Household and Family Characteristics; March 1992." In *Current Population Reports,* series P-20, no. 467. U.S. Bureau of the Census. Washington, DC: U.S. Government Printing Office.

Rodgers, Harrell R. 1996. *Poor Women, Poor Children: American Poverty in the 1990s.* Armonk, NY: M. E. Sharpe.

Shireman, Joan F. 1995. "Adoptions by Single Parents." *Marriage and Family Review* 20(3/4):367–388.

Sorenson, Elaine, and Mark Turner. 1996. "Barriers in Child Support Policy: A Literature Review." Paper LB-SB-96-04. Philadelphia: National Center on Fathers and Families, University of Pennsylvania.

Spencer, Rich. 1989. "Child Support Collections Jump in '88." *The Washington Post,* 8 December.

Steinbock, Marcia R. 1995. "Homeless Female-Headed Families: Relationships at Risk." *Marriage and Family Review* 20(1/2):143–159.

United Nations. 1995. *Living Arrangements of Women and Their Children in Developing Countries.* New York: United Nations.

U.S. Bureau of the Census. 1992. "Money, Income and Poverty Status of Families and Persons in the United States: 1991." Washington, DC: U.S. Government Printing Office.

———. 1995a. "Income, Poverty, and Valuation of Noncash Benefits: 1993." In *Current Population Reports,* series P-60, no. 188. Washington, DC: U.S. Government Printing Office.

———. 1995b. "Who Receives Child Support?" Statistical Brief. Washington, DC: U.S. Bureau of the Census.

———. 1996a. *Statistical Abstract of the United States: 1996.* Washington, DC: U.S. Government Printing Office.

———. 1996b. "Income, Poverty, and Valuation of Noncash Benefits: 1994." In *Current Population Reports,* series P60–189. Washington, DC: U.S. Government Printing Office.

U.S. Congress, Joint Economic Committee, Subcommittee on Fiscal Policy. 1976. *Studies in Public Welfare Paper No. 20, Handbook of Public Income Transfer Programs: 1975.* Washington, DC: U.S. Government Printing Office.

U.S. Congressional Budget Office. 1990. *Sources of Support for Adolescent Mothers.* Washington, DC: U.S. Congressional Budget Office.

U.S. Department of Commerce. 1984. "Household and Family Characteristics: March 1983." Series P-20, no. 388, May. Washington, DC: U.S. Department of Commerce.

U.S. Department of Health and Human Services. 1995. *Report to Congress on Out-of-Wedlock Childbearing.* Washington, DC: U.S. Department of Health and Human Services.

———. 1997. "Clinton Administration Moving Forward on the Promise of Welfare Reform." Fact Sheet. Washington, DC: U.S. Department of Health and Human Services, press office.

U.S. Women's Bureau. 1993. *Women Who Maintain Families.* Washington, DC: U.S. Department of Labor, Women's Bureau.

———. 1969. *1969 Handbook on Women Workers,* Bulletin 294. Washington, DC: U.S. Government Printing Office.

Ventura, Stephanie J., Joyce A. Martin, Selma M. Taffell, T. J. Mathews, and Sally C. Clarke. 1995. "Advance Report of Final Natality Statistics, 1993." *Monthly Vital Statistics Report* 44(3):Supplement.

———. 1996. "Advance Report of Final Natality Statistics, 1994." *Monthly Vital Statistics Report* 44(11):Supplement 1–88.

Virginia Coalition for the Homeless. 1995. "Shelter Provider Survey, 1995." Richmond: Virginia Coalition for the Homeless.

Wattenberg, Esther. 1993. "Paternity Actions and Young Fathers." In *Young Unwed Fathers: Changing Roles and Emerging Policies,* ed. Robert Lerman and Theodora Ooms. Philadelphia: Temple University Press.

Waxman, Laura, and Remy Trupin. 1997. "A Status Report on Hunger and Homelessness in America's Cities." Washington, DC: U.S. Conference of Mayors.

Wilson, W., and K. Neckerman. 1986. "Poverty and Family Structure: The Widening Gap Between Evidence and Public Policy Issues." In *Fighting Poverty: What Works and What Doesn't,* ed. S. Danziger and D. Weinberg. Cambridge, MA: Harvard University Press.

Wright, Skelly. 1970. "Poverty, Minorities, and Respect for Law." *Duke Law Journal* 425:437–438.

Directory of Organizations 5

This chapter describes organizations, listed alphabetically, that are involved in working with single parents. Some of these groups operate at the international or regional level, some are national in scope, and some provide services in local communities.

**Adoption Resource Exchange
for Single Parents**
P.O. Box 5782
Springfield, VA 22150-9998
(703) 866-5577
Fax: (703) 912-7605
e-mail: aresp@aol.com

The Adoption Resource Exchange for Single Parents (ARESP) advocates for the adoption of older and special needs children by single men and women. Staff members offer assistance and information on adoption, including assisting prospective parents in the process of finding children to adopt and gathering resources of interest to single adoptive parents. A quarterly newsletter, *ARESPnews*, is published.

Adoptive Families of America
2309 Como Ave.
St. Paul, MN 55108

(612) 645-9955 or (800) 372-3300
Fax: (612) 645-0055

Adoptive Families of America is a nonprofit organization with over 20,000 members throughout the country. Committed to helping all people touched by adoption, the organization offers a list of adoptive parent support groups throughout the country, a how-to booklet for the prospective parent(s), and a selection of adoption and multicultural resources. Staff members operate a helpline for individual consultation and access to the Family Support Network. They advocate for the equitable treatment of adoption in legislation and the media. Staff members promote equitable treatment of adoptive families in law and regulation by consulting with the U.S. Congress and several federal agencies. A bimonthly magazine, *Adoptive Families,* contains articles written by adoptive parents and adoption professionals that provide up-to-date information and practical parenting tips.

**The Association for Children
for Enforcement of Support, Inc.**
2260 Upton Ave.
Toledo, OH 43606
(419) 472-6609 or (800) 738-ACES

Founded in 1984, the Association for Children for Enforcement of Support (ACES) is a nonprofit organization that advocates for child support. It is dedicated to assisting disadvantaged children affected by the failure of their parents to meet legal and moral child support and/or visitation obligations. With chapters in 47 states, ACES provides educational information concerning child support and visitation, including legal rights and remedies, which agency to contact for assistance, local and interstate methods available under current law to collect current and back child support, and the methods available under current law to resolve visitation problems. Staff members have successfully advocated for federal laws that make it a federal crime to cross state lines to avoid paying child support and that require that child support enforcement orders include provisions for health insurance coverage. They have initiated wage withholding for child support. Staff members also conduct seminars on child support and its collection. Publications include a national newsletter and books such as *How to Collect Child Support.*

Big Brothers Big Sisters of America
230 N. 13th St.
Philadelphia, PA 19107-1538
(215) 567-7000
Fax: (215) 567-0394
e-mail: bbbsa@aol.com
Internet: http://www.bbbsa.org

With over 500 independent agencies in all 50 states, Big Brothers Big Sisters of America offers mentoring activities for boys and girls, usually from single-parent families. The organization pairs a volunteer with a child based on the child's specific needs and any common interest the two can share. These volunteers serve as role models and help young people to increase their self-confidence, to reach their highest potential, and to see their future as positive and successful. Big Brothers Big Sisters focuses particularly on helping children at risk of failing in school or engaging in dangerous behavior. Over 1 million children in thousands of communities throughout the country have been helped by this program. Publications include *The Correspondent*, a magazine published quarterly by the national organization.

Center on Fathering
325 N. El Paso St.
Colorado Springs, CO 80903
(719) 634-7797 or (800) 693-2334
Fax: (719) 634-7852

The Center on Fathering provides programs and services that strengthen, support, and encourage fathers to be actively involved in the care and nurturance of their children. Staff members provide timely and competent service to fathers and fathers-to-be, supplying them with the personal and social skills necessary to help them fulfill their responsibilities. An extensive library of books, audio and video tapes, manuals, computer software, and various other interactive and multimedia materials provides fathers and other interested clients with information to help them understand the responsibilities of being a father. Referrals are made to qualified providers of therapy, and for housing, legal, and other appropriate services. Classes, workshops, and seminars on a variety of topics are offered. Outreach activities include recreational activities, outings, and crisis intervention. Volunteer mentors, who are experienced fathers from the community, receive training so that they can participate in the "Fathering Partners" mentoring program, functioning as sponsors who are in frequent contact with participating fathers.

Center for Law and Social Policy
1616 P St., NW, Suite 150
Washington, DC 20036
(202) 328-5140
Fax: (202) 328-5195
e-mail: info@clasp.org or HN3088@handsnet.org
Internet: http://www.clasp.org

The Center for Law and Social Policy (CLASP) was founded in 1968 with the help of Supreme Court Justice Arthur Goldberg. A national public policy and law organization, the Center has focused on the problems of low-income families with children. CLASP conducts education, policy research, and advocacy activities on income support issues at both the state and federal levels, including welfare reform, child care, work force development, and child support enforcement. Staff members track and analyze federal proposals and legislation, and provide training and technical assistance to advocates, administrators, and officials. They conduct audio conferences for advocates and officials and manage the electronic Federal Welfare Watch and Family Economic Security Forums as part of the HandsNet Children, Youth and Family Initiative. Publications include *CLASP Update*, a periodic report concerning the latest developments on family and child poverty issues; *Welfare-to-Work Grants and Other TANF-Related Provisions in the Balanced Budget Act of 1997, The New Framework: Alternative State Funding Choices Under TANF,* and *Proposed TANF Regulations re Child Support Cooperation and Good Cause.*

Child Care Law Center
22 Second St., 5th Floor
San Francisco, CA 94105
(415) 495-5498
Fax: (415) 495-6734

A national nonprofit legal services organization founded in 1978, the Child Care Law Center continues to advocate for the expansion of child care options, particularly for low-income families. It believes that children should be safe and nurtured when they are in a child care program outside the home. Using legal tools to encourage the development of high-quality, affordable child care for every child in the country, the staff members provide legal representation, information resources, legal support, educational activities, and pro bono attorneys. Staff members help develop public policy concerning major child care issues. They also advocate for new child care funding and the improvement of regulatory standards and enforcement practices that govern child care settings. They promote the growth of child care options by helping to remove legal impediments such as overly burdensome zoning, planning, and building codes. Caregivers are supported through the strengthening of due process and employment rights of child care workers and providers. Publications include *Child Care as Welfare Prevention; Recruiting Welfare Recipients for Child Care Work: Not a Panacea;* and *Regulation-Exempt Family Child Care in the Context of Publicly Subsidized Child Care: An Exploratory Study.*

Child Trends, Inc.
4301 Connecticut Ave., NW, Suite 100
Washington, DC 20008
(202) 362-5580
Fax: (202) 362-5533

Child Trends is a national nonprofit organization dedicated to studying children, youth, and families by conducting research and collecting and analyzing data. Major research areas include teenage pregnancy and childbearing, the effects of poverty and welfare on children, and other issues related to parenting and family structure. With support from the U.S. Department of Health and Human Services, Child Trends staff and other researchers work with states and other groups to improve the measurement of child outcomes in state welfare evaluations and in other state data systems. Publications include *The Many Faces of Nonmarital Childbearing, America's Children: Key National Indicators of Well-Being,* and *Postponing Second Teen Births in the 1990s.*

Child Welfare League of America
440 First St., NW, Suite 310
Washington, DC 20001
(202) 638-2952
Fax: (202) 638-4004

The Child Welfare League focuses on improving care and services for abused, neglected, or dependent children, youth, and their families. The League provides consultation services, conducts research, maintains a library and information services, develops standards for child welfare practice, and administers special projects. Publications include *Child Welfare: Journal of Policy, Practice, and Program,* presenting articles for child welfare professionals on topics such as foster care, adoption, teenage pregnancy, and day care.

Children, Youth, and Family Consortium
University of Minnesota
201 Coffey Hall
1420 Eckles Ave.
St. Paul, MN 55108
(612) 625-7248
Fax: (612) 626-1210
e-mail: cyfcec@maroon.tc.umn.edu

The Children, Youth, and Family Consortium was established in 1991 to unite the knowledge, experience, and resources of the University of Minnesota with the resources of Minnesota communities to help improve the well-being of Minnesota children, youth, and families. The program enhances the ability of individuals and organizations to address the critical health, education, and social policy concerns that are relevant to children, youth, and families. Over 8,000 individuals and organizations participate in the Consortium, which coordinates several national initiatives, including an annual conference on family policy issues moderated by Vice President Al Gore. An extensive Internet resource has been developed, which includes research, expert perspectives, and discussion groups that address current issues that affect children and families (see chapter 7).

Children's Defense Fund
25 E St., NW
Washington, DC 20001
(202) 628-8787 or (800) CDF-1200
Fax: (202) 662-3510

The Children's Defense Fund (CDF) was founded to provide a strong and effective voice for all children, to educate the nation about the needs of children, and to encourage the support of children before they get sick, drop out of school, or get into trouble. The Violence Prevention Project is CDF's most recent effort to provide a safe start for all children in America. The project focuses on federal legislation, public education, and community mobilization in order to begin to curb the cycle of violence plaguing our schools, families, and communities. Publications include *The State of America's Children*, published annually.

Children's Rights Council
220 Eye St., NW, Suite 140
Washington, DC 20002-4362
(202) 547-6227
Fax: (202) 546-4272

The Children's Rights Council (CRC) is concerned with the healthy development of children whose parents are divorced or separated. Staff members look for ways to strengthen families during marriage through education and advocacy activities. In cases of divorce, they work for mediation, parenting education, and joint custody. With chapters in 31 states, the CRC publishes a quarterly newsletter; has resources available on parenting and protecting children; has a nationwide directory of groups that provide mediation, parenting, and legal help; and works with state legislatures, Congress, and the courts to protect access and visitation rights.

Coalition on Human Needs
1000 Wisconsin Ave., NW
Washington, DC 20007
(202) 342-0726
Fax: (202) 338-1856
e-mail: chn@chn.org

The Coalition on Human Needs is an alliance of more than 170 national organizations working together to promote public policies that address the needs of low-income and other vulnerable populations. Member organizations include civil rights, religious, labor, and professional groups and other organizations concerned with the well-being of children, women, the elderly, and people with disabilities. The Coalition acts as a clearinghouse for information on poverty and human needs issues. Washington-based legislative advocates meet biweekly to share information and develop collaborative strategies to impact national policy on low-income issues, many of interest to single parents. A major initiative was launched in 1998 focusing on the major challenge facing low-income families; that is, improving the employment options for low-skilled individuals. Publications include the *Directory of National Human Needs Organizations; The Human Needs Report*, which is a bimonthly legislative newsletter; fact sheets; and action alerts.

Committee for Mother and Child Rights, Inc.
210 Ole Orchard Drive
Clear Brook, VA 22624
(540) 722-3652
Fax: (540) 722-5677

A national organization, the Committee for Mother and Child Rights offers emotional support and guidance for mothers with child custody problems. The Committee was founded by four mothers who experienced contested child custody. They believe that maternity is not a woman's only destiny and that women are entitled to equal opportunities in areas in which men and women have the same potential.

Committee for Single Adoptive Parents
P.O. Box 15084
Chevy Chase, MD 20815
(202) 966-6367

As a national membership organization, the Committee provides information on agencies that accept single men and women as adoptive parents and the names of state and local groups that help single adoptive parents. Single people planning on adopting a child are provided with a list of recommended books and names of single adoptive parents living in their states. Publications include *Handbook for Single Adoptive Parents*.

Family Resource Coalition
200 S. Michigan Ave., 16th Floor
Chicago, IL 60604
(312) 341-0900
Fax: (312) 341-9361

The Family Resource Coalition works to develop a new societal response to children, youth, and their families. This response is aimed at strengthening and empowering families and communities to help prevent problems before they arise. Families, communities, government, social service institutions, and businesses should work together to provide healthy, safe environments for children and families. The Coalition builds networks and strengthens connections among those in the family support field, offers technical assistance and consulting services, undertakes public education and advocacy efforts, develops a knowledge base of family support issues, and provides resources and publications.

Gay and Lesbian Parents Coalition International
4938 Hampden Lane, #336
Bethesda, MD 20814
(301) 907-2647
Fax: (301) 907-4739

The Coalition provides support, education, advocacy activities, and resources for gays and lesbians in child-nurturing situations. They promote broader understanding of alternative parenting concerns within the general community, encourage communications and cooperation among all groups and individuals, and gather, compile, and disseminate educational and other information about gay and lesbian parenting and related issues. A list of resources for gay men and lesbians interested in parenting includes information on adoption agencies, artificial insemination, attorneys, books for children, books for parents, bookstores, infertility, Internet resources, relevant organizations, surrogacy, videos, and other materials.

Institute for Women's Policy Research
1400 20th St., NW, Suite 104
Washington, DC 20036
(202) 785-5100
Fax: (202) 833-4362
Internet: http://www.iwpr.org

Established in 1987, the Institute for Women's Policy Research (IWPR) is a nonprofit, independent scientific research organization set up to inform and stimulate debate on issues of critical importance for women. The Institute is national and international in scope and is committed to addressing the full spectrum of issues that affect women and families. The organization conducts research concerning issues of race, ethnicity, and class and specifically addresses policies that help women achieve self-sufficiency and autonomy. Staff members work with policy makers and scholars throughout the country to design and execute research studies, and to publicize research findings. Policy areas that are emphasized include poverty and welfare, family and work, health care and domestic violence, and employment. Publications include *The Status of Women in the States,* which provides baseline statistics from each state and the District of Columbia concerning politics, economics, health, and demographics; and *Welfare That Works: The Working Lives of AFDC Recipients,* which analyzes factors that increase the likelihood that single mothers who receive AFDC also engage in paid employment. A biennial conference is held on topics of critical interest to women. The IWPR Information Network publicizes and disseminates research and findings.

Lambda Legal Defense and Education Fund, Inc.
120 Wall St., Suite 1500
New York, NY 10005-3904
(212) 809-8585
Fax: (212) 809-0055

The Lambda Legal Defense and Education Fund is a national organization that focuses on achieving full recognition of the civil rights of lesbians, gays, and people with HIV/AIDS. Lambda was founded in 1973 and is the oldest and one of the largest lesbian and gay legal organizations in the country. The national office is in New York, and regional offices are located in Los Angeles, Chicago, and Atlanta. Among the projects that Lambda works on are several that can help single parents and their children. Fair treatment for lesbian and gay families is sought; these families frequently are denied legal protection in areas such as custody, adoption, guardianship, and inheritance. Staff attorneys defend gay parents whose relationships with their children are threatened because of homophobia.

Lavender Families Resource Network
P.O. Box 21567
Seattle, WA 98111
(206) 325-2643

This program serves as a clearinghouse of relevant information and support to help gay and lesbian adults enjoy parenthood.

Lesbians, gay fathers, coparents, and children are included as members and can participate in all programs. Referral files are maintained for a variety of resources and support groups for parents and for children. Their newsletter, *Mom's Apple Pie*, informs lesbians and gay families about the specific issues that affect child-rearing patterns. Current services include personal and emotional support; 24-hour voice mail service; prelegal advice; referrals to attorneys, expert witnesses, mediators, and other professionals; resource files containing current literature, case law, and legal strategies; limited financial assistance; information on donor insemination, child rearing, adoption, and foster parenting; support group information; and public education activities. Although programs and activities do not focus on single parents, many of the parents who participate in programs are single parents and the network includes single parents in all aspects of their services.

MELD
123 N. Third St., Suite 507
Minneapolis, MN 55401-1664
(612) 332-7563
Fax: (612) 344-1959

MELD was founded as a result of an investigation in 1973 into ways that families can be strengthened. MELD's parenting education programs value and model the philosophy that parents can learn from each other, they can provide support for each other, and they should be free to make informed choices. In 1975 MELD piloted five groups of new parents; their programs now include nine groups of parents helping parents. These specific groups include new parents, young mothers, parents of children with special needs, growing families, new families, Hmong parents, young dads, deaf or hard-of-hearing parents, and African-American Young Mothers. Each program provides the most useful information in a supportive environment. Most of these programs provide services to parents during pregnancy and the child's first two years. Experienced parents volunteer their time to help facilitate the groups. Their programs for young mothers and for young fathers focus on single parents; their program that focuses on parents of children with special needs also has many single-parent participants.

National Adoption Information Clearinghouse
P.O. Box 1182
Washington, DC 20013-1182
(703) 352-3488 or (888) 251-0075
Fax: (703) 385-3206
e-mail: naic@calib.com
Internet: http://www.calib.com/naic

The Clearinghouse is a major source of information concerning adoption in the United States and is funded by the Children's Bureau, Administration for Children and Families, within the U.S. Department of Health and Human Services. Staff members are experts in adoption, child welfare, law, information management, and library science and are available to answer questions from professionals, adoptive and birth parents, adopted children, policy makers, journalists, educators, and the public. The Clearinghouse maintains a database of several thousand documents; a group of experts on a variety of aspects of adoption; directories of services; lists of organizations that provide adoption-related services, support, training, and education; a catalog of audiovisual and electronic resources on adoption; lists of federal discretionary grants for adoption programs; and summaries and copies of federal and state laws and case laws on adoption.

**National Association of Child Care
Resource and Referral Agencies**
1319 F St., NW, Suite 810
Washington, DC 20004-1106
(202) 393-5501
Fax: (202) 393-1109

This association promotes the growth and development of quality resource and referral services and leads the effort to build a diverse, high-quality child care system accessible to all families. Technical consultation and resources are provided to member child care resource and referral agencies. Individual families, including almost 1.5 million in 1994, turn to the Association for referrals and/or consultations about child care. Parent workshops, distribution of consumer education materials, and cooperation with the media to inform the public concerning child care issues are offered. A database consisting of over 310,000 child care programs throughout the country provides information to families on child care providers, school-age programs, and child care centers. Many member agencies work with community groups to plan for child care, support families in their search for child care, compile and share information with parents and child care providers, support individuals and programs that care for children, and build connections in communities and states to develop policies on family and children's issues.

National Campaign to Prevent Teen Pregnancy
2100 M St., NW, Suite 300
Washington, DC 20037
(202) 857-8655
Fax: (202) 331-7735
Internet: http://www.teenpregnancy.org

Founded in 1996, the National Campaign to Prevent Teen Pregnancy is a nonprofit organization that is supported primarily by private donations. The Campaign provides national leadership in the fight to raise awareness of the issue of teenage pregnancy and to attract new voices and resources to the cause. The group's mission is to prevent teenage pregnancy by supporting moral values and encouraging behavior that is consistent with a pregnancy-free adolescence. Staff members support and initiate state and local action, ensure that local community efforts are based on the best information available, and lead a national discussion on the role of religion, culture, and public values in an effort to build common ground in the fight against teenage pregnancy.

National Center for Children in Poverty
Columbia School of Public Health
154 Haven Ave.
New York, NY 10032-1180
(212) 304-7100
Fax: (212) 544-4200 or (212) 544-4201
Internet: http://cpmcnet.columbia.edu/dept/nccp

Founded in 1989 at the Columbia School of Public Health, the National Center for Children in Poverty (NCCP) identifies and promotes strategies that will reduce the number of young children living in poverty in the United States. NCCP provides demographic statistics about child poverty; identifies programs, policies, and practices that help young children and their families living in poverty; disseminates information; challenges policy makers to help reduce the consequences of poverty on young children; and brings together public and private groups to assess current strategies that have been established to lower the poverty rate for young children and improve their lives.

National Center for Fathering
10200 W. 75th St., Suite 267
Shawnee Mission, KS 66204
(913) 384-4661
Fax: (913) 384-4665
e-mail: dad@fathers.com
Internet: http://www.fathers.com

The National Center for Fathering is a nonprofit education and research center that was founded in 1990 to champion the role of fathers and to help men become more involved with children. The Center offers a variety of services including several resources to help men become better fathers. These resources include *Today's Father*, a quarterly magazine that offers practical advice, anecdotes, and inspiration. Their website provides articles, poll results, and information on training opportunities. Trainers conduct courses for fathers who have had contact with the legal system. Briefings are held to help local communities develop a comprehensive father initiative.

National Center for Missing and Exploited Children
2101 Wilson Blvd., Suite 550
Arlington, VA 22201-3052
(703) 235-3900 or (800) 843-5678 (for reporting information on missing or exploited children)
Fax: (703) 235-4067
Internet: http://www.missingkids.com

The National Center for Missing and Exploited Children is a private, nonprofit organization that spearheads national efforts to locate and recover missing children. Many of these children are the victims of parental kidnapping. The Center was established in 1984 by a congressional mandate and works in cooperation with the U.S. Department of Justice and Delinquency Prevention to coordinate the efforts of law enforcement, social service agencies, elected officials, judges, prosecutors, educators, and the public and private sectors. Providing a national voice, advocating for those too young to vote or speak up, and mobilizing efforts to protect children, the Center has four branch offices located in

Tustin, California; Lake Park, Florida; Rochester, New York; Columbia, South Carolina; and another office as part of the Adam Walsh Children's Fund in Lake Park, Florida. Through March 1997 the Center has participated in the recovery of over 35,000 children, worked on more than 56,000 cases, and handled over 1 million telephone calls. More than 140,000 law enforcement officers have been trained throughout the country in techniques for finding and recovering lost or missing children. Publications include *Family Abduction,* which offers step-by-step information for parents who have experienced a family abduction, and *Selected State Legislation,* which includes parental kidnapping statutes and model state legislation.

National Council for Single Adoptive Parents
P.O. Box 15084
Chevy Chase, MD 20825
(202) 966-6367 (phone and fax)

The National Council for Single Adoptive Parents was founded in 1973 to inform and assist single people who want to adopt a child. As a nonprofit corporation, the Council supports the rights of adoptable children to become members of loving families. Publications include the *Handbook for Single Adoptive Parents,* which provides potential adoptive parents with information concerning how to adopt a child from the United States or from a foreign country. Laws and regulations, ways to find the children they want, how to avoid dead ends, ideas on financing adoptions, where to find child care, how to manage money, and necessary medical care are some of the topics covered. Studies that confirm the success of single-person adoption are discussed. Other resources are suggested, and include books, periodicals, and names of support groups.

National Head Start Association
201 N. Union Street
Alexandria, VA 22314
(703) 739-0875
Internet: http://www.nhsa.org

The National Head Start Association (NHSA) is a nonprofit membership organization that represents the children and staff of Head Start programs in the United States. NHSA provides a national forum to enhance Head Start services for poor children, up to the age of five years, and their families. The organization actively works to expand and improve Head Start programs throughout the country. Annual training conferences are conducted. A wide variety of publications are developed and are available to the public.

National Men's Resource Center
P.O. Box 800-SP
San Anselmo, CA 94979-0800
e-mail: menstuff@aol.com
Internet: http://www.menstuff.org

The National Men's Resource Center is an organization that focuses on promoting positive changes in male roles and men's relationships and provides a variety of resources to meet this goal. It has developed *Menstuff*, a resource directory on the Internet that lists over 2,500 men's services and publications and offers information on events that are of interest to men. The organization assists local groups in developing local resource hotlines and calendars. Staff members assist bookstores in developing men's studies sections, encourage the development of men's studies programs on college campuses, and offer antihazing programs for fraternities. Conflict resolution and self-esteem building, appropriate forms of emotional release, and cooperation with women's communities are promoted.

National Organization of Single Mothers
P.O. Box 68
Midland, NC 28107
(704) 888-2337
Fax: (704) 888-1752
e-mail: solomother@aol.com

Founded in 1991, the National Organization of Single Mothers (NOSM) is a nonprofit organization that helps single parents meet the challenges of daily life. NOSM has provided help and advice to over 20,000 single mothers and their families, suggesting ways that they can successfully raise children while taking good care of themselves. Program activities include working closely with other agencies, establishing additional regional chapters, expanding research on single families, and promoting educational events and special projects. Members network with each other, providing mutual support and access to local and national resources. A bimonthly newsletter, *SingleMOTHER*, offers a variety of information on relevant topics, such as parenting and self-help tips, advice on money and time management, coparenting, child support, custody, uninvolved fathers, adoption, donor insemination, dating, legal issues, and updates on books, resources, and trends. If a member wants to start a community single mother support group, NOSM provides a packet of information including a group director's guide and a listing of other single parents in the area.

National Resource Center for Youth Services
College of Continuing Education
University of Oklahoma
202 W. 8th St.
Tulsa, OK 74119-1419
(918) 585-2986
Fax: (918) 592-1841
Internet: http://www.nrcys.ou.edu

The National Resource Center for Youth Services provides comprehensive, experience-based professional training and educational materials. Its goal is to enhance the quality of life for the nation's at-risk youth and their families by improving the effectiveness of human services. The Center offers information, training materials, and programs on a variety of topics of interest to children and families, including single parents and teenage pregnancy.

NOW Legal Defense and Education Fund
99 Hudson St.
New York, NY 10013-2871
(212) 925-6635
Fax: (212) 226-1066
Internet: http://www.nowldef org

The NOW Legal Defense and Education Fund (NOW LDEF) is a nonprofit organization supported by foundations, corporations, and individuals. Staff members focus on the major social and economic justice concerns on the women's rights agenda by defining the issues and bringing them to public attention. Equality for women and girls in the workplace, the schools, the family, and the courts is promoted through litigation, education, and public information programs. A variety of resource kits and publications are available and include topics such as child custody, child support, teenage parents, and violence against women.

Under the new federal welfare law, states can adopt the so-called Family Violence Option, which was developed by NOW LDEF. The Family Violence Option allows states to waive temporarily strict time limits, stringent work requirements, and paternity establishment for welfare recipients who are victims of domestic violence. The organization has distributed an education packet on the Family Violence Option to state governors, state welfare agencies, over 800 state legislators, and hundreds of individuals who called for technical assistance and legal analysis. Staff members helped prevent a mandated "family cap" in the new welfare law. The cap would have denied benefits to newborn children born into welfare.

Office of Child Support Enforcement
Administration for Children and Families
U.S. Department of Health and Human Services
370 L'Enfant Promenade, SW
Aerospace Building
Washington, DC 20447
(202) 401-9373
Fax: (202) 401-5559

This office helps individual states develop, manage, and operate their child support enforcement programs effectively and according to federal law. Most of the state programs' operating costs are paid for by this office. Policy guidance and technical help are provided to enforcement agencies, audits and educational programs are conducted, research is supported, and ideas for program development are shared. Regional offices are located in Boston, New York, Philadelphia, Atlanta, Chicago, Dallas, Kansas City, Denver, San Francisco, and Seattle. Their addresses and phone numbers are provided below. Publications include *Handbook on Child Support Enforcement*, which provides valuable information for the parent having problems collecting child support.

OCSE Program Manager
Administration for Children and Families
John F. Kennedy Federal Building
Room 2000
Boston, MA 02203
(617) 565-2478

OCSE Program Manager
Administration for Children and Families
Federal Building, Room 4048
26 Federal Plaza
New York, NY 10278
(212) 264-2890

OCSE Program Manager
Administration for Children and Families
P.O. Box 8436
Philadelphia, PA 19104
(215) 596-4370

OCSE Program Manager
Administration for Children and Families
101 Marietta Tower, Suite 821
Atlanta, GA 30323
(404) 331-2180

OCSE Program Manager
Administration for Children and Families
105 W. Adams St.
20th Floor
Chicago, IL 60603
(312) 353-4237

OCSE Program Manager
Administration for Children and Families
1200 Main Tower, Suite 1050
Mail Stop A2
Dallas, TX 75202
(214) 767-3749

OCSE Program Manager
Administration for Children and Families
601 E. 12th St.
Federal Building, Suite 276
Kansas City, MO 64106
(816) 426-3584

OCSE Program Manager
Administration for Children and Families
Federal Office Building, Rm. 325
1961 Stout St.

Denver, CO 80294
(303) 844-3100

OCSE Program Manager
Administration for Children and Families
50 United Nations Plaza
Mail Stop 351
San Francisco, CA 94102
(415) 437-8459

OCSE Program Manager
Administration for Children and Families
2201 Sixth Ave.
Mail Stop RX-70
Seattle, WA 98121
(206) 615-2547

Parents Without Partners International
401 N. Michigan Ave.
Chicago, IL 60611-4267
(800) 637-7974
e-mail: pwp@sba.com
Internet: http://parentswithoutpartners.org

Founded in 1957 by two single parents, Parents Without Partners (PWP) is an international, nonprofit membership organization devoted to the welfare and interests of single parents and their children. With over 400 chapters PWP has over 63,000 members in the United States and Canada. Most members have teenage children, the average length of membership is four years, and members come from all walks of life. All chapters offer a variety of activities, including educational activities, family activities, and adult social/recreational activities. Many chapters also conduct community service programs that include community outreach, fund-raising for national or local charities, and cooperative exchanges. At the international level, staff members advocate for single parents and their children on Capitol Hill, at various conferences, national coalitions, and in workshops. Legislative policies and priorities are supported. An annual international convention offers workshops on single parenting and instruction on how to run PWP chapter programs.

Single Mothers by Choice
P.O. Box 1642
Gracie Square Station
New York, NY 10028
(212) 988-0993
e-mail: mattes@pipeline.com
Internet: http://www.parentsplace.com/readroom/smc

The nonprofit group Single Mothers by Choice (SMC) was founded in 1981 by Jane Mattes, a single mother and psychotherapist, to provide support and information to single women who have become, or are planning to become, single mothers. Members are found throughout the United States as well as in Canada. They focus on sharing information and resources. Opportunities are provided to members to take part in anonymous research projects and participate in media interviews. A quarterly newsletter provides information and networking for all members. An all-day workshop for women who are thinking about becoming single mothers is offered several times each year. Members can also participate in a private e-mail group and can register their child(ren) in a sibling registry, which is composed of children conceived through anonymous donor insemination.

Single Parent Resource Center
31 E. 28th St.
New York, NY 10016
(212) 951-7030
Fax: (212) 951-7037

The Single Parent Resource Center provides a variety of programs for single parents and their children. Its Access Family Program offers parents and children a safe environment where they can rebuild their families following incarceration or alcohol or narcotic dependency. Most of the children are in foster care and don't have many positive memories of their mothers before they left. The KIDSCLUB program conducts prevention activities for children in homeless shelters; they work with the children to prevent them from falling into the same traps that their parent(s) have fallen into. The newest program, in collaboration with WomenCare, is a mentoring program for incarcerated women. Publications include the *PARENT-PAK*, a series of eight pamphlets that provide information about issues of concern to single parents, including struggles for power within the family, moving life forward, reducing stress and tension, the other parent, getting organized, and sex, love, and intimacy.

Single Parents Raising Kids, Inc.
P.O. Box 0288
Rockville, MD 20848-0288
(301) 598-6395
Internet: http://www.corphome.com/spark

Single Parents Raising Kids (SPARK) is an organization for single parents living in Montgomery County, Maryland, and surrounding areas. Its mission is "to build a community where single parents can share the knowledge and provide the mutual support needed to experience a rewarding life for ourselves while raising our children to be competent and well-adjusted people." Program activities include family, educational, and social events.

Single Parents Society
527 Cinnaminson Ave.
Palmyra, NJ 08065
(609) 582-9808 (NJ)
(215) 928-9433 (PA)

As a nonprofit, nonsectarian, educational organization, the Single Parents Society encourages and assists single parents in working together with their children. Activities include dances, weekly socials, family activities, day and other trips, discussions, and sports activities. A monthly newsletter provides information on activities to all members.

Solo Parenting Alliance
139 23rd Ave. South
Seattle, WA 98144
(206) 720-1655
Fax: (206) 328-8658
e-mail: solo@accessone.com

The Solo Parenting Alliance is a nonprofit organization that was founded in 1990 by single parents looking for help and support in raising their children. The Alliance allows parents of all ages and walks of life to support each other and share their hard-earned wisdom as they face the challenges of raising healthy children.

The program promotes support networks, self-determination, and self-sufficiency. A "family homeshare" program that helps solo parents find affordable housing and support through shared housing is offered. Other activities and programs include parenting workshops, solo parenting classes, family outings, field trips to sporting events, a parenting resource center, referral information, informal social gatherings, and volunteer opportunities. The group publishes *Solo Connections*, a quarterly newsletter.

Welfare Warriors
Mothers Organizing Center
2711 W. Michigan
Milwaukee, WI 53208
(414) 342-6662
Fax: (414) 342-6667

Founded in 1986, the Welfare Warriors are a multiracial group of mothers living in poverty who must rely on public support to raise their children. Their primary purpose is to combat the stereotypes and social stigma that they face on a daily basis. They call themselves the Welfare Warriors because they are "fighting for the lives of mothers and children, struggling to survive in a system not working for us." Activities include education and advocacy. A quarterly newsletter, *Welfare Mothers Voice*, educates mothers about systemic problems that cause poverty, provides support and a forum for welfare mothers to be heard, and encourages mothers to create their own organizations to fight for social justice. *Mothers Survival Self-Help Manual*, a book that describes the laws, policies, and philosophies controlling public benefits, was published by the group. In 1990 the MOMS' Line was started and provides a daily help line staffed by mothers living in poverty. In 1992 Welfare Warriors founded the MaGoD project (Mothers and Grandmothers of the Disappeared Children) to provide support and legal advocacy to mothers whose children have been removed by Social Services. Another project, Mothers and Youth Volunteers, brings together mothers and their children to work for social justice while helping to strengthen family bonds and to develop their organizing, office, newspaper, and computer skills.

Selected Print Resources 6

This chapter contains descriptions of published books, manuals, journal articles, and other print resources that focus on issues of importance to single parents. Views on single-parent families and the effect that single parents have on society vary widely, and the selection of materials cited in this chapter attempts to reflect these divergent views.

Books

Anderson, Joan. *The Single Mother's Book: A Practical Guide to Managing Your Children, Career, Home, Finances, and Everything Else.* Atlanta: Peachtree Publishers, 1990. Resources, index. ISBN 0-934601-84-4.

Anderson is a former day care center director and a facilitator for the Single Mother's Group at Vanderbilt University. In this book she draws on her own experiences as a single mother and provides the reader with a wealth of information for single mothers. The changing American family is discussed, along with the various ways that women become single mothers. Individual chapters focus on ex-partners and their relatives, legal concerns, raising healthy children, children and community, teenagers, child care, life with Dad, taking care of yourself, job searches, resumes, working, finances, personal and home security, fixing things around the house, managing space and time, updating one's social life, and romance. Appendices provide information on starting a single mother's group.

Arendell, Terry. *Mothers and Divorce: Legal, Economic, and Social Dilemmas.* Berkeley: University of California Press, 1986. Bibliography, index. ISBN 0-520-05708-2.

Popular beliefs that divorced women and their children have enough safeguards to protect them and their interests are incorrect, according to Arendell. Arendell interviewed a random sample of 60 divorced mothers living in northern California. These women had been considered to be in the middle class while they were married. Seven popular assumptions about divorce are examined: divorce is equally hard on men and women, children from divorced families are likely to have serious problems, reform in divorce laws has given equality to women, community property laws treat wives and husbands equally, divorced fathers pay heavily to support their ex-wives and their children, divorce provides opportunities for personal growth and development, and problems following divorce are temporary because most people remarry. Arendell suggests that research contradicts these assumptions and, based on the research the author conducted, believes that women are hurt—especially economically—by divorce more often than men. This book offers a focused sociological examination of the real experiences of divorced women.

———. *Fathers and Divorce.* Thousand Oaks, CA: Sage Publications, 1995. References, index. ISBN 0-8039-7188-5.

Most research on divorce and single-parent families has focused on the mothers. Little has been written about the fathers and their experiences, including experiences as single fathers with custody and other legal issues. Arendell interviewed 75 divorced fathers living in various parts of New York state and talked with family attorneys, mediators, and mental health workers. In this book she discusses the results of her interviews, including how the fathers manage their situation and relationships. Individual chapters focus on men and divorce, divorce in the context of family and gender, injustices of divorce, former relations with spouses, traditional fathers, neotraditional fathers, parenting partnerships with former wives, innovative fathers, and major policy issues concerning fathers and divorce.

Barker, Richard W. *Lone Fathers and Masculinities.* Brookfield, VT: Ashgate Publishing, 1994. Bibliography. ISBN 1-85628-522-7.

Most research concerning single-parent families focuses on single mothers. This book helps to fill the gap in knowledge concerning single fathers. Barker studied single fathers living in northern England. These fathers were either divorced or widowed. The literature concerning single fathers is reviewed. The research design is described and findings are discussed. Specific topics include the different routes to single fatherhood, fathers' relationships with their children, housework, paid employment, economic positions of single fathers as well as single parents in general, extended family relationships, the sexual lives of single fathers, community relations, and relationships with social workers and other social health and welfare professionals. A final chapter considers the conclusions that can be drawn from this research. Brief descriptions of the fathers in the study are provided in an appendix.

Barnes, Annie S. *Single Parents in Black America: A Study in Culture and Legitimacy.* Bristol, IN: Wyndham Hall Press, 1987. Bibliography. ISBN 1-55605-023-2.

Barnes has conducted several research studies concerning urban, black single mothers and fathers. This book presents findings from studies in two low-rent housing developments in Norfolk, Virginia. The author's purpose is to "describe relationships important to black single mothers and fathers through their own eyes and what they would do if they could start life over" (p. 1). Specific topics include the principle of legitimacy, the culture of poverty model, unwed single mothers, why single motherhood, reactions to becoming single mothers, single fatherhood, and home sex education. Five studies of black single parenthood are described. Finally, the author presents models for pregnancy prevention, including youth advocates for singlehood without parenthood, human sexuality training in schools, a parental model for improving family relations and pregnancy prevention, and home sex education for fatherhood prevention.

Bartholet, Elizabeth. *Family Bonds: Adoption and the Politics of Parenting.* Boston: Houghton Mifflin Company, 1993. Notes, index. ISBN 0-395-51085-6.

Bartholet, a lawyer, a professor at Harvard Law School, and a formerly married mother of one, decided that she wanted to have another child even though she was no longer married. Unable to conceive, she tried every medical treatment available to help her become pregnant, from surgery, to fertility drugs, to sexual intercourse, to in vitro fertilization. Nothing worked and she finally decided to adopt a child. In this book Bartholet describes her experiences pursuing adoption. The book is written for other people who are struggling with many of the same issues she faced, for single people and others who are classified as marginal parents by the system, for those people who are thinking about adoption, and for those who are in a position to make or influence public policy. The barriers to transracial adoption that have been created by adoption agencies, the many problems faced by single people who want to adopt, her experiences adopting children from a foreign country (Peru), the stigma associated with adoption, and her experiences with in vitro fertilization are all described and discussed.

Blankenhorn, David. *Fatherless America: Confronting Our Most Urgent Social Problem.* New York: Basic Books, 1995. Notes, index. ISBN 0-465-01483-6.

According to Blankenhorn, approximately 40 percent of children in America live in homes in which there is no father. He believes that fatherlessness is "the most harmful demographic trend of this generation. . . . It is also the engine driving our most urgent social problems, from crime to adolescent pregnancy to child sexual abuse to domestic violence against women" (page 1). Not only is American society experiencing the absence of fathers in many families, many people no longer believe in the importance of fathers. Part I discusses fatherlessness, including the diminishment of American fatherhood, and the belief that fathers are not necessary in the process of raising children. Part II examines the cultural script of fatherhood, including the unnecessary father, the old father, new father, deadbeat dad, visiting father, the sperm father, and the stepfather. Part III focuses on fatherhood and examines the good family man and the need for a father for every child.

Blau, Melinda. *Families Apart: Ten Keys to Successful Co-parenting.* New York: G. P. Putnam's Sons, 1993. Resources, bibliography, index. ISBN 0-399-13895-1.

Based on 10 principles of successful coparenting, Blau provides specific suggestions for helping the single parent maintain emotional health and protect his or her children. The author suggests that parents can put aside their differences for their children's sake, maintain contacts between ex-spouses and their new families, and get through disagreements without a lot of pain and frustration. The 10 keys to successful coparenting include healing after divorce, acting maturely, listening to the children, respecting each other as parents, dividing parenting time, accepting each other's differences, communicating about and with the children, stepping outside traditional gender roles, anticipating and accepting change, and knowing that coparenting is forever. Appendices provide information on a sample parenting agreement and resources concerning divorce and raising children; resources include print material and organizations.

Boumil, Marcia Mobilia, and Joel Friedman. *Deadbeat Dads: A National Child Support Scandal.* Westport, CT: Praeger, 1996. Bibliography, index. ISBN 0-275-95125-1.

In recent years more and more policy makers and state legislatures are realizing the importance of tracking down deadbeat fathers to force them to help support their children. The burden on states and the federal government to provide support for these families is growing and many people believe that the fathers must be held responsible for supporting their children. This book explores many of the important issues surrounding deadbeat fathers and explains who they are and why they do not help support their children. States are now required to find ways to locate absent parents and force them to meet their obligations through several available means, including withholding wages, intercepting tax refunds, or placing liens on property. Individual chapters focus on the growing number of deadbeat fathers, the psychological consequences of divorce and absent fathers, the effect of fault and no-fault divorce laws on child support, contesting paternity, legal guidelines for establishing and enforcing child support awards, child custody alternatives, characteristics of deadbeat dads, and social relationships, economic responsibility, and the deadbeat epidemic.

Burns, Ailsa, and Cath Scott. *Mother-Headed Families and Why They Have Increased.* Hillsdale, NJ: Lawrence Erlbaum Associates, 1994. References, author index, subject index. ISBN 0-8058-1440-X.

The number of households headed by women has increased dramatically in the past 20 years. This book explores the reasons why so many more families throughout the Western world are currently headed by women. The authors pay particular attention to the United States, the former Soviet Union, and Sweden because of the high prevalence of families headed by mothers. Practices in these countries are contrasted with Japan, where few single-parent families exist. Chapters focus on the ease of obtaining divorces in many areas, the contribution of out-of-wedlock births and why they have increased, divorce in non-European countries, widows, various theories of parenting, feminist and decomplementary theories (i.e., "how the interests of women and men have lost much of their complementary nature," page 183) of parenting, and final conclusions. The book provides a valuable resource in offering a variety of theories for the growth in female-headed households, a cross-cultural perspective, and an excellent examination of current literature and research on this topic.

Chambers, Diane. *Solo Parenting: Raising Strong and Happy Families.* Minneapolis: Fairview Press, 1997. Appendix, resource guide. ISBN 1-57749-008-8.

This book offers the single parent many specific and helpful guidelines for raising a family alone. Divided into three parts, chapters in the first part present information to help prepare the reader for single parenthood, how to overcome the fear often associated with becoming a single parent, how to examine each parent's current situation, and ways to turn negative emotions into positive attitudes. Part II emphasizes self-development, addressing career goals, financial concerns, and self-esteem, and helps the reader deal with many parenting issues. Part III helps parents help their children succeed and discusses discipline and responsibility, financial welfare, and improving the future. An appendix offers helpful worksheets on finances, spending habits, setting spending priorities, assets and liabilities, income and expenses, networking, and the expectations and consequences of being a single parent.

Clapp, Genevieve. *Divorce and New Beginnings: An Authoritative Guide to Recovery and Growth, Solo Parenting, and Stepfamilies.* New York: John Wiley & Sons, 1992. Selected sources. ISBN 0-471-52631-2.

Written as a survival guide for parents following divorce, this book offers practical advice to all divorced parents, whether they remain single or remarry. The author provides practical information on the basic issues facing divorced parents, including many legal and financial issues. Ways to deal with the stress of a divorce, combat depression, deal with anger, and let go of the marriage are described in Part I. Part II provides information on ways to help the children survive a divorce. Building a rewarding single life is the focus of Part III, including creating a new life for parent and children, the benefits and problems of solo parenting, ways to be a successful single parent, parenting styles and discipline, and other problems associated with being a single parent. Part IV examines part-time parenting for parents without custody and Part V discusses problems that may occur for stepfamilies.

Dickerson, Bette J. *African American Single Mothers: Understanding Their Lives and Families.* Thousand Oaks, CA: Sage Publications, 1995. Index. ISBN 0-8039-4911-1.

Many misconceptions exist concerning African-American single mothers and their families, including the stereotypes that they are inferior, not productive, and dysfunctional. In this book Dickerson and other contributors set out to disprove these misconceptions. Issues facing African-American single mothers that affect all aspects of their lives are discussed. The effects of many elements of African heritage that have carried over into the current lives of African-Americans and events of the period of slavery are presented. The view of unwed motherhood as sinful according to Western Christianity is examined along with belief and value systems carried over from Africa. Various concepts and perspectives that affect African-American teenage single mothers are discussed. The role of the mass media in portraying white middle- and upper-class single mothers as living an alternative lifestyle while seeing African-American single mothers as deviant and wrong is presented along with suggestions for more accurate portrayals. The impact of the legal system on single mothers is examined, including the image of the African-

American woman as the cause of societal problems, rather than as the victim. Problems that children face in single-parent families are examined, along with a discussion of the strengths that sustain these families. The supportive role of grandmothers in extended families is evaluated. Finally, strategies that could lead to policy changes and improvement of the quality of life for these families are explored.

Dodson, Fitzhugh. *How to Single Parent.* New York: Harper and Row, 1987. ISBN 0-06-015492-6.

As a clinical psychologist, Dodson works with children and adults and understands many of the challenges of being a single parent. He believes that single parents must take care of themselves as well as their children, by taking time to have a life of their own. In this book he provides practical advice on how to survive divorce, how to tell children about divorce or the death of a parent, how to help children cope with separation, child-raising skills, how to deal with custody and visitation, taking care of oneself, dating, and how to find a mate.

Dowd, Nancy E. *In Defense of Single-Parent Families.* New York: New York University Press, 1997. Notes, references, index. ISBN 0-8147-1869-8.

Single-parent families can be as successful as two-parent families. However, they face strong social and legal stigmas that work to undermine them. Dowd believes that the justifications for stigmatizing these families are based primarily on myths that are used to rationalize harshly punitive social policies. In this book she describes these myths and social policies and her belief that children are the ones who are most likely hurt by these policies. Part I describes the myths creating the stigma and the realities of single parenthood. Part II discusses the impact of laws on single-parent families and individual chapters focus on divorced single parents, nonmarital single-parent families, and single parents as positive role models. Part III examines legal reform, discussing policies for single-parent families and legal strategies. Dowd suggests that social policy should be centered around the welfare and equality of all children.

Edin, Kathryn, and Laura Lein. *Making Ends Meet: How Single Mothers Survive Welfare and Low-Wage Work.* New York: Russell Sage Foundation, 1997. References, index. ISBN 0-8175-4229-3.

Unskilled single mothers and their children have the highest poverty rate in America. With the new time limits on welfare, more single mothers will have to find jobs to support themselves and their families. This book focuses on the experiences of single mothers and is based on research conducted by the authors in Boston, Charleston, Chicago, and San Antonio. The authors found that most single mothers had trouble supporting themselves and their families on welfare or when they worked. Low-wage jobs may provide more income than welfare but also entailed more expenses such as child care, transportation to and from work, and clothing expenses, often for uniforms or for specific items to meet a specific dress code. Many low-wage jobs do not provide health insurance or provide it only for the employee, not the family. The authors conclude that while "current welfare-to-work programs might move women into jobs in the short term, these mothers and their children will experience much material hardship if they remain trapped in jobs that pay $5, $6, or $7 an hour and offer few benefits" (page 235).

Engber, Andrea, and Leah Klungness. *The Complete Single Mother: Reassuring Answers to Your Most Challenging Concerns.* Holbrook, MA: Adams Publishing, 1995. Resources, recommended reading, bibliography, index. ISBN 1-55850-553-9.

In order to combat stereotypes about single mothers and to provide encouragement when the challenges of single motherhood seem overwhelming, Engber and Klungness wrote this book. Full of valuable information for single mothers, individual chapters focus on how women can become single mothers (i.e., through divorce, through donor insemination, adoption, widowhood); dealing with childbirth, an infant, emotional and physical health, financial matters and housing; gaining confidence to raise a child alone (e.g., child care, parenting at various stages, explanations of the father's absence, raising daughters and raising sons); relating to others (e.g., custody and coparenting, child support, problems with ex-partners, sex and dating, relationships, remarriage, and balancing work and family). Lists of resources, recommended reading, and a bibliography provide additional sources of information.

Ferrara, Frank. *On Being Father: A Divorced Man Talks about Sharing the Responsibilities of Parenthood.* Garden City, NY: Doubleday & Company, 1985. ISBN 0-385-19128-6.

Ferrara has written this book to provide advice to single fathers because "most formerly married men are pretty poorly equipped to be single men again, much less single fathers. They've gotten used to having a wife around—that convenient person who seems to know all about children, knows all the things he hasn't bothered about" (page xii). He discusses everything he learned about how to cope with being a suddenly single father. Individual chapters focus on the gift of parenting, the period between separation and divorce, re-creating the family, running the home as a single father, dealing with the children's mother, the opposite sex, separation and work, being a weekend father, being a long-distance father, a father's almanac, and putting it all together.

Gardner, Richard A. *The Boys' and Girls' Book about One-Parent Families.* New York: G. P. Putnam's Sons, 1978. ISBN 399-12181-1.

As a leading child psychiatrist, Gardner provides an excellent source of information for children living with only one parent. The book is divided into three parts. Part I examines issues of importance to children whose parents are divorced. Part II discusses the major issues of living with a mother who has never married. Part III helps children who are suffering from the loss of a parent through death. Gardner discusses such major issues as how to handle grief over the missing parent, how to cope when a parent has sleep-over dates with the opposite sex, dealing with such feelings as jealousy or fear when a parent is dating someone who also has children, and what to do when a parent becomes overly dependent on a child. Children are encouraged to speak up about issues that concern them—to talk with their parent about their feelings. This book provides a good starting point for discussions between parents and children.

Gordon, Linda. *Pitied But Not Entitled: Single Mothers and the History of Welfare 1890–1935.* New York: Free Press, 1994. Index. ISBN 0-02-912485-9.

Gordon provides the reader with an excellent overview of social welfare in the United States. She focuses on the history of welfare from 1890 to 1935 and the impact of welfare on single mothers. "Welfare" once referred to a hope for a good life and well-being. Today, this word evokes images of slums, single mothers, and juvenile delinquents. Gordon examines the transformation of welfare from something good to something bad. Individual chapters focus on defining welfare, facts concerning single mothers, single mothers as a social problem, the state as caretaker, the social work perspective, black women and welfare, social insurance and the sexual division of labor, relief policies during the Depression, New Deal social movements, the legislative process, and welfare and citizenship. An appendix offers a list of prominent leaders in the welfare reform movement.

Gregg, Chuck. *Single Fatherhood.* New York: Sulzburger & Graham Publishing, 1995. Selected resources, index. ISBN 0-945819-57-9.

According to Gregg, 1.4 million single fathers are the primary caregivers for their children in the United States in the mid-1990s. As one of those single fathers, and as a result of his experiences in dealing with the many aspects of being a single parent, he wrote this book to provide information to other single fathers. He dispels many negative attitudes and beliefs about single fathers, including the belief that most single fathers do not have financial problems, can usually find someone to take care of the major household duties, will get remarried quickly, are not capable of caring for a toddler or preschooler, and should not be trusted with raising a young daughter. He provides other single fathers with information on getting organized; having fun with the children; planning trips; nurturing children's nutritional, social, and educational needs; how to grow with the children; balancing traditional male roles and the emotional demands of parenthood; how to avoid anger, denial, guilt, and shame about being a single parent; how to form and maintain supportive relationships; and how to benefit from support networks and professional guidance.

Greif, Geoffrey L. *Single Fathers.* Lexington, MA: Lexington Books, 1985. References, related bibliography, index. ISBN 0-669-09594-X.

Most of the literature on single parents focuses on single mothers. This book, however, is the result of a study of single fathers and provides the reader with an enlightening examination of single fathers based on the results of a survey of 1,100 single fathers. Providing insights into the day-to-day activities and struggles facing men raising their children alone, Greif describes how fathers handle the many aspects of parenting. Individual chapters focus on the phenomenon of single fathers, custody in perspective, reasons for divorce, reasons that fathers receive custody, housekeeping and child care arrangements, balancing the demands of work and child rearing, fathers' relationships with their children, adjusting to being single again, the relationship of the ex-wife with the father and children, experience with the legal system and child support, mothers with custody, children of single fathers, and conclusions.

————. *The Daddy Track and the Single Father.* Lexington, MA: Lexington Books, 1990. References, index. ISBN 0-669-19849-8.

This book is based on the results of a national survey completed in 1988 of over 1,100 separated and divorced single fathers. Greif provides the reader with an overview of single fathers and their experiences and suggests specific ways to help fathers cope with the problems they encounter in raising their children alone. The experiences of single fathers with housekeeping, child rearing, working, socializing, dealing with ex-wives, and working within the court system are described. The experiences of many single fathers are included in the hope of helping other single fathers cope with their situation.

Greif, Geoffrey L., and Mary S. Pabst. *Mothers without Custody.* Lexington, MA: Lexington Books, 1988. References, index. ISBN 0-669-13024-9.

Based on a study of noncustodial mothers, Greif and Pabst provide an enlightening examination of mothers who do not have custody of their children. Most people cannot understand how a mother can give up custody of her children—society is much more accepting of a father who does not have custody. This book explains societal attitudes toward mothers without custody and helps the reader understand why some mothers do not have custody of their children. The experiences of three noncustodial mothers are described, along with how custody decisions of the study subjects were made, the mothers' relationships with their children and with their ex-husbands, life as a noncustodial mother, child support, and experiences with the court system. Comparisons between noncustodial mothers and noncustodial fathers are made. Descriptions of how these mothers sought help from legal, social, and mental health professionals are provided. Some of the children provide insights into their experiences. Conclusions are discussed.

Greywolf, Elizabeth S. *The Single Mother's Handbook.* New York: Quill, 1984. Index. ISBN 0-688-02261-8.

This book is the result of a research project in which women shared their experiences. The Stress and Families Project was developed at Harvard University as a result of a grant from the Mental Health Services branch of the National Institute of Mental Health. Mothers with at least one child were interviewed about their early lives, experiences with institutions (from welfare to hospitals), views on parenting, experiences of discrimination, the men in their lives, and their political beliefs on a wide range of topics. Half of the women were single mothers. Greywolf discusses many of the issues and challenges facing these mothers. Specific topics include the stresses of single motherhood, how to regain emotions after separation and divorce, ways to prevent stress buildup, maintaining a healthy body and mind, nutritional guidelines and needs, ways to handle time efficiently, steps for a happier home life, day care concerns, welfare, sex and the single parent, and job and career development. This book is a good source of information and support for the single mother.

Hao, Lingxin. *Kin Support, Welfare, and Out-of-Wedlock Mothers.* New York: Garland Publishing, 1994. Bibliography, index. ISBN 0-8153-1571-6.

Since the 1960s the structure of the American family has undergone major changes. Young single mothers are bearing the brunt of these changes, many living in poverty with their young children, unable to find ways to get off welfare. These mothers must find ways to provide economic support to their families as well as emotional nurturing that is critical to healthy children. The author of this book compares the public and private support systems that help these families and their effects on the marriage, fertility, education, and employment of out-of-wedlock mothers. The role that the family plays in influencing fertility decisions of young women, ways that parents may attempt to influence the fertility decisions of their daughters as well as their childbearing behavior, and the influence of family support and AFDC (Aid to Families with Dependent Children) on out-of-wedlock births are explored. The sociological and economic literature concerning illegitimate births, family support, welfare, and labor force participation is reviewed; hypotheses are developed and tested; and findings are discussed. Implications for further research are examined.

Hardey, Michael, and Graham Crow, eds. *Lone Parenthood: Coping with Constraints and Making Opportunities in Single-Parent Families.* Toronto: University of Toronto Press, 1991. Bibliography, index. ISBN 0-8020-2824-1.

In contemporary British society single parents find themselves in a marginal position, often financially disadvantaged. Hardey and Crow have gathered an excellent group of experts to examine the position of single parents in British society. Topics discussed include lone parenthood and demographic change, housing strategies, patterns of health and illness, income and employment, day care, family policy as an antipoverty measure, becoming a lone parent, conflicting experiences of lone parenthood, and the transition from lone-parent family to stepfamily.

Harris, Kathleen Mullan. *Teen Mothers and the Revolving Welfare Door.* Philadelphia: Temple University Press, 1997. Bibliography, index. ISBN 1-56639-499-6.

Many people believe that the welfare system encourages women to stay at home and have more children in order to increase the amount of their benefits; the belief is that teenage mothers are especially susceptible to this type of irresponsible behavior. In this revealing book Harris describes her research concerning teenage mothers and their relationship to welfare. She studied long-term patterns of urban black teenage mothers in Baltimore and their receipt of welfare over two decades. She found that the "vast majority of teenage mothers treat public assistance not as a destination but as a way station to work. On occasion they cycle back onto welfare but largely because the escape routes from public assistance are uncertain." The book provides information concerning adolescent mothers and poverty, data and methods of the research study, patterns of welfare receipt, entry into the welfare system, routes of exit from the system, return to welfare, and implications for future welfare policy. Appendices provide information on the reliability of the data and the methods of analysis.

Josephson, Jyl J. *Gender, Families, and State: Child Support Policy in the United States.* New York: Rowman & Littlefield, 1997. References, index. ISBN 0-8476-8371-0.

Over the past 30 years families, family policy, and the law have changed drastically. Increasing rates of children living in poverty and the growing number of divorces, out-of-wedlock births, and single women–headed families have led policy makers and legislators to seek solutions to the problems created by these increasing numbers. In this book Josephson explores family policy, social policy, and law in the United States. She examines ideas concerning family-state relations, political institutions in the United States, how child support policy reflects state interests, goals of federal child support law and policy, selected state child support policy (Maryland and Texas), child support policy in practice in Maryland and Texas, the role of gender in child support policy, and child support policy in relation to state purposes. Appendices provide the reader with information on the legislative history of federal child support laws and child support laws in Maryland and Texas, a list of interviews conducted, and detailed information regarding the data collection methods, the survey, and study results.

Kamerman, Sheila B., and Alfred J. Kahn. *Mothers Alone: Strategies for a Time of Change.* Dover, MA: Auburn House, 1988. Index. ISBN 0-86569-183-5.

During the 1980s the composition of single-mother families as well as their needs changed. Kamerman and Kahn describe the changes that occurred, the importance of single-mother families, and the public perception of the needs of these families. They examine the difficult public policy choices that faced legislators, policy makers, scholars, and concerned citizens. Options that are explored include an antipoverty strategy, a categorical single-mother strategy, a family policy that focuses on young children, and a universal strategy that focuses on integrating work and family life. The implications of the possible options provided are discussed. The intended audience includes concerned citizens, policy makers, public officials, and experts in the field.

Kissman, Kris, and Jo Ann Allen. *Single-Parent Families.* Newbury Park, CA: Sage Publications, 1993. References, index. ISBN 0-8039-4322-9.

While professionals working with families are becoming increasingly aware of varying forms of the family, including single-parent families, the literature on family-centered practice contains very little information concerning single-parent families. This book attempts to fill this gap. The authors describe and discuss issues that are important in working with single parents and that are based on factors such as the gender, ethnicity, age, and sexual orientation of the head of the household. The focus is on mother-headed families, families that face economic hardships, and the mistaken belief that women are not able to effectively head these families. Individual chapters focus on family life cycle, the external environment, support for family and partners, extrafamilial support, ethnic families, adolescent parents, single father–headed families, noncustodial parenting, and policy perspectives.

Leslie, Marsha R., ed. *The Single Mother's Companion: Essays and Stories by Women.* Seattle: Seal Press, 1994. ISBN 1-878067-56-7.

Leslie has gathered a group of strong, motivated women who offer essays concerning single motherhood. This book provides a "forum for single mothers to read and to write about their lives from their own varied and unique perspectives" (page xii). Some women describe their experiences of single motherhood in the 1970s, having a child after an illustrious career, or leaving an abusive situation. Economic struggles are described. Contributors include former U.S. Senator Carol Moseley-Braun, author Barbara Kingsolver, and *New York Times* reporter Sheila Rule.

Leving, Jeffrey M., with Kenneth A. Dachman. *Fathers' Rights: Hard-Hitting and Fair Advice for Every Father Involved in a Custody Dispute.* New York: Basic Books, 1997. Index. ISBN 0-465-02443-2.

For divorced fathers, seeking visitation and other rights concerning their children can be difficult. As a men's rights attorney for over 15 years, Leving provides divorced fathers with a clear road map to help them with their legal rights. All aspects of the custody process are described. Individual chapters focus on custody, joint custody, access to children, protection, interference, support, enforcement of support orders, choosing an attorney, working with an attorney before the divorce is final, temporary custody, and strengthening the father-child bond. Issues surrounding negotiating with a spouse, mediation, arbitration, and shared parenting are examined. The litigation process is described, including planning, discovery, witnesses, dealing with sexual abuse allegations, the trial, and eleventh-hour settlements. Life after divorce is described, raising issues of visitation and litigation that may follow the divorce decree. Issues of paternity, including establishing paternity and contesting adoption, are discussed. Finally, recommendations are presented and an appendix provides a list of support groups for fathers seeking custody following a divorce.

Ludtke, Melissa. *On Our Own: Unmarried Motherhood in America.* New York: Random House, 1997. Bibliography, index. ISBN 0-679-42414-8.

A former correspondent for *Time* magazine, Ludtke frequently wrote about families and children. In this book she examines the many issues surrounding unmarried women having children. Growing out of her own desire to have a child even though she was not married, Ludtke began reading everything she could find about unmarried motherhood, but found that talking with unmarried mothers provided her with greater insight into the emotions that these women face in deciding to bear a child and raise it alone. She talks with women from all backgrounds, from the well-off to those surviving month to month on public assistance. They are teenage mothers as well as older women who decided to have a child in their forties. Ludtke tells these women's stories, alternating between two sets of unmarried mothers that receive a great deal of public discussion: teenagers and older women. The stories of the women portrayed in this book help the reader understand the many issues, including emotional and financial, that these women face and demonstrate that a decision to bear and raise a child while unmarried is not a simple one.

Marindin, Hope, ed. *The Handbook for Single Adoptive Parents.* Chevy Chase, MD: Committee for Single Adoptive Parents, 1992.

Practical advice for single people who want to adopt a child is provided in this excellent resource, containing original articles as well as reprints of relevant articles. Domestic and intercountry adoption, adoption by gay men and lesbians, legal aspects of adoption, and ways to make adoption affordable are discussed in a section on the mechanics of adoption. A section on ways to manage once a person has adopted a child focuses on medical and financial aspects of adoption, including a resource list of support groups, organizations, publications, and websites. Advice on ways to cope when adopting children with special needs is provided in a section on handling challenges. Firsthand accounts of adoption experiences provide insight into the problems, challenges, and rewards of becoming a single parent. The final chapter describes two research studies of adoption by single persons; the results of the studies indicate that the overwhelming majority of single parents have positive experiences and that children adopted into single-parent homes have fewer problems than children adopted into two-parent homes, although both groups of adopted children display some serious emotional and behavioral problems.

Marston, Stephanie. *The Divorced Parent: Success Strategies for Raising Your Children after Separation.* New York: William Morrow, 1994. Suggested reading list, resources, index. ISBN 0-688-11323-0.

As a family therapist and seminar leader, Marston has experienced divorce and single parenthood firsthand. In this book Marston dispels the myth that a single-parent home is a broken one. She offers the reader practical advice as well as specific tools for raising healthy and well-adjusted children. Individual chapters focus on helping children cope with divorce and its aftermath, games parents play, how to stop the battle with an ex-spouse, how to build a parenting partnership, ways to communicate that will encourage cooperation, dealing with difficult ex-spouses, ways to keep both parents involved with the children, choosing an attorney and other legal issues, the money factor, what children have to say about divorce and single parents, and healing oneself and one's children.

Mathes, Patricia G., and Beverly J. Irby. *Teen Pregnancy and Parenting Handbook.* Champaign, IL: Research Press, 1993. ISBN 0-87822-333-9.

This is an excellent resource book that is written in language that adolescents can easily read and understand. The authors present a realistic picture of teenage pregnancy and parenting. Topics covered include decisions about pregnancy or termination, development of the fetus, diet and nutrition, child development during the first year, birth control methods, single parenting issues, completing school, and other topics of interest to pregnant teenagers. Recommended as a student manual for teen pregnancy and parenting groups, a discussion guide that accompanies the book provides suggested assignments, group activities, and guidelines for working effectively with teenagers.

Mattes, Jane. *Single Mothers by Choice: A Guidebook for Single Women Who Are Considering or Have Chosen Motherhood.* New York: Times Books, 1994. Appendices, recommended reading list, index. ISBN 0-8129-2246-8.

Choosing to become a mother without the presence of a father in the home is a difficult decision. For many reasons, many women have decided to bear or adopt a child alone. This book describes the experiences of Jane Mattes as a single mother and her attempts to find answers to the many questions she had concerning single motherhood. She invited other single mothers to her home to help each other find answers and support. The group grew into the national organization Single Mothers by Choice, with over 20 chapters throughout the country. This book provides answers to many of the questions Mattes and other single mothers had. Part One focuses on making the decision to have a child and carrying it out and includes information on conceiving a child, legal rights, artificial insemination, fertility problems, and adopting a child. Part Two focuses on the experience of actually being a single mother, and includes information on pregnancy, birth, postpartum, preparing for questions about the father and other questions young children will have, special child development issues for children of single mothers, legal and moral aspects, and the social life of a single mother by choice. Appendices offer information on sperm banks that work with single women, resources for adoption, two examples of an agreement with a known donor, and support groups.

McLanahan, Sara, and Gary Sandefur. *Growing Up with a Single Parent: What Hurts, What Helps.* Cambridge, MA: Harvard University Press, 1994. Notes, index. ISBN 0-674-36407-4.

Many people, experts as well as the general public, are concerned about the effects on children of living with only one parent. Many people believe that children who are raised by single parents are at risk for all types of problems, from leaving school early to getting in trouble with the law. In this book McLanahan and Sandefur focus on whether children who grow up with a single mother or a mother and stepfather are worse off than children with similar characteristics who grow up with both of their biological parents. The authors also examine answers to the question of whether children from divorced families would be better off if their parents had stayed together.

Merritt, Sharyne, and Linda Steiner. *And Baby Makes Two: Motherhood without Marriage.* New York: Franklin Watts, 1984. Index. ISBN 0-531-09847-8.

Merritt and Steiner present and discuss the results of a nationwide informal study concerning single motherhood. They found women throughout the United States who had children while single: one quarter of them got pregnant intentionally, one quarter "invited an accident" (page 2), one quarter became pregnant by accident, and one quarter adopted a child. The book focuses on the women's feelings and experiences and covers topics such as the decision to have a child while single, becoming a mother, adoption, artificial insemination, pregnancy, coping, the child's welfare, the rights of the father, finances, physical support, the support of family and friends, psychological aspects, and the effects of single parenting. An appendix provides information on the legal aspects of single parenting, including establishing paternity, custody, child support, adoption by a stepfather, contracts, wrongful death statutes, inheritance, and artificial insemination.

Millar, Jane. *Poverty and the Lone Parent: The Challenges to Social Policy.* Brookfield, VT: Gower Publishing Company, 1989. Bibliography, index. ISBN 0-566-05770-0.

Single parents, especially single mothers, face many challenges in their lives, no matter where they live. As in many countries, the number of single parents is growing in Great Britain. This book analyzes the living standards of single-parent families in Great Britain and examines social policies meant to alleviate many of the pressures on these families. The number of single-parent families in Great Britain and other countries is examined. Income support policies and results of family finances and resources surveys, including income and living standards, dependence on the state, and the persistence of poverty are discussed. A comparative analysis of employment, maintenance, and social security policies regarding single-parent families in EEC countries, Nordic countries, Australia, Canada, and the United States is presented. Finally, the main findings of the Family Finances Survey/Family Resources Survey (FFS/FRS) are discussed along with the options available for developing policies that will benefit single-parent families.

Miller, Dorothy C. *Women and Social Welfare: A Feminist Analysis.* New York: Praeger, 1990. Bibliography, index. ISBN 0-275-92973-6.

According to Miller, many of the social welfare policies that have been developed in the United States are based on the traditional nuclear family in which the father works and the mother stays at home to raise the children. When the Social Security Act was passed in 1935 divorce was not common and women were not expected to support their families. Miller believes that "the social welfare system has been designed to perpetuate a system in which women's place is in the nuclear family" (page 3). The relationships of women to men as well as women's status as mothers are stronger variables than "work ethic principles in shaping social welfare policies. Thus married women with their husbands are rewarded better than women without men, whether they be divorced, widowed, or never married, not only in poverty-related policies, but those related to the middle class as well" (page 4). Individual chapters focus on theories that may explain the differences in Western society in treating gender issues, an examination of AFDC, child support and child custody issues, the problems facing elderly women, and suggestions for reforming social welfare policy in the United States.

Miller, Naomi. *Single Parents by Choice: A Growing Trend in Family Life.* New York: Plenum Press, 1992. Select directory of resources, notes, index. ISBN 0-306-44321-X.

In recent years an increasing number of people have intentionally decided to become single parents. Many of these parents are older, educated, financially secure, and successful in a number of professions. As a clinician and expert in family relations, Naomi Miller examines this new group of single parents. She provides the reader with interesting insights into being a single parent.

Four groups of single parents are discussed: single biological mothers, single adoptive mothers or fathers, divorced parents, and gay and lesbian parents. Based on interviews with many single parents, this book offers the reader a fascinating insight into the struggles, problems, frustrations, and joys of raising a child independently.

Morton, Marian J. *And Sin No More: Social Policy and Unwed Mothers in Cleveland, 1855–1990.* Columbus: Ohio State University Press, 1993. Bibliography, index. ISBN 0-8142-0602-6.

Tracing the care of unmarried mothers in Cleveland from 1855 to 1990, Morton offers a fascinating history of single motherhood in the United States. She explores the ways that the changing dynamics of social welfare, religion, and race have affected choices related to single motherhood and responses to this important social issue. The history of unwed motherhood and the public attitudes and social policies toward unwed mothers have changed over the years and this book helps the reader understand these attitudes and policies. Individual chapters focus on the Cleveland Infirmary (or poorhouse), private sectarian refuges and maternity homes, the professionalization of social work, the movement of childbirth from the home to the hospital, how Salvation Army Rescue and other social welfare organizations and policy makers worked to help black unwed mothers, and the provision of services to poor, often black, mothers by public hospitals.

Mulroy, Elizabeth A. *The New Uprooted: Single Mothers in Urban Life.* Westport, CT: Auburn House, 1995. Bibliography, index. ISBN 0-86569-038-3.

Many books about single parents focus on family relations, divorce, teenage pregnancy, and welfare reform. Mulroy provides a different approach to the study of single parents: she examines how single mothers from a variety of backgrounds experience their two roles as sole family breadwinners and sole resident parents. This book offers information on the quality of life, life choices, and chances of single mothers and their families. It provides a comprehensive picture of life for a single mother, including the social and physical environments experienced by a single mother. This book is divided into three parts. Part I offers background information on single-parent families. Part II discusses the findings of Mulroy's qualitative study of single mothers and includes the ways that single mothers "attempt to meet their three most basic needs: personal safety from a violent relationship with an ex-husband or partner, an affordable housing unit, and a job with benefits that pays a living wage" (page 14). The transition to a more stable family situation is discussed in Part III.

Pearson, Carol Lynn. *One on the Seesaw: The Ups and Downs of a Single-Parent Family.* New York: Random House, 1988. ISBN 0-394-56496-0.

This book provides an entertaining look at raising children as a single parent. Carol Lynn Pearson met her future husband in a play at Brigham Young University, married him a year later, and together they had four children. He was a homosexual but hoped that marriage would help him change. It did not. They divorced and he later died of AIDS, cared for by his ex-wife in her home. Pearson describes life after marriage in a house with two sons, two daughters, and a variety of animals. She describes the joys of single parenting as well as the challenges. This book offers a delightful look at a single-parent family that has the financial means to enjoy life.

Polakow, Valerie. *Lives on the Edge: Single Mothers and Their Children in the Other America.* Chicago: University of Chicago Press, 1993. Notes, index. ISBN 0-226-67183-6.

Many single mothers and their children live in poverty in the United States today. Based on interviews and observation as well as library research, this book provides a compelling examination of these single mothers and their children. Polakow begins by reviewing the history of childhood and prevailing attitudes toward children in Western Europe and the United States. Part Two focuses on an examination of public attitudes and public policy toward single mothers, presents the stories of individual single mothers and their children, and is based on interviews conducted with women living in Michigan between 1989 and 1991. Part Three focuses on the children of poor single mothers, discussing poor children and public child care, Head Start programs, and preschool programs for at-risk children, providing portraits of the classroom experiences of five at-risk children and the attitudes of teachers and other students toward these children. In an afterword Polakow reflects on the future of single mothers and their children, and suggests that universal health care, affordable housing, child allowances and maternity/parental leave, a national child care system, and equity in education are ways to improve the lives of single mothers and their children who are living in poverty.

Popenoe, David. *Life without Father: Compelling New Evidence That Fatherhood and Marriage Are Indispensable for the Good of Children and Society.* New York: The Free Press, 1996. Notes, index. ISBN 0-684-82297-0.

In recent years a growing trend to strengthen the family, especially the role of the father, is occurring throughout the United States. This book analyzes the father's role in American society, drawing on resources from the social sciences, history, and evolutionary psychology. Popenoe "examines the nature and meaning of fatherhood and reviews the trends, the evidence, and the social consequences of the removal of fathers from families and the lives of their children" (page 1). The decline of fatherhood and marriage, the costs of fatherlessness, fathers in history, and the reasons why fathers are important are discussed. The final chapter offers ways to reclaim fatherhood and marriage and includes suggestions for restoring some cultural propositions, reestablishing marriage, redefining the father's role in the family, and government action, including welfare reform, promarriage values, divorce reform, and rebuilding local communities.

Popenoe, David, Jean Bethke Elshtain, and David Blankenhorn, eds. *Promises to Keep: Decline and Renewal of Marriage in America.* Lanham, MD: Rowman and Littlefield, 1996. Index. ISBN 0-8476-8230-7.

Many experts on the family believe that in the United States the institution of marriage and the family is in trouble, replaced with a culture of divorce and unwed parenthood. The essays in this book, written by lawyers, theologians, social scientists, policy makers, and activists, explore the problems facing families today and suggest ways to strengthen the family. Part One explores the decline of the American family, values and attitudes toward the family, myths of marriage and family, comparative perspectives on marriage and divorce, and conservative, liberal, and feminist views toward the decline of the family. Part Two examines religious, legal, and clinical dimensions of the declining family, including Christian family theory, postmodern family law, law and the stability of marriage, and parenting from separate households. Part Three presents suggestions for re-creating marriage.

Part Four presents the report of the Council on Families in America on the state of marriage in America.

Renvoize, Jean. *Going Solo: Single Mothers by Choice.* Boston: Routledge and Kegan Paul, 1985. ISBN 0-7102-0065-X.

In many cases women in long-term marriages or relationships probably give less thought to the impact of a child on their lives than unmarried women who deliberately choose to become pregnant. Renvoize believes that all women should be more aware of what motherhood involves. In this book, the results of interviews with mothers, prospective mothers, gynecologists, therapists, and other professionals in Great Britain, the United States, and Holland provide the basis for an examination of single parenthood. Part 1 examines the growing phenomenon of single parenthood by choice, the women's movement, men's images and desires, reasons why women choose single parenthood, and marriage and family today. Part 2 looks at the various ways to become pregnant, the problems and joys of parenthood, children, fathers' relationships with children, and the views of professionals toward single parenthood. Part 3 offers the views of single mothers regarding their experiences.

Riley, Julia. *Living the Possible Dream: The Single Parent's Guide to College Success.* Boulder, CO: Johnson Books, 1991. Bibliography, index. ISBN 1-55566-086-X.

This comprehensive guidebook is written for any single parent who wants to earn a college degree. Major issues that a single parent faces when searching for and attending a college are discussed, including overcoming the fear associated with going to college, sources of financial aid, finding good child care, study skills, parenting skills, and coping with social service agencies and college bureaucracy. A list of child care referral agencies throughout the country and state-by-state lists of sources of assistance are provided.

Rodgers, Harrell R., Jr. *Poor Women, Poor Children: American Poverty in the 1990s.* Armonk, NY: M. E. Sharpe, 1996. Bibliography, index. ISBN 1-56324-607-4.

This is an excellent resource book with lots of statistics concerning women, children, and poverty. Single mothers and their families are the focus of many of these statistics, because many single mothers find themselves in financial trouble. The problems of increasing poverty levels among women and their children are discussed in this book. The primary causes and consequences of the growing numbers of poor single mothers and their children are presented. Existing welfare, social, and private-sector programs developed to help those in poverty are assessed. Policy alternatives and new welfare approaches are discussed. Individual chapters focus on an empirical analysis of the changing population of those living in poverty, causes of poverty among women and children, social welfare programs for women in several European countries, and a critical analysis of attempts at reforming welfare in the United States.

Rodgers, Joann Ellison, and Michael F. Cataldo. *Raising Sons: Practical Strategies for Single Mothers.* New York: New American Library, 1984. Bibliography, index. ISBN 0-453-00470-9.

Easy to read, this book is written by a behavioral psychologist and an award-winning science writer and single mother of two sons. They provide valuable information for single mothers who are raising sons without their fathers living at home. Intimate interviews with single mothers and their sons provide the basis for suggestions to mothers on how to help their sons grow up with a sense of responsibility, self-worth, and dignity. Chapters provide information on how to cope with the view that mothers cannot raise "real" men; what and how to talk with boys about sex, drugs, and drinking; methods of effective discipline; ways to make the transition into adulthood smooth; and reasons for ensuring that sons have good male role models in their lives.

Sander, Joelle. *Before Their Time: Four Generations of Teenage Mothers.* New York: Harcourt Brace Jovanovich, 1991. ISBN 0-15-111638-5.

Four women in one family, representing four generations, tell their stories about life as poor, black women trying to survive in a harsh environment. Sander has done an excellent job of telling the stories of these women. About the repetitive cycle of teenage pregnancy and parenthood, this book provides the reader with an inside look at the lives of these women. Leticia Johnson, the youngest, begins by describing her life, her long-term boyfriend, her pregnancies, and her children. Sexually abused by her stepfather, Leticia is scared and confused about sex. Her mother, Denise

Benjamin, tells about her early life and how she became pregnant. Rena Wilson, Denise's mother, describes what her life was like before pregnant girls were allowed to be out in the world. Finally, Louise Eaton, Rena's mother and Leticia's great-grandmother, explains to the reader what her life was like, how she became pregnant before she was married, and how she handled all these experiences. Sander has woven a poignant story, providing the reader with insight into the problems of teenage pregnancy. The final chapter of the book brings the reader up-to-date with the lives of all four women and discusses the implications of the experiences of these women in relation to the problem of teenage pregnancy in the United States.

Schein, Virginia E. *Working from the Margins: Voices of Mothers in Poverty.* Ithaca, NY: ILR Press (Cornell University Press), 1995. References, index. ISBN 0-87546-341-X.

Many people believe that welfare benefits have been abused by many recipients who should be required to go out and get a job. The welfare reforms enacted in 1996 supported this belief. Schein examines single mothers and their experiences with welfare and poverty. She believes that reducing welfare rolls may not reduce poverty, that "evaluations of welfare-to-work programs look more at reductions in welfare payments and expenditures to the state than the significance of any earnings increases to the participants" (page 7). Because of the low wages that many of these mothers earn as well as jobs that often do not provide health benefits, many women see no benefits to working. Schein believes that "we need to learn more about the women and to understand their current circumstances within the context of their lives" (page 10). She provides this understanding; 30 women from rural and urban areas were interviewed. They were all single mothers who were raising at least one child 18 years old or younger, receiving some type of public assistance, and who had had some type of work experience. She introduces the reader to these women, describing the emotional and psychological stress that they face in their daily lives, and provides the reader with a better understanding of the relationship between single mothers and poverty.

Sidel, Ruth. *Keeping Women and Children Last: America's War on the Poor.* New York: Penguin Books, 1996. Notes, bibliography, index. ISBN 0-74-024663-0.

A sequel to *Women and Children Last: The Plight of Poor Women in Affluent America* (1992), this book reexamines the plight of poor women and children in America. Sidel focuses on the attempts by the federal government to dismantle the welfare system, targeting single mothers. She believes that politicians have waged a successful campaign to portray female-headed families as the cause of many of America's current social ills, stigmatizing these women to divert attention from the severe problems facing America today. Full of statistics, this book examines current trends and shows that children are the real victims of poverty. Sidel believes that

> the designation of poor single mothers as the cause of America's ills deflects attention from the severe economic and societal problems we face and our unwillingness to deal with those problems: the growing gap between rich and poor; widespread employment insecurity; increasing political apathy and alienation; extraordinary levels of violence, particularly among our young people; and our rapidly deteriorating infrastructure. This strategy in effect shifts blame from the affluent and powerful to the poor and powerless." (page xviii)

Sidel examines the assault on the female-headed family, who the poor are, targeting welfare recipients for stigmatization, teenage mothers, poor children, and ways to return to caring about all people.

Solinger, Rickie. *Wake Up Little Susie: Single Pregnancy and Race before* **Roe v. Wade.** New York: Routledge, 1992. Bibliography, index. ISBN 0-415-90448-X.

Before abortion was legalized as a result of the U.S. Supreme Court's ruling in *Roe v. Wade* in 1973, white unwed mothers had very different experiences from black unwed mothers. Solinger explores these differences, and argues that unwed mothers were used by politicians, social service personnel, the media, and the public to explain the causes of many social problems, depending on the race of the mother. The book explores the background of welfare and abortion politics during the Reagan-Bush era. Race "was the most accurate predictor of an unwed mother's parents' response to her pregnancy; of society's reaction to her plight; of where and how she would spend the months of her pregnancy; and most important, the most accurate predictor of what she would do with the 'fatherless' child she bore, and of how being mother to such a child would affect the rest of her life" (page 18). Theories of race, gender, motherhood, and social stability were tested using single mothers and their experiences. Many public initiatives and attitudes encouraged white women to give up their babies. On the other hand, social welfare policies were based on the assumption that black women would keep their babies and would need to be restricted from having additional babies.

Swain, Shurlee, and Renate Howe. *Single Mothers and Their Children: Disposal, Punishment, and Survival in Australia.* New York: Cambridge University Press, 1995. Bibliography, index. ISBN 0-521-47443-4.

The history of unmarried, single motherhood in Australia is presented in this book. The period from 1850, when the colony of Victoria was separated from New South Wales, to 1975, when illegitimacy was abolished as a legal category, is covered. Women who became single mothers are introduced. The circumstances of conception, decisions single mothers had to face—including telling family members and deciding whether to have an abortion or marry the father—are examined. Pregnancy and birthing options that these mothers faced created their own problems along with the choices that were open to mothers concerning the "disposing" of their children (abortion, adoption, etc.). Death, separation, and survival are the focus of individual chapters. The struggles that many of these women and their advocates went through to improve their lives and change public policy are discussed.

Taylor, Dorothy L. *The Positive Influence of Bonding in Female-Headed African American Families.* New York: Garland Publishing, 1993. References, index. ISBN 0-8153-1127-3.

The African-American family has long been known as having a tradition of support through an extended family. The primary focus of this book is "the relationship between the behavior of children and the natural support systems unique to African-American female-headed households" (page xvi). Many studies have been conducted to determine whether a relationship exists between juvenile delinquency and various economic or social factors. This book provides data from a study to understand the relationship between female-headed households and juvenile delinquency by exploring bonding factors in female-headed households. A review of the literature, theoretical perspectives, study methodology, preliminary analysis, findings, and conclusions are presented.

Terdal, Leif, and Patricia Kennedy. *Raising Sons without Fathers: A Woman's Guide to Parenting Strong, Successful Boys.* Secaucus, NJ: Carol Publishing Group, 1996. Bibliography, index. ISBN 1-55972-342-4.

In this resource book Terdal and Kennedy focus on the problems that many single mothers face in raising their sons without a father. The authors believe that boys may be affected more negatively than girls by the absence of a father in the home. Many suggestions apply to both sons and daughters, such as how to tell the children about an impending divorce and ways to deal with financial difficulties. Part I examines the problems that sons face without fathers and suggests solutions to several common problems. Part II examines fatherless parenting, how to parent in a positive way, how to discipline, and positive school experiences. Ways to improve financial status, issues of abuse, and finding positive role models are discussed in Part III. Positive outcomes and survival techniques are presented in Part IV. Finally, an appendix offers a list of organizations to help single mothers, including programs that provide services such as mentoring, parenting, peer counseling, therapeutic activities, recreational activities, conflict resolution, life and social skills, and work opportunities.

Tippins, Sherill, and Prudence Tippins. *Two of Us Make a World: The Single Mother's Guide to Pregnancy, Childbirth, and the First Year.* New York: Henry Holt and Company, 1996. Appendices, index. ISBN 0-8050-3780-2.

An excellent resource book for single mothers, this book provides information concerning medical, social, financial, emotional, and legal aspects of being a single mother. The authors suggest ways to encourage family support, work out a child custody agreement, develop a support network, deal with discrimination in all areas of life, and develop a sound financial plan for the future.

Practical advice from experts in the field is provided, and personal testimonies are offered from women who are single parents. Appendices offer information on resources, recommended readings, state child support enforcement offices, a sample donor agreement, and a sample coparenting agreement.

Wartman, William. *Life without Father: Influences of an Unknown Man.* New York: Franklin Watts, 1988. ISBN 0-531-15074-7.

When Wartman was only two years old, his father died of a brain tumor at the age of 31 years. Growing up, he and his two sisters missed out on the experiences of having a father as well as many memories. His mother rarely talked about her husband, preferring to ignore the children's many questions. When Wartman turned 31 he believed he was dying of a brain tumor, just as his father had died. When he finally was diagnosed as hypoglycemic (no brain tumor) he set out on a search to find out about his own father and the experiences that other fatherless children had growing up. He found that many people initially agreed to talk with him, but when the time for the interview approached, they backed down, not wanting to bring up many negative memories. He describes his attempts to learn about his own father as well as the experiences of some of the other people who grew up without a father who were willing to talk with him. He discusses the feelings of sensitivity and denial that surround the very personal issue of not knowing one's biological father.

Wassil-Grimm, Claudette. *Where's Daddy? How Divorced, Single and Widowed Mothers Can Provide What's Missing When Dad's Missing.* Woodstock, NY: Overlook Press, 1994. Bibliography. ISBN 0-87951-541-4.

This book provides readers with an understanding of what it is like to live in a single-parent family. Written for single mothers, Wassil-Grimm's book helps these women provide safe and secure homes for their children and keep noncustodial fathers financially and emotionally involved with their children. Individual chapters focus on various aspects of single motherhood and the lack of a father in the home. These aspects include the role of the father, reasons why fathers don't get involved with their children, ways to involve the father, early fatherhood, motivating unwed fathers, the death of a father, what's missing when a father is missing from the family, how to get child support, boyfriends, stepfathers, creative custody choices, and ways for mothers to cope with their situations.

Watnik, Webster. *Child Custody Made Simple: Understanding the Laws of Child Custody and Child Support.* Claremont, CA: Single Parent Press, 1997. Glossary, index. ISBN 0-9649404-0-X.

An excellent guide for people looking for answers to questions concerning child custody and child support. Child custody and visitation information focuses on where laws come from, laws of child custody and visitation, the reality of child custody, and deciding and modifying child custody. Part II examines parenting plans, and includes information on negotiating a parenting plan, making decisions, creating a schedule, finding and hiring a lawyer, and working with a lawyer. Part III discusses going to court, including courts and jurisdiction, pretrial, and trial. Alternatives to courts and lawyers focus on negotiation, alternative dispute resolution, and representing oneself. Legal problems that may occur include the mistreatment of children, kidnapping, custodial interference, moving away, establishing paternity, and collecting child support. A final section on child support examines relevant laws, calculating child support, and modifying support. An appendix provides information concerning state laws on child custody.

Zucchino, David. *Myth of the Welfare Queen.* New York: Scribner, 1997. Index. ISBN 0-684-81914-7.

For approximately six months, Zucchino followed the lives of several unmarried welfare women living in North Philadelphia in order to answer questions about what these women did all day, and how they spent their welfare checks, managed their finances, fed and clothed their children, obtained medical care, and whether they could find jobs. He wanted to know "whether anyone among a class of women so despised by mainstream America attempted to improve their circumstances and to raise their children for lives beyond poverty. I wanted to know whether such women were worthy more of contempt or compassion, or something in between" (page 13). Zucchino found women who spent most of their time looking for food and clothing and for a safe home for their children. He expertly tells their stories, letting the reader into their lives, exposing their vulnerabilities, and helping the reader understand the situations in which they find themselves. They work valiantly to make a better life for their children, finding themselves and their families off welfare and sometimes back on welfare. Some of their children break out of the cycle of poverty, with lots of hard work, but these women continue to fear for the future.

Journal Articles

Bowen, Gary L., Dennis K. Orthner, and Laura I. Zimmerman. **"Family Adaptation of Single Parents in the United States Army: An Empirical Analysis of Work Stressors and Adaptive Resources."** *Family Relations* 42 (1993):293–304.

From a sample of 238 single parents serving on active duty in the U.S. Army, this study examines the contribution of work stressors, family and community resources, and army support resources in the lives of these single parents. Results indicate that the ways that single parents adapt to the requirements of the military lifestyle are influenced by the availability of family members and community and army resources. These factors are more important than the work-related stresses that these parents face. The authors suggest recommendations for policy and practical application.

Bumpass, Larry, and Sara McLanahan. **"Unmarried Motherhood: Recent Trends, Composition, and Black-White Differences."** *Demography* 26, no. 2 (1989):279–286.

The authors used the National Survey of Family Growth (1982) to study the extent to which racial differences in premarital birthrates are related to differences in the socioeconomic status, family structure, and residential characteristics of the parents. The researchers found that black women who come from high-risk backgrounds are three times more likely to experience a premarital birth than black women who come from low-risk backgrounds. Bumpass and McLanahan explain that racial differences in premarital births exist because black women are more likely to come from high-risk backgrounds and because black women from low-risk backgrounds are more likely to have a premarital birth than white women from low-risk backgrounds.

Campbell, Marian L., and Phyllis Moen. **"Job-Family Role Strain among Employed Single Mothers of Preschoolers."** *Family Relations* 41 (1992):205–211.

Some studies have suggested that two critical predictors of job tension are being a single mother and having a preschool child. Although few studies have examined this issue, this study looks at data from a sample of employed single mothers of young children to find out what factors influence job and family strain in these families. The authors found that, after interviewing 224 single mothers, the most important factor considered in the effect of work on role strain originated in the workplace. The mothers' attitude toward work was the most important factor, followed by work time and work satisfaction. Family variables that proved important in contributing to role strain included the number of children and the age of the children. Child care variables were not found to be significant factors in role strain.

Cheung, Chau-kiu, and Elaine Suk-ching Liu. **"Impacts of Social Pressure and Social Support on Distress among Single Parents in China."** *Journal of Divorce and Remarriage* 26, no. 3/4 (1997):65–82.

Using a sample of 301 single parents in Guangzhou, China, the authors examine the relationships between single parenthood and distress and social support. There are very few single-parent families in China (only 2.5 percent of all households). Divorce and widowhood account for most single-parent families. Social pressure is often put on single parents concerning their custodial role. Widowhood generally leads to higher depression than divorce. The authors suggest that programs be set up to educate the public concerning the problems faced by single parents and social networking skills of single parents should be enhanced to help them gain social support from family and friends.

DeMaris, Alfred, and Geoffrey L. Greif. **"The Relationship between Family Structure and Parent-Child Relationship Problems in Single Father Households."** *Journal of Divorce and Remarriage* 18 (1992):55–77.

The authors studied 912 single-father households to determine the influence of number, sex distribution, age distribution, and age spacing of children on the severity of the problems between parents and children. According to the single fathers, preadolescent girls are the most desirable age-sex combination to raise, compared to raising both preadolescent and adolescent girls, children of both sexes, or boys only. Family size and age spacing appeared to have no effect on parent-child relationships. Other predictors of the quality of the parent-child relationship included the method of obtaining custody, social support, marital conflict, and father involvement in child care during the marriage.

Downey, Douglas B. **"The School Performance of Children from Single-Mother and Single-Father Families: Economic or Interpersonal Deprivation?"** *Journal of Family Issues* 15 (1994): 129–147.

Using a nationally representative sample of eighth graders from the National Longitudinal Study of 1988, Downey examined the school performance of children from single-mother, single-father, and two-parent families. The sample consisted of 3,483 children from single-mother families, 409 children from single-father families, and 14,269 children in two-parent families. According to the findings, there was no significant difference between the performance of children from single-father families and children from single-mother families. However, Downey found that children from two-parent families performed consistently better in school than children from single-parent families. Findings suggest that financial resources, or the lack of these resources, may help in understanding the problems that children from single-mother families encounter in school. The lack of interpersonal parental resources helps explain the problems children from single-father families face in school.

Downey, Douglas B., and Brian Powell. **"Do Children in Single-Parent Households Fare Better Living with Same-Sex Parents?"** *Journal of Marriage and the Family* 55 (1993):55–71.

Some researchers have suggested that children who live in single-parent families have better lives and better chances of success if they live with a parent of the same sex. In this study, Downey and Powell used data from the National Educational Longitudinal Study of 1988 to examine this theory. They found little evidence to support this theory.

Goldberg, Wendy A., Ellen Greenberger, Sharon Hamill, and Robin O'Neil. **"Role Demands in the Lives of Employed Single**

Mothers with Preschoolers." *Journal of Family Issues* 13 (1992): 312–333.

The authors examine several factors that are associated with the well-being of single mothers and their perceptions of the behavior of their children. A mailed survey was completed by 76 single employed mothers who had a preschool-age child. Factors that were found to be most important in the well-being of the mothers related to the mothers' work and family roles and included their beliefs concerning the consequences of maternal employment for children and their perceptions concerning quality of child care. The level of stability and amount of resources in the mothers' lives were related to levels of depression. Single mothers' perceptions of their children were associated with the recency of their single parenthood, the quality of their work lives, and the ways that work and family roles interact.

Greif, Geoffrey L. **"Children and Housework in the Single Father Family."** *Family Relations* 34 (1985):353–357.

The author studied 1,136 fathers who were members of Parents Without Partners and who were raising their children by themselves following separation or divorce. Over time the children tended to assume more responsibilities and participate more in housework. Fathers with teenage daughters received more help than fathers raising teenage sons. Also examined was the use of outside help, as well as daughters becoming mother substitutes and taking on housekeeping and child care responsibilities. Among the recommendations were that fathers not overburden their children when they ask for help with housework, that fathers may feel guilty about breaking up the family, that fathers don't have to prove to the world that they are competent parents, and that daughters who are acting as mother substitutes may need some help with housework.

Gringlas, Marcy, and Marsha Weinraub. **"The More Things Change . . . Single Parenting Revisited."** *Journal of Family Issues* 16, no. 1 (1995):29–52.

This study investigated the maternal and preschool child functioning in homes headed by single mothers. An original sample consisted of 42 mother-child pairs, 21 children from single-parent families and 21 children from two-parent families. This study followed up with this same sample seven years later; the authors found 28 of the original 42 mother-child pairs, including 14 single mothers and 14 married women and their children. Child functioning was measured using maternal and teacher reports of behavior problems, social competence, and academic performance. Maternal functioning was measured using parenting, social supports, and stress levels. Teachers reported that preadolescent children of single mothers had more behavior problems, lower social competence, and poorer school performance than children of married mothers. Single mothers were still less satisfied with emotional supports and also reported higher levels of stress.

Groze, Victor K., and James A. Rosenthal. **"Single Parents and Their Adopted Children: A Psychosocial Analysis."** *Families in Society* 72 (1991):67–77.

The authors conducted a study of single- and two-parent adoptive families by sending a survey to families who had finalized their adoption of a special needs child. Adoptive family functioning was described, focusing on emotional, behavioral, educational, and ecological areas. Fifteen percent of all adoptions in the study were to single parents. Single parents were more likely to have adopted older children, nonwhite children, and mentally retarded children; girls were more likely to be adopted by single parents. Many special needs adopted children do exhibit serious behavioral difficulties; children in single-parent families experienced fewer problems than children adopted into two-parent families. No significant differences were found in the performance of children in school. Finally, single parents found parent support groups more helpful than two-parent families did. The authors conclude that single-parent adoption is good for children; they are an untapped resource, especially for providing homes to children with special needs—for example, older children, physically challenged children, children of mixed or minority ethnicity, siblings, and children with emotional and/or behavioral problems.

Hall, Leslie D., Alexis J. Walker, and Alan C. Acock. **"Gender and Family Work in One-Parent Households."** *Journal of Marriage and the Family* 57, no. 3 (1995):685–692.

Using data from the 1987–1988 National Survey of Families and Households, the authors compared 1,433 mothers and 128 fathers in single-parent families. They focused on the time these parents spent with their children and the time they spent on housework. Fathers were hypothesized to spend less time in talking privately with their children and more time playing with them, as well as less time in feminine household tasks and more time in masculine household tasks. The hypotheses were supported by the findings, indicating that the child-rearing practices of parents are predictable according to the gender of the parent.

Hao, Ling-xin, and Mary C. Brinton. **"Productive Activities and Support Systems of Single Mothers."** *American Journal of Sociology* 102, no. 5 (1997):1305–1344.

In this study the authors examine a theoretical framework that would predict the role that family support plays in single mothers' decisions to participate in outside work or school activities. Using data from the National Longitudinal Survey of Labor Market Experience, Youth Survey, 1979–1992, Hao and Brinton examined education and employment histories of young single mothers over time. They found that women who spent less time as single mothers (under six years) were more likely to participate in productive activities, that is, work or school/training programs. Single mothers who live with other family members are more likely to be looking for a job. However, once a single mother is enrolled in a training program or is working, the actual working/training conditions are more critical to her staying at the job or in school than whether she is living with other family members. Policy implications of these and other findings are discussed.

Harris, Kathleen Mullan. **"Teenage Mothers and Welfare Dependency: Working Off Welfare."** *Journal of Family Issues* 12, no. 4 (1991):429–518.

Harris examines the ways that teenage single mothers are able to work their way off of welfare. The study was based on data from the Baltimore study, which followed a group of teenage black mothers for 17 years after the birth of their first child. Young mothers were quite active in the labor market. Findings suggest that education contributes to finding a job and helps in finding a high-paying job. As the young mothers gained more job experience, they were more likely to get off welfare. When mothers stayed on welfare, it was often because of problems finding child care. Implications for the new welfare reform legislation are discussed.

Hogan, Dennis P., Ling-xin Hao, and William L. Parish. **"Race, Kin Networks, and Assistance to Mother-Headed Families."** *Social Forces* 68, no. 3 (1990):797–812.

The relationships among kin networks, child care, and financial support for single-mother families were examined in this study, based on data from a nationally representative sample of black and white American mothers who were single or currently married in 1984. Black mothers were found to have better access to extended family members than white mothers, their child care was more often provided by family members, and they often received at least one-half of their income from people other than their husbands. Young black single mothers were more likely to live with adult family members and have access to free child care. Not all mothers benefitted from extended family networks; almost one-third of single black mothers did not have extended family support.

Jayakody, Rukmalie, Linda M. Chatters, and Robert J. Taylor. **"Family Support to Single and Married African American Mothers: The Provision of Financial, Emotional and Child Care Assistance."** *Journal of Marriage and the Family* 55 (1993):261–276.

Family-based support networks can often provide a single parent with financial, emotional, child care, and other types of assistance to help them survive. This study examined the relationship between marital status and the kin-network support provided. The region in which the family lived, the age of the family members, household structure, and proximity to family members were all found to play a role in the provision of assistance by extended family members.

Lee, Mo-Yee, and Chi-Kwong Law. **"Child Care Practices of Single Parent Families in Hong Kong."** *International Journal of Sociology of the Family* 24 (1994):45–59.

The authors attempt to understand the child care patterns of single-parent families in Hong Kong. The sample consisted of 311 single-parent families and 268 two-parent families. The authors hypothesized that single parents would have less time to spend in child care and homemaking activities and would see child care as more problematic than two-parent families. They also hypothesized that the relationship between the employment status of single parents and time spent and perceived problems in child care would be negative. Their data supported these hypotheses. The authors suggest that existing work policies and child care policies should be reconsidered in light of these findings to help both single-parent and two-parent families.

Letiecq, Bethany L., Elaine A. Anderson, and Sally A. Koblinsky. **"Social Support of Homeless and Permanently Housed Low-Income Mothers with Young Children."** *Family Relations* 45 (1996:265–272.

Family homelessness, especially among single mothers and their children, has been increasing in recent years. The social support systems of 92 homeless and 115 permanently housed low-income mothers were examined in this study. The authors found that homeless mothers had considerably less contact with friends and family members, could count on fewer people to help with child care, and believed that their social networks were less helpful in raising their children than housed mothers. Homeless mothers were found to be significantly more transient than housed mothers, that is, they moved more often and stayed for a shorter amount of time in any one place. Single mothers who spent a shorter time in temporary housing received more help in raising their children than mothers who spent a great deal of time in temporary housing. Implications for policy and practice are discussed.

Macpherson, David, and James B. Stewart. **"The Effects of Extended Families and Marital Status on Housing Consumption by Black Female-Headed Households."** *Review of Black Political Economy* 19 (1991):65–83.

The authors examined the factors that affect the housing characteristics of black females in order to determine how housing consumption is affected by marital status and the existence of extended families living within one housing unit. Based on the number of people living in black single-mother households that do not contain extended family members, the authors conclude that their homes are not crowded. However, in black female-headed households in which extended family members also live, the results are different. These families live in what the authors refer to as crowded conditions. Young black single mothers who are separated and live in the South are most likely to live in crowded households.

McLanahan, Sara, and Karen Booth. **"Mother-Only Families: Problems, Prospects, and Politics."** *Journal of Marriage and the Family* 51 (1989):557–580.

Three aspects of mother-only families are discussed in this article. These aspects include economic and social well-being, consequences for children, and the role of these families in the politics of gender, race, and social class. The authors found that economic insecurity is high in single-mother families due to the low earning ability of single mothers, the lack of child support from nonresidential parents, and limited public benefits. Children in single-mother families also appear more likely to become single parents themselves. Several factors contribute to lower socioeconomic mobility, including economic deprivation, parental practices, and neighborhood conditions. The authors suggest that single-mother families have become the focus of quite a bit of negative publicity, that they have become the standard for a wider set of struggles concerning the changes in women's roles, the relationship between the state and the family, and class and racial inequality.

Meyer, Daniel R., and Steven Garasky. **"Custodial Fathers: Myths, Realities, and Child Support Policy."** *Journal of Marriage and the Family* 55 (1993):73–89.

Even though the number of single-father families is growing, many people believe that there are few custodial fathers. The authors examine five myths concerning single fathers: that there are not very many of them, that most of them have remarried, that many are widowers and very few have never been married, that they have high incomes, and that they primarily receive custody of older boys. The authors believe that current child support policies should be reexamined in order to treat both parents equally.

Olson, Myrna R., and Judith A. Haynes. **"Successful Single Parents."** *Families in Society* 74 (1993):259–267.

The authors conducted in-depth interviews with 26 single parents who were identified in a two-state region of the Midwest in order to explore the dynamics of successful single parents. The authors defined successful single parents as those who conveyed a positive attitude toward their parental role and who also appeared competent in that role. The authors discovered several characteristics that were indicative of being a successful single parent. These characteristics included accepting the responsibilities of being a single parent, making these responsibilities a priority, providing consistent and nonpunitive discipline, emphasizing open communication, fostering individuality within a supportive family unit, recognizing the need for self-nurturance, and dedicating time to rituals and traditions.

Plotnick, R. D. **"The Effect of Social Policies on Teenage Pregnancy and Childbearing."** *Families in Society* 74, no. 6 (1993): 324–328.

Social policies in the United States can significantly affect teenage pregnancy and childbearing outcomes. Policies that focus on providing tangible family planning services and that improve access to and the cost of abortion have stronger and more consistent effects on teenage sexual behavior than those policies that attempt to change personal attitudes and values. The author suggests that increases in welfare benefits may offer an incentive for pregnant teenagers not to bother getting married. Teenage pregnancy and childbearing rates may be reduced indirectly through policies that improve educational and earnings opportunities for teenagers. Plotnick suggests that better economic prospects may lead teenagers to believe that they have something to gain if they do not become parents.

Richards, Leslie N., and Cynthia J. Schmiege. **"Problems and Strengths of Single-Parent Families: Implications for Practice and Policy."** *Family Relations* 42 (1993):277–285.

This study is based on data from a study of 60 single mothers and 11 single fathers. The types of family problems and strengths that these parents have identified in interviews are described and discussed. The article focuses on the three primary problems that these single parents face, the personal or family strengths that were identified as being helpful to these parents, whether they thought single parenting became easier over time, and if and how the single fathers perceived their experiences as parents were different from the experiences of single mothers. Single fathers often reported more problems with their former spouses than single mothers, and single mothers reported more financial problems than single fathers. Both single mothers and fathers found that role and task strain and developing a social life were problems that they faced. Approximately two-thirds of both single mothers and fathers found single parenting easier over time. Policy implications of these findings are discussed.

Sandfort, Jodi R., and Martha S. Hill. **"Assisting Young, Unmarried Mothers to Become Self-Sufficient: The Effects of Different Types of Early Economic Support."** *Journal of Marriage and the Family* 58 (1996):311–326.

This study examines a sample of young, unmarried mothers from the Panel Study of Income Dynamics, focusing on how different types of economic support received soon after the birth of their first children contribute to their ability to become self-sufficient over time. Economic support included AFDC payments, food stamps, and child support, as well as shared housing and the assistance of relatives. Receipt of child support is the only type of economic support that is a consistent predictor of later self-sufficiency. Young, unmarried mothers are a diverse group; many of them are able to gain work experience after the birth of their first child, while others are not. The young woman's behavior following an early pregnancy is important in determining her future ability to be self-sufficient. Women who are able to continue in school, gain some work experience, and postpone additional children are more able to become self-sufficient.

Shireman, Joan F. **"Adoptions by Single Parents."** *Marriage and Family Review* 20 (1995):367–388.

Many people believe that single-parent adoptions are less advantageous to the children involved than adoption by two-parent families. As a result many of the children adopted by single parents are older children and those who are difficult to place; some of these children may have emotional or behavioral problems. If a single parent wants to adopt a young child or infant, he or she may find it easier to adopt a child from a foreign country. Shireman reviews the literature concerning single-parent adoption and looks at the findings of a longitudinal study on single-parent adoption. She finds that single parents who adopt are usually fully capable of carrying out parental responsibilities. Important factors in successful single parenting of adopted children include continuing support from family and friends, the community, and from the agency handling the adoption. These factors are important because single parents do not have another adult, a spouse, to help with the many responsibilities involved. Children who are adopted by single parents appear as well adjusted as those adopted by two-parent families.

Siegel, J. M. **"Pathways to Single Motherhood: Sexual Intercourse, Adoption, and Donor Insemination."** *Families in Society* 79, no. 1 (1998):75–82.

Using quantitative and qualitative analyses, Siegel examined whether single women who become mothers in different ways experienced the same concerns about becoming a mother, as well as whether the way the mother becomes pregnant is related to the level of coping and satisfaction that mothers have with motherhood. Three groups of single mothers were studied: those who conceived through sexual intercourse, mothers who adopted, and mothers who conceived through donor insemination, as well as one group of married women who conceived through sexual intercourse. Single mothers thought more about the role of a father in their children's lives than married women who conceived through sexual intercourse. A smaller group of the single mothers who conceived through sexual intercourse and whose pregnancies were unplanned were the most worried about becoming single mothers. The author concludes that single motherhood by itself is not problematic; the adjustment to single motherhood is influenced by whether the choice to become a single mother is made before or after a woman becomes pregnant.

Simons, Ronald L., Jay Beaman, Rand D. Conger, and Wei Chao. **"Stress, Support, and Antisocial Behavior Traits as Determinants of Emotional Well-Being and Parenting Practices among Single Mothers."** *Journal of Marriage and the Family* 55, no. 2 (1993):385–398.

Many people have suggested that single mothers are under an intense emotional strain in trying to raise their children without the support and encouragement of a father. Simons and his associates studied 209 recently divorced women, examining the differences in how single parents function. The findings suggest that there are two ways in which single parents adjust poorly to single parenting.

Inadequate financial resources and lack of an adequate social support network explain many of the reasons why single mothers may exhibit psychological distress and problems with child rearing.

Steinbock, Marcia R. **"Homeless Female-Headed Families: Relationships at Risk."** *Marriage and Family Review* 20 (1995):143–160.

National as well as state laws in the United States have an effect on the child-rearing abilities of single mothers. These laws and their effects are described in this article. The legal system's response to domestic violence, and its role in the increasing number of homeless women and their children who need to find a safe place to live are discussed. The article describes the problems that women have with poverty or domestic violence that can lead to becoming homeless. Some single mothers lose their children when they lose their housing; many of the children are placed in foster care. The foster care system and its response to homeless families and maternal substance abuse are described. Policy implications are discussed.

Stewart, Dana G. **"Single Custodial Females and Their Families: Housing and Coping Strategies after Divorce."** *International Journal of Law and the Family* 5 (1991):296–317.

In a study of the effects of the no-fault divorce law in Manitoba enacted in 1986, Stewart examines the effects of divorce on the income, consumption, and standard of living of divorced persons and their children. All of the divorced couples had, prior to the divorce, owned their homes and had at least one dependent child under the age of 18 years. The focus of the study was on 50 single mothers with custody. The study examined postdivorce housing arrangements and satisfaction, neighborhood satisfaction, child custody, child support, and levels of self-sufficiency. The author suggests that policies that advocate financial counseling as part of the divorce process should be supported.

Voegeli, Wolfgang, and Barbara Willenbacher. **"Children's Rights and Social Placement: A Cross-National Comparison of Legal and Social Policy towards Children in One-Parent Families."** *International Journal of Law and the Family* 7 (1993):108–124.

A child's right to an adequate standard of living and education is based upon the child's place in society. This placement is easier for children from two-parent families. For children from one-parent families, their place in society is dependent on many environmental factors. Data for this study were obtained in Germany. The purpose of the study was to determine the factors that influence the social placement of children in single-parent families. Individual family factors are important, and include factors such as self-esteem, cultural aspirations, family size, and sex of the child. Social factors also play a significant role; these factors include employment opportunities, availability of child care services, child support, and access to the educational system.

Walters, Lynda Henley, and Carla Rae Abshire. **"Single Parenthood and the Law."** *Marriage and Family Review* 20 (1995): 161–188.

Most of the laws that affect single parents focus on continuing the relationship between parent and child following a divorce. Many of these same laws apply to never-married parents. State statutes are the laws that apply most often to single-parent families; many states have similar laws regarding the single parent and child. The status of these laws and the experiences that single parents have with these laws are discussed by the authors, who base their discussion on information from social scientists, legal commentators, and appellate opinions in the areas of child support, child custody, tax law, and court involvement in welfare reform. Gender discrimination is fairly common throughout the legal environment. The authors suggest that to preserve the best interests of the child, conflicting attitudes and beliefs should be resolved, myths and stereotypes should be explored and destroyed, and equality for parents should be promoted.

Selected Nonprint Resources 7

This chapter provides annotated descriptions of videos and films that focus on single parents and sources of information that can be found on the Internet.

Video Resources

Children of Divorce

Type: VHS
Length: 30 minutes
Cost: $195.00
Source: The Bureau for At-Risk Youth
135 Dupont St.
P.O. Box 760
Plainview, NY 11803-0760
(800) 99-YOUTH (800-999-6884)
Fax: (516) 349-5521
e-mail: info@at-risk.com
Internet: http://www.at-risk.com

This video presents the impact of divorce from the child's perspective. Many children from varying ages, ethnic groups, and backgrounds share their personal experiences of divorce in order to help other children who are experiencing the same situation and feelings. One of the goals of the video is to make parents aware of the feelings their children may be experiencing

233

as a result of their parents' divorce. The ultimate goal is to ease the communication between parents and children during divorce. The video is appropriate for all ages and for in-service training. A leader's guide is included.

Daddy Doesn't Live with Us
Type: VHS
Length: 14 minutes
Date: 1994
Cost: $99.95
Source: Sunburst Communications
101 Castleton Street
P.O. Box 40
Pleasantville, NY 10570
(800) 431-1934
Fax: (914) 769-2109
e-mail: service@nysunburst.com

This video helps children in families that have experienced separation or divorce understand that the breakup is not their fault. Children are shown that they cannot control what their parents do. Using a storyteller to convey the message, the video uses one child's experience with family breakup to show children in similar situations that it's okay to feel sad. Kevin thinks that it is his fault that his mom and dad fight all the time and that his dad is moving out. Kevin's uncle Brian helps him to understand that his parents' breakup is not his fault. Ways are suggested to help children feel better. The video is for children in kindergarten through second grade. A teacher's guide and 12 student worksheets come with the video.

Decisions: Teens, Sex and Pregnancy
Type: VHS
Length: 26 minutes
Cost: $95.00
Source: The Bureau for At-Risk Youth
135 Dupont St.
P.O. Box 760
Plainview, NY 11803-0760
(800) 99-YOUTH (800-999-6884)
Fax: (516) 349-5521

e-mail: info@at-risk.com
Internet: http://www.at-risk.com

Currently, over 1 million teenagers become pregnant each year. Approximately 50 percent will decide to keep their babies, 45 percent will choose abortion, and 5 percent will give up their children for adoption. Most teenagers do not know the problems that young mothers face. This documentary video tells the stories of three teenage mothers after they learned they were pregnant and describes the decisions that they made concerning their children. The video offers insight for both boys and girls about the consequences of sex. A leader's guide and set of masters come with the video. For students from seventh to twelfth grade.

The Firefighter: Single Parenting and Its Effect on Children
Type: VHS
Length: 25 minutes
Date: 1993
Cost: $95.00
Source: National Resource Center for Youth Services
            College of Continuing Education
            University of Oklahoma
            202 W. 8th St.
            Tulsa, OK 74119-1419
            (918) 585-2986
            Fax: (918) 592-1841

Part of the series *Working It Out at Madison,* this video is set at Madison High School. A talented group of actors from a variety of backgrounds bring to life the many problems and challenges that are experienced by young people today. This video presents Penny, a child of a single parent. Penny finds herself afraid that her single parent might become involved with someone who could become her stepparent. Penny is afraid of being abandoned. Comes with a leader's guide.

Four Pregnant Teenagers: Four Different Decisions
Type: VHS
Length: 51 minutes
Date: 1987
Cost: $198.95

Source: Sunburst Communications
101 Castleton St.
P.O. Box 40
Pleasantville, NY 10570
(800) 431-1934
Fax: (914) 747-4109
e-mail: service@nysunburst.com

This video dramatizes the difficult decisions that unwed pregnant teenagers face concerning their future and the future of their children. Vignettes present the four possible decisions that pregnant women face about their children. Here, Kim decides to have her baby and give it up for adoption; Joanne decides to keep her child and raise it without the help or presence of the father; Leslie and her boyfriend decide to get married; and Amanda reluctantly chooses to have an abortion. This video helps students weigh the emotional, ethical, and financial problems that they may face if they become pregnant.

I'm Not Ready for This
Type: VHS
Length: 18 minutes
Cost: $198.00
Source: National Resource Center for Youth Services
College of Continuing Education
University of Oklahoma
202 W. 8th St.
Tulsa, OK 74119-1419
(918) 585-2986
Fax: (918) 592-1841

The audience for this video is primarily teenagers who have just become, or are about to become, parents. The video focuses on Janine, who is a junior in high school and finds herself pregnant. She finds that she is no longer like her friends. They are still just teenagers having fun, while she has more serious things to think about. This video focuses on several issues, including the challenges, conflicts, and options facing teenage parents; the importance of staying in school; proper prenatal and infant health care; the importance of not trying to deal with all the challenges alone; and the role of the father.

Kids and Divorce
Type: VHS
Length: 21 minutes
Date: 1996
Cost: $99.95
Source: Sunburst Communications
101 Castleton St.
P.O. Box 40
Pleasantville, NY 10570
(800) 431-1934
Fax: (914) 747-4109
e-mail: service@nysunburst.com

Children often have a difficult time dealing with the divorce of their parents. This video, for children in grades two through five, provides poignant insights into the feelings and experiences of children of divorce. First-person accounts provide valuable insights into the children's feelings about their parents' divorce. Set in a nonthreatening environment of a peer support group, children talk freely about the variety of emotions divorce can arouse. They recall problems at school or home. They urge viewers from divorced families to find someone to talk to, and emphasize that divorce is never the fault of the child. A teacher's guide is included.

New Beginnings: Skills for Single Parents and Stepfamily Parents
Type: VHS
Length: 30 minutes
Cost: $285.00
Source: Center for the Improvement of Child Caring
11331 Ventura Blvd., Suite 103
Studio City, CA 91604-3147
(800) 325-CICC or (818) 980-0903
Fax: (818) 753-1054

This video-based program focuses on the needs of single and stepfamily parents. Developed by Don Dinkmeyer, Gary D. McKay, and Joyce L. McKay, the easy-to-use audiovisual training format creates an interactive learning environment in which parents can discuss the challenges they face, share experiences, try out new ideas, and receive support, feedback, and encouragement from other group members. The program is designed to be presented in eight sessions and covers such topics as self-esteem, relationships, behavior, emotional development, communication, decision making, discipline, and personal and family challenges. It can be used as either an audio or video-based program. An Instructor's Kit includes a video discussion guide, a 222-page *New Beginnings* book, a set of four audiocassettes, a 178-page leader's manual, and a "Rules for Group Discussion" poster. A parent's manual can also be purchased for $11.95.

Practical Parenting Series: Single Parenting
Type: VHS
Length: 30 minutes
Date: 1995
Cost: $99.00
Source: Research Press
            Dept. 98
            P.O. Box 9177
            Champaign, IL 61826
            (217) 352-3273 or (800) 519-2707
            Fax: (217) 352-1221
            e-mail: rp@researchpress.com

This video is part of a series developed for use with parenting groups. Dramatized scenes of real-life situations are intermixed with a lively narration by actor Dick Van Patten. This video focuses on the unique challenges facing single parents, including parental roles, parent-child bonding, communication, discipline, and financial pressures. A facilitator's guide is included. The video is for parents of children of any age.

Real People: Pregnancy and Teens
Type: VHS
Length: 20 minutes
Date: 1995
Cost: $149.95
Source: Sunburst Communications
            101 Castleton St.
            P.O. Box 40
            Pleasantville, NY 10570
            (800) 431-1934

Fax: (914) 747-4109
e-mail: service@nysunburst.com

Television broadcast journalist Jane Pauley hosts this video, which makes the case for preventing teenage pregnancy by telling the poignant stories of several pregnant and parenting teenagers as they talk about their lives and problems. Cynthia, 16 years old, pregnant and a school dropout, is living on her own because her mother will not let her live at home. Irma is 19 years old and has a 17-month-old son; she hopes to get her diploma with the help of a parenting program at school. Irma and other teenage mothers participating in the parenting program share their experiences with a group of students. They explain why they became pregnant. If they were given a second chance, they agree that they would have used some form of birth control. Two other teenagers appearing in the video, Tiffany and Jenna, explain why they are committed to abstinence. A teacher's guide is included.

Real People: Teen Mothers and Fathers Speak Out
Type: VHS
Length: 27 minutes
Date: 1995
Cost: $189.95
Source: Sunburst Communications
            101 Castleton St.
            P.O. Box 40
            Pleasantville, NY 10570
            (800) 431-1934
            Fax: (914) 747-4109
            e-mail: service@nysunburst.com

Part of the series of videos especially for minority and urban teenagers in grades seven through twelve, this video presents in-depth interviews with real teenage mothers and fathers. The teenagers examine the reasons for their pregnancies. The video can help teenagers question their own motivations and behavior. A teacher's guide is included.

The Single Parent Family: A Challenge for Children
Type: VHS
Length: 20 minutes
Cost: $49.95

Source: The Bureau for At-Risk Youth
            135 Dupont St.
            P.O. Box 760
            Plainview, NY 11803-0760
            (800) 99-YOUTH (800-999-6884)
            Fax: (516) 349-5521
            e-mail: info@at-risk.com
            Internet: http://www.at-risk.com

Many children have a difficult time understanding the ramifications of living in a single-parent family. This video details the single-parent experience from the child's point of view. Many of the common problems are described along with the adjustments that children must make to help deal with these problems. Special emphasis is placed on uncomfortable feelings, including anger, guilt, loneliness, rejection, and disappointment. A comprehensive facilitator's guide is included.

The Single Parent Family: A Challenge for Parents
Type: VHS
Length: 20 minutes
Cost: $49.95
Source: The Bureau for At-Risk Youth
            135 Dupont St.
            P.O. Box 760
            Plainview, NY 11803-0760
            (800) 99-YOUTH (800-999-6884)
            Fax: (516) 349-5521
            e-mail: info@at-risk.com
            Internet: http://www.at-risk.com

Many parents find the adjustment to being a single parent difficult and challenging. This video describes many of the problems that are common to all single parents and their families and makes suggestions that can help these families adjust to their new lives. The emotions that parents feel, the shortage of money, parent exhaustion, support systems, social life, dating, and remarriage are covered by this video. Parents learn how a single-parent family impacts the child and what steps should be taken to be a successful single parent.

Single Parenting

Type: VHS
Length: 30 minutes
Cost: $99.00
Source: The Bureau for At-Risk Youth
135 Dupont St.
P.O. Box 760
Plainview, NY 11803-0760
(800) 99-YOUTH (800-999-6884)
Fax: (516) 349-5521
e-mail: info@at-risk.com
Internet: http://www.at-risk.com

This video focuses on ways to minimize the adverse effects that a divorce or death in the family may have on children. It provides positive techniques to effective single parenting. As part of the Bureau's *Practical Parenting* series, this video is appropriate for parenting workshops, PTA groups, counseling groups, hospitals, high schools, libraries, and religious centers. A leader's guide is included.

Stories of Change

Type: VHS
Length: 57 minutes
Date: 1991
Cost: $250.00
Source: Future Educational Films
121 W. 27th St., Suite 902
New York, NY 10001

This award-winning video profiles the lives of four women from different backgrounds. Anna, Angelina, Mink-Floa, and Anitra have surmounted incredible odds, including divorce, poverty, discrimination, substance abuse, single parenting, and cultural stereotypes and barriers. Each woman describes her experiences, the ways she has overcome problems in her life, and how she has become stronger. The film was sponsored by the Ford Foundation and the California Council for the Humanities. The audience includes college-age students and adults.

Teen Moms Talking: Preventing Teen Parenthood
Type: VHS
Length: 30 minutes
Cost: $149.95
Source: The Bureau for At-Risk Youth
135 Dupont St.
P.O. Box 760
Plainview, NY 11803-0760
(800) 99-YOUTH (800-999-6884)
Fax: (516) 349-5521
e-mail: info@at-risk.com
Internet: http://www.at-risk.com

The purpose of this video is to make teenagers think twice about teenage sex and pregnancy. In a frank examination of the challenges that face teenage parents, this video presents dramatic vignettes that provide firsthand messages from teenage mothers. In their own words they describe their experiences as teenage mothers; they talk about telling their parents, telling their partners, and the reactions of their friends to their pregnancies. Other topics discussed include finances, school and careers, responsibility and commitment, and the major changes that transform their lives forever.

Teenage Parenting
Type: VHS
Length: 30 minutes
Cost: $99.00
Source: The Bureau for At-Risk Youth
135 Dupont St.
P.O. Box 760
Plainview, NY 11803-0760
(800) 99-YOUTH (800-999-6884)
Fax: (516) 349-5521
e-mail: info@at-risk.com
Internet: http://www.at-risk.com

This video provides teenagers with a realistic picture of the responsibilities of raising a child. The consequences of sexual activity are explored and the myths about pregnancy explained. One teenager is followed throughout her pregnancy to show the viewers what happens in real life. As part of the Bureau's *Practical Par-*

enting series, this video is appropriate for parenting workshops, PTA groups, counseling groups, hospitals, high schools, libraries, and religious centers. A leader's guide is included.

Internet Resources

Big Brothers Big Sisters of America
http://www.bbbsa.org

Big Brothers Big Sisters of America offers mentoring activities for boys and girls, usually from single-parent families. Its website contains information on local agencies, contributions, current news, results from a study on the impact of Big Brothers Big Sisters on the children they serve, the vision and mission statement, and other areas of interest.

Center for Law and Social Policy (CLASP)
http://www.clasp.org

A national public policy and law organization, the Center focuses on the problems of low-income families with children. CLASP conducts education, policy research, and advocacy activities on income support issues at both the state and federal levels, including welfare reform, child care, work force development, and child support enforcement. Its website provides a wealth of information, including links to law libraries, other legal resources, the U.S. Congress, Supreme Court cases, state and federal laws, and other U.S. and foreign legal resources. Links are also available to law journals, magazines, and law schools. Law-related search engines, law-related discussion groups, and e-mail discussion lists are available.

Child Trends, Inc.
http://www.childtrends.org

Child Trends is a nonprofit research organization dedicated to studying children, youth, and families. Study topics include teenage pregnancy and childbearing, the effects of welfare and poverty on children, parenting, and fatherhood. Its website provides information on the background and purpose of the program, current research projects, abstracts of recent papers, a list of publications, press releases, job announcements, facts-at-a-glance, and links to other data sources.

Child Welfare League of America
http://www.cwla.org

The Child Welfare League's website provides a great deal of information concerning vulnerable children and their families. The site describes the purpose of the organization, its advocacy activities, the major areas in which it is working to benefit children, a list and description of publications available from the organization, a calendar of events, consultation services, member agencies, and corporate partners. A news and events segment provides up-to-date information on current affairs. Among the organization's activities is the Florence Crittenton Adolescent Pregnancy Prevention and Parenting Division. The activities and projects of this program are described on the website.

Children, Youth and Family Consortium
http://www.cyfc.umn.edu

The Children, Youth and Family Consortium (CYFC) brings together research and resources to address a variety of critical issues that face children and families. An extensive Internet resource, the Consortium Electronic Clearinghouse provides information concerning the health, education, and welfare of children, youth, and families, including articles and research materials on topics from practical parenting to formulating policies and designing and implementing programs. Special sections focus on specialized topics. AdoptINFO offers research-based information on a variety of topics including policy issues, search and reunion, adoption subsidy, special needs children, legal issues, parent support groups, how to adopt, and race and adoption. FatherNet includes conference proceedings, research, and policy and opinion documents concerning social, economic, and policy factors that support or hinder men's involvement in the lives of children. MediaForum includes conference proceedings from The Family and the Media conference in 1995, related research, and policy and opinion documents discussing social, economic, and policy factors related to the media's influence on children and families. An electronic bulletin board is available for online discussion of relevant issues. Family Friendly Workplace addresses the delicate balance between family and work and includes articles, research, policy, opinion documents, and links to related websites. Other theme areas available through the Clearinghouse include young children, adolescents, family and parenting, diversity, a calendar of events, background information on CYFC, new material, links to related websites, and a listing of experts on children, youth, and family issues.

Independent Adoption Center
http://www.adoptionhelp.org/nfediac

The Independent Adoption Center is one of the largest open adoption programs in the United States. A nonprofit organization, the Center focuses primarily on counseling and support. This website provides information about the Center's programs, including information concerning single-parent adoptions.

Institute for Women's Policy Research
http://www.iwpr.org

The Institute works to inform and stimulate the debate on issues of importance to women. It conducts credible research and contributes to public education and awareness concerning the economic needs of women. The website includes information about the organization's program, activities, publications, current research, welfare reform, available resources, employment possibilities, and membership. The organization's current research program focuses on four policy areas, including labor market and employment, poverty and welfare, family and work, and health care policy, and information concerning these areas is included on the website.

Kids Campaign
http://www.kidscampaign.com

Created to provide information to a variety of people, including parents, grandparents, educators, businesses, community leaders, policy makers, the media, volunteers, religious leaders, and service providers, this website offers feature stories, news of the campaign, and information on networking for single parents.

Men's Issues
http://www.vix.com/pub/men/

The Men's Issues Page attempts to cover the men's movement as completely as possible. Its goals are to maintain comprehensive reference lists of organizations, books, periodicals, Web links, and other related resources and to serve as an online reference source for statistics, studies, and other items of interest. Topics of relevance to single parents include fathering and fatherlessness, battered men, and single fathers. The single fathers site provides information on child support, including commentary, legal cases, statistics, and relevant legislation; paternity; and custody, including relevant legislation, legal cases, and studies.

Moms Online
http://www.momsonline.com

Moms Online is a virtual community of mothers working together to create a friendly site on the Internet. Their website provides information and advice as well as a place to "hang out" and receive moral support and encouragement. Information is provided on why the site was started, who the staff members are, hot tips on a variety of subjects, a "mom of the week" profile, relevant news, the opportunity to ask professionals about issues of importance to mothers, and other helpful information.

National Adoption Center
http://nac.adopt.org/single

The National Adoption Center website provides a wealth of information concerning adoption. A section on books on adoption offers a wide variety of materials concerning all aspects of adoption. A section called Adoption Quest offers information on how to adopt, sources for financial assistance, resources, adopting special needs children, adoption parenting issues, and race and culture. Photo listings provide data on children to adopt, and information packets are also available.

National Adoption Information Clearinghouse
http://www.calib.com/naic

The Clearinghouse was established in 1987 by the U.S. Congress to provide information on all aspects of adoption to professionals as well as to the general public. Information is provided on infant and intercountry adoption, and the adoption of children with special needs. An adoption literature database, a database of adoption experts, lists of adoption agencies, adoptive parent support groups and search support groups, and excerpts and full texts from state and federal laws on adoption are some of the resources available. The website provides access to much of this information.

National Campaign to Prevent Teen Pregnancy
http://www.teenpregnancy.org

The National Campaign to Prevent Teen Pregnancy provides national leadership in the fight to raise awareness of the issue of teenage pregnancy and to attract new voices and resources to the cause. This site provides information concerning the Campaign and its major activities, lists of publications, upcoming events, and a variety of other resources, including links to related sites, facts and statistics concerning teenage pregnancy, 10 tips for parents, and resources available to parents. The capability to search the website is also available.

National Center for Children in Poverty
http://cpmcnet.columbia.edu/dept/nccp

The National Center for Children in Poverty identifies and promotes strategies that can reduce the number of children living in poverty in the United States. It alerts the public to demographic statistics concerning child poverty, and research focusing on the impact of poverty on children and their families. The Center's website provides information about the organization and its activities, news releases, what's new in the field of child poverty, and child poverty facts. State and local information is provided, along with quite a bit of information on child care, welfare reform, and families under stress. The Center newsletter is available. A list of publications is available along with information on the research forum.

National Center for Fathering
http://www.fathers.com

The National Center for Fathering was developed to inspire and equip men to be better fathers by providing resources for men who want to strengthen their fathering skills. Staff members have developed a large database containing information relevant to fathers. Their website provides site information, practical tips, hot topics, available print materials, ways to contact other fathers, humor, subscription information, recent research findings on fathering, information about the Center's program, and how to get help. Links to other relevant sites concerning parenting, including single parenting, are provided.

National Fathering Initiative
http://www.register.com/father

The National Fathering Initiative, started in 1994, works to counter the growing problem of fatherlessness by promoting responsible fatherhood. The group's public education campaign highlights the importance of fathers to the well-being of children. Its website provides information on the Initiative, a catalog of available materials, online resources, tips from fathers, membership information, and links to other relevant websites.

National Head Start Association
http://www.nhsa.org

The National Head Start Association provides a national forum to enhance Head Start services for poor children and their families. This site offers information on the activities of the program, including government affairs, publications, meetings and other upcoming events, public relations activities, partnerships, services provided, research and evaluation activities, and membership information.

National Men's Resource Center
http://www.menstuff.org

This website offers a wealth of information on male roles and relationships. The National Men's Resource Directory lists over 2,600 men's services and publications. Lists of several hundred men's events are also available. Publications are broken down by important issues, including single fathers. Information is available concerning international activities, other relevant groups and their activities, resources that are available, what's new in the field, issues of importance to men and their relationships, and links to other relevant sites.

National Organization of Single Mothers
http://www.parentsplace.com/readroom/nosm

The nonprofit National Organization of Single Mothers is committed to helping single parents meet the many challenges of daily life. This site provides information on the National Organization of Single Mothers, suggestions, Internet tools, connections to other relevant sites on the Web, a newsletter, a calendar of upcoming events, and information on membership. A question-and-answer column offers information on relationships with fathers, reentering the dating scene, tips for single parents with latchkey kids, sending children to day care for the first time, child support, and what to do when school forms ask about a child's father.

National Parent Information Network
http://www.npin.org

This site is a project sponsored by two ERIC clearinghouses—the ERIC Clearinghouse on Urban Education and the ERIC Clearinghouse on Elementary and Early Childhood Education. Other ERIC system components and collaborating organizations also provide information resources. The site provides information to parents and those who work with parents and facilitates the exchange of parenting information.

National Resource Center for Youth Services
http://www.nrcys.ou.edu

This organization's website provides information about the Center, its training and educational programs, available publications and videos, and other program information. The page provides links to other related sites, including search engines, virtual libraries, government agencies, librarians and information specialists, and topical links to information on abuse, teenage pregnancy, conflict and violence, adoption, and other related topics.

NOW Legal Defense and Education Fund
http://www.nowldef.org

As the nation's oldest legal advocacy organization for women and girls, the NOW Legal Defense and Education Fund focuses on the major social and economic justice concerns on the women's rights agenda by defining the issues and bringing them to public attention. The organization's website provides information on publications, research, and other resources of interest to women. Legal docket highlights are available, as well as links to other relevant organizations.

Parent Soup
http://www.parentsoup.com

The Parent Soup website contains information on all aspects of parenting. People must join to gain access to discussion groups, chat rooms, and bulletin boards but membership is free.

Parents Place
http://www.parentsplace.com

This site provides a great deal of information for parents of all kinds, including single parents. Links are offered to other parenting programs. Members can participate in chat rooms and can access many of the site's bulletin boards. Users can direct questions to a variety of experts, including pediatricians, family therapists, and nutritionists.

Parents without Partners International
http://www.parentswithoutpartners.org

The website for this program provides basic information; a listing of international and local events; online support that includes resources, research, and articles for single parents; a listing of chapters throughout the world; links to related sites; and a "members only" page that provides specific services.

Research Forum on Children, Families,
and the New Federalism
http://www.researchforum.org

The Research Forum encourages collaborative research and policy on welfare reform and child well-being. Its clearinghouse, available through the website, includes an online database with summaries of 40 welfare research projects, including specific information on their Fragile Families Project, Teenage Parent Demonstration Program, and Florida's Family Transition Program. The Forum is adding a database that will include a broader range of welfare and income security research; plans have been developed to include information on general research on child and family well-being. The site also includes a calendar of events, information on updates and their review process, a glossary, information on contacting the Forum, and links to related sites.

Single African American Fathers' Exchange
http://www.saafe.com

The Single African American Fathers' Exchange (SAAFE) is a clearinghouse for single fathers. This webpage provides information on becoming more capable and involved as parents, offering ideas that have been developed to help single fathers. A variety of resources and other information are available to help men cope with their responsibilities as single fathers. Around the House offers in-depth articles that examine practical approaches to single parenting. Kids-n-Stuff looks at the experiences of children and their environment. The Book Room lists titles of books of interest to single fathers. The Learning Tree discusses education issues. The Resource Guide offers information about and links to federal, state, and local resources and social programs that can help single parents in areas of child care and home management. Additional links are provided to other sites on single parenting, single fatherhood, culture, news, and other areas of interest to single parents.

Single and Custodial Fathers Network
http://www.single-fathers.org

The Single and Custodial Fathers Network helps fathers meet the challenge of being custodial parents. The Network provides information and supportive resources to fathers and their families. The website provides information about the services the Network provides, how to join, parenting issues, work issues, research, and links to related sites.

Single Fathers' Lighthouse
http://www.qnet.com/~rlewis3

This webpage developed by a single father offers information on cooking for a family, humor, inspirational items, and information on custody, visitation, and other legal issues. Links to other single-parent resources are provided, with personal notes and comments. E-mail and Listserv offer ways to learn more about single parenting and meet other single parents.

Single Mothers by Choice
http://www.parentsplace.com/readroom/smc

This Internet site provides a variety of information concerning single mothers. Advice to women about single motherhood, an online newsletter, membership form, and description of the book *Single Mothers by Choice*, written by Jane Mattes, the founder of this organization, are available.

Single Parent Resource
http://www.parentsplace.com/readroom/spn/index.html

The Single Parent Resource is an online forum that focuses on issues that single parents find important. The material included at this site is gathered from single parents who share support and solutions to questions asked about single parenting. Online features include selected articles, quotes from kids concerning things they wish their parents knew, why and how the newsletter began, and ordering information for resources and pamphlets.

Single Parents Association
http://www.neta.com/~spa/story.html

This association is a membership organization that provides education, resources, friendships, and entertainment activities for single parents and their children. Its website provides information on the program's mission, testimonials, how they differ from other single-parent programs, how to start a chapter, parenting tips, frequently asked questions, and links to other relevant sites.

Single Parents Raising Kids, Inc. (SPARK)
http://www.corphome.com/spark

SPARK is an organization of single parents living in Montgomery County, Maryland, and surrounding areas. Program activities include family, educational, and social events. The website provides information about the organization, orientation dates, e-mail, and links to other relevant organizations.

Sole Mothers International
http://home.navisoft.com/solemom

In 1995 Diane Chambers started this online organization to address the common problems and concerns of single mothers. Her webpage has links to several relevant organizations and state agencies. The National Coalition for Child Support Reform information site investigates current child support practices and hopes to uncover unfair and irresponsible enforcement practices and make recommendations to state and federal governments regarding a reform plan. The link to the home page of the Federal Office of Child Support Enforcement provides valuable information on child support enforcement in individual states. Links are also provided to many state child support pages, the Bureau of Family Support Operations of the Los Angeles County District Attorney's Office, the California Child Support Advocacy Group, and many private child support collection agencies. Another section entitled "legal-ease" helps individuals become better acquainted with self-help legal resources for a variety of circumstances.

Solo: A Guide for the Single Parent
http://pages.prodigy.com/Solo/guide.htm

This is an online magazine that focuses on issues of importance to single parents. The first issue in September 1995 was distributed to support groups, advance subscribers, and selected newsstands and was quickly sold out. Started by a single mother and published quarterly, *Solo* is designed to address relevant issues in finance, law, child psychology, custody disputes, coping strategies, and success stories. The site includes subscription information, sample articles, current topics of interest, planned future articles, support groups and other resources, websites of interest, advisors and contributors, and information for commercial advertising.

U.S. Administration for Children, Youth, and Families
http://www.acf.dhhs.gov/programs/acyf

The Administration for Children, Youth, and Families administers federal programs focusing on social services that promote development of children and their families, protective services for children at risk, child care for working families, and adoption of children with special needs. The agency's website provides the starting point for finding a great deal of information concerning children and their welfare. A staff directory is available, along with information on the various geographic regions, answers to frequently asked questions, the organizational structure, and various programs. Within this program is the child support enforcement office, with its own website (http://www.acf.dhhs.gov/ACFPrograms/CSE), which provides much information concerning child support issues. Also found is a link to the Children's Bureau home page (http://www.acf.dhhs.gov/programs/cb/).

U.S. Bureau of the Census
http://www.census.gov

An excellent resource for social, economic, and demographic data concerning the population of the United States. Census statistics, reports, and links to other related sites are available. A search engine helps navigate through this site and find information on specific topics.

U.S. Federal Statistics
http://www.fedstats.gov

This website provides access to over 70 government agencies that produce statistics of interest to the general public. Maintained by the Federal Interagency Council on Statistical Policy, this site provides a wide range of information, including fast facts, a site map, and directions on how to search the site for the information needed.

U.S. Women's Bureau
http://www.dol.gov/dol/wb

The Women's Bureau provides a wealth of information concerning the status and experiences of women in the United States. The website contains statistics and data, a searchable library, a news room, descriptions of the programs and services the Bureau provides, information on child care, equal pay issues, educational resources, and regional information. Links are available to dozens of other sites, including other government sites, as well as some private sites.

Index

255